Pra

Published in conjunction with
the British Association of Social Workers

THE BRITISH ASSOCIATION OF SOCIAL WORKERS

Social work is at an important stage in its development. The profession is facing fresh challenges to work flexibly in fast-changing social and organisational environments. New requirements for training are also demanding a more critical and reflective, as well as more highly skilled, approach to practice.

The British Association of Social Workers (www.basw.co.uk) has always been conscious of its role in setting guidelines for practice and in seeking to raise professional standards. The concept of the *Practical Social Work* series was conceived to fulfil a genuine professional need for a carefully planned, coherent series of texts that would stimulate and inform debate, thereby contributing to the development of practitioners' skills and professionalism.

Newly relaunched, the series continues to address the needs of all those who are looking to deepen and refresh their understanding and skills. It is designed for students and busy professionals alike. Each book marries practice issues and challenges with the latest theory and research in a compact and applied format. The authors represent a wide variety of experience both as educators and practitioners. Taken together, the books set a standard in their clarity, relevance and rigour.

A list of new and best-selling titles in this series follows overleaf.
A comprehensive list of titles available in the series, and further details about individual books, can be found online at:
www.palgrave.com/socialworkpolicy/basw

Series standing order ISBN 978–0–333–80313–4

You can receive future titles in this series as they are published by placing a standing order. Please contact your bookseller or, in the case of difficulty, contact us at the address below with your name and address, the title of the series and the ISBN quoted above.

Customer Services Department, Macmillan Distribution Ltd, Houndmills, Basingstoke, Hampshire, RG21 6XS, UK

Practical social work series
Founding Editor: Jo Campling

New and best-selling titles

Robert Adams *Empowerment, Participation and Social Work* (4th edition)
Sarah Banks *Ethics and Values in Social Work* (4th edition)
James G. Barber *Social Work with Addictions* (3rd edition)
Christine Bigby and Patsie Frawley *Social Work Practice and Intellectual Disability*
Suzy Braye and Michael Preston-Shoot *Practising Social Work Law* (3rd edition)
Veronica Coulshed and Audrey Mullender with David N. Jones and Neil Thompson
    Management in Social Work (3rd edition)
Veronica Coulshed and Joan Orme *Social Work Practice* (5th edition)
Lena Dominelli *Anti-Racist Social Work* (3rd edition)
Celia Doyle *Working with Abused Children* (4th edition)
Gordon Jack and Helen Donnellan *Social Work with Children*
Tony Jeffs and Mark K. Smith (editors) *Youth Work Practice*
Joyce Lishman *Communication in Social Work* (2nd edition)
Paula Nicolson, Rowan Bayne and Jenny Owen *Applied Psychology for Social Workers*
    (3rd edition)
Michael Oliver, Bob Sapey and Pam Thomas *Social Work with Disabled People*
    (4th edition)
Joan Orme and David Shemmings *Developing Research-Based Social Work Practice*
Terence O'Sullivan *Decision Making in Social Work* (2nd edition)
Mo Ray and Judith Phillips *Social Work with Older People* (5th edition)
Michael Preston-Shoot *Effective Groupwork* (2nd edition)
Steven Shardlow and Mark Doel *Practice Learning and Teaching*
Jerry Tew *Working with Mental Distress*
Neil Thompson *Anti-Discriminatory Practice* (5th edition)
Alan Twelvetrees *Community Work* (4th edition)

For further companion resources visit www.palgrave.com/socialwork/basw

Gordon Jack
and
Helen Donnellan

Social Work with Children

palgrave
macmillan

First published 2013 by
PALGRAVE MACMILLAN

Palgrave Macmillan in the UK is an imprint of Macmillan Publishers Limited, registered in England, company number 785998, of Houndmills, Basingstoke, Hampshire RG21 6XS.

Palgrave Macmillan in the US is a division of St Martin's Press LLC, 175 Fifth Avenue, New York, NY 10010.

Palgrave Macmillan is the global academic imprint of the above companies and has companies and representatives throughout the world.

Palgrave® and Macmillan® are registered trademarks in the United States, the United Kingdom, Europe and other countries

ISBN 978–0–230–30814–5

This book is printed on paper suitable for recycling and made from fully managed and sustained forest sources. Logging, pulping and manufacturing processes are expected to conform to the environmental regulations of the country of origin.

A catalogue record for this book is available from the British Library.

A catalog record for this book is available from the Library of Congress.

Brief contents

Contents

Preface

Underpinning frameworks

In this book we draw together knowledge from contemporary theory, research, policy and practice in order to develop a critical approach to social work with children in a wide range of settings and across the four countries of the UK.

Social workers employed in any branch of children's services and any organizational setting will routinely be involved in assessing the needs of children experiencing problems in order to determine the actions or services required to promote their well-being and safeguard them from harm. Even in apparently straightforward cases, practitioners are likely to be faced with a lot of information, often from a wide range of different sources, which can quickly become overwhelming without the help of appropriate organizing frameworks. That is why we have based this book on a combination of what are arguably the two most important organizing frameworks used in social work practice with children today – human ecology and child development.

Ecological theory was originally developed within the biological sciences to explain the relationships between living organisms and their environments, with the earth consisting of a number of *systems* – plants, animals, humans, the physical environment – involved in constant processes of mutual interaction, with changes in one system capable of affecting each of the others. Following its original formulation, ecological theory was adapted to explain the process of human development, with a similar systems approach used to understand the ways in which people both shape and are shaped by their surroundings (Bronfenbrenner, 1979). Since then, comprehensive reviews of the research evidence (e.g. Belsky and Jaffee, 2006; Cicchetti and Valentino, 2006) have confirmed that developmental outcomes for children depend upon interactions between the characteristics, often referred to as 'risk and protective factors', of the child, their parents and their wider family and community circumstances, as well as the society in which they are all embedded.

Ecological theory serves to remind us that individuals and their environments can never be understood separately from one another – development always needs to be considered within the context in which it is taking place. It is for this reason that we have organised the material in the first three chapters of the book, which cover children's development from 0–18 years, using an ecological framework, considering the contributions made by the child, the parents, and the wider family and environment, as well as the interactions between them. This approach mirrors the assessment frameworks used in social work with children and families throughout the UK (e.g. DH/DfEE/HO, 2000).

Ecological theory also reminds us that most social problems are the product of interactions between various factors in different spheres of people's lives, pointing the way to the issues that will need to be addressed (often simultaneously) for preventive and early intervention strategies to be effective. It therefore informs much of the material presented in Part II of the book as well, which examines social work practice with different groups of children.

Structure of the book

Part I: The knowledge base

Chapters 1, 2 and 3 cover children's development and relationships at different stages in their lives, roughly equating to their pre-school, primary and secondary school years. Each of these chapters uses an ecological framework to examine children's innate contribution to their own development, alongside that of their parents and the wider family and environmental conditions in which they are growing up, considering the interactions which occur, for example, between the characteristics of their family, school and neighbourhood, their biological and cognitive development, and their social and emotional behaviour.

Part II: Professional practice

In **Chapter 4** we look at the issues involved in **working with 'children in need'**, including the reasons for children being 'in need', the effects on parents and children of living in disadvantaged circumstances, and different approaches to the assessment of needs and the provision of effective services, with an emphasis on prevention and early intervention.

In **Chapter 5** we examine the role of social workers in **safeguarding and promoting the welfare of children**, considering the extent, causes and effects of child abuse and neglect, as well as official responses to it, including the development of child protection legislation, policy and procedures across the UK, preventive and therapeutic programmes and interventions, and the role of communities and wider society in safeguarding children.

Chapter 6 is concerned with **children looked after away from home by local authorities and with leaving care**. The chapter covers the characteristics of 'looked after children', the issues involved in prevention, reunification with families, and promoting the quality of care, including the role of education and the regulations governing visits, care plans and reviews. We also consider some of the specific knowledge needed for working effectively with children in foster care, residential care, placed for adoption, and leaving care.

In **Chapter 7** we consider the disadvantages and social exclusion commonly experienced by **children with disabilities** and their families, and the policies and approaches to practice which attempt to address these issues, including the way that social work practice is based on a synthesis of medical and social models of disability, the development of integrated approaches to assessment and services provision, and the importance of communication skills.

In **Chapter 8**, which focuses on **social work with young offenders**, we consider the extent of children's antisocial and offending behaviour, as well as the risk and protective factors involved and the youth justice policies and systems which have been developed in different parts of the UK to address these issues, including evidence about the effectiveness of the main interventions and programmes currently in use.

In **Chapter 9** we consider how to promote **children's mental health** and respond appropriately when problems arise. We include information about the prevalence, persistence and consequences of mental health problems in childhood, as well as the key role of schools in promoting children's mental health and working with pupils who have less severe problems. We end by considering the work undertaken with vulnerable groups of children and those who have more severe problems, including the use of cognitive behavioural therapy and parenting programmes.

Whilst the six chapters which make up Part II of the book focus on practice with the main groups of children with whom social workers are likely to be engaged, there are inevitably other groups of children whom it has not been possible to feature in this way. However, this does not mean that they have been excluded altogether, with information about children who are acting as carers, for example, being included in Chapters 3 and 9, and consideration of some of the issues involved in working with children from different ethnic groups, including refugee and asylum-seeking children, threaded throughout the book.

In a book intended to be useful to social workers and other practitioners working with children and families in different parts of the UK, consideration has also had to be given to the balance between a UK-wide and a more country-specific focus. The way that this issue has been addressed is generally to provide a UK-wide perspective, with country-specific information (or sign-posting to more detailed sources) provided where appropriate. To give an example, while much of the material included in Chapter 6 about working with children in need applies equally across the whole of the UK, the different approaches to dealing with young offenders across the UK means that more country-specific material is included in Chapter 8 which deals with this area of practice.

Practice pointers, key messages and additional resources

Each chapter contains a number of **practice pointers,** designed to stimulate reflection on readers' own skills, knowledge and experience in relation to important issues, prompting consideration of questions relevant for social work practice with children. Each chapter concludes with a summary of the **key messages for practice,** drawn from the information presented, and a final section identifying **additional resources** which offer further practical help and guidance.

Terminology

It is also worth pointing out some of the decisions that have been made about the terminology used throughout the book, in order to make it more readable and to cut down on unnecessary repetition. Most obviously, perhaps, readers will notice that we have generally referred to children across the whole age range (0–18 years) simply as 'children', rather than the composite phrase 'children and young people', although we use more specific terms (e.g. 'infants', 'adolescents') when these are appropriate. In a similar way, we also use the single word 'parents' to include not only birth parents but also other 'caregivers', with more specific terms (e.g. 'step-parents', 'foster carers') used when they are relevant.

PART I

The Knowledge Base

Introduction: an overview of childhood in the UK today

An ecological framework

As discussed in the Preface, research demonstrates that the well-being of children depends on interactions between their individual characteristics, those of their parents, and the wider family and environmental circumstances in which they live (e.g. Belsky and Jaffee, 2006). To give one simple example, parents may not be providing a child with appropriate guidance and boundaries, perhaps failing to deal effectively with misbehaviour in the home, or allowing the child more freedom away from the home than the child is capable of exercising responsibly. This is likely to affect adversely not only children's social and emotional development, but also their learning at school and relationships in the community. Every aspect of children's behaviour and development is interconnected in this way, with the characteristics of the child, parents, and the wider family and environmental circumstances being in a constant state of interaction. This *ecological* approach to understanding human development (Bronfenbrenner, 1979) provides the framework for the three chapters that make up Part I of the book, which examine the development of children in relation to their individual, family and community characteristics and circumstances, at different stages in their lives.

However, before going on to look in detail at the development of individual children at different stages in their lives, it is important to consider some of the wider issues in society that set the context for childhood in the UK today.

Families in the UK: a story of change and continuity

First of all, it is important to recognise that concepts such as 'family' and 'childhood' are *socially constructed*, with their meanings contested and dependent on who is doing the defining, and the historical, political, cultural, social and economic perspectives on which they are drawing (Jenks, 1982; Fox Harding, 1996). This makes it imperative that social work practice is founded on reliable sources of knowledge, such as the General Household Survey (GHS), which has been undertaken by the Office for National Statistics on an annual basis since 1970. The GHS published in 2010 reveals that people living in what are often uncritically referred to as 'traditional families', comprising a couple with dependent children, are now in a minority in the UK, having fallen from just over half of the population in 1961 to just over a third by 2009. However, this still means that more than three-quarters of dependent children were living with both of their parents at that time. Whilst a decline in the popularity of marriage means that the proportion of children born outside of marriage has steadily increased since the 1970s, reaching 45 per cent of all live births in 2008, two-thirds of such births were registered by parents living at the same address. Children not living with both parents were usually living with one parent (most often the mother), or one parent and a step-parent. However, as ecological theory suggests, variations in family form and household composition do not occur by chance, but are strongly influenced by the wider circumstances of different groups within society. In 2009, for example, largely as a result of underlying demographic and socio-economic factors, a greater proportion of dependent children from the Asian and Asian British ethnic group in the UK were living in married couple families than those from a white background (86 compared to 62 per cent), whereas more than half of black and black British dependent children lived with a lone parent, compared with only one in seven of those from an Asian background, who were the least likely to do so (ONS, 2010).

More than one in three children in the UK now experience the divorce or separation of their parents before the age of 16 (Walker, 2009). Studies in which children have been interviewed following family breakdown (e.g. Dunn and Deater-Deckard, 2001) reveal that they would have liked more information about what was happening, as well as greater opportunities to express their feelings and views. Most children go through a period of unhappiness when their parents separate or divorce, but given sufficient support and stability the majority adjust successfully to their changed circumstances (Rodgers and Pryor, 1998; Mooney et al., 2009). The risk factors associated with poorer outcomes for children following family breakdown include poor parent–child relationships prior to the separation, and high levels of parental distress or conflict, financial hardship and multiple changes in family structure and circumstances after the separation (Maclean, 2004). The child's age when parental separation occurs can also play a part, with teenagers often finding it more difficult to adjust to becoming part of a step-family, for instance, than younger children (Hawthorne et al., 2003). However, a number of protective factors may also be significant, with on-going family support (particularly that provided by grandparents), for example, often playing an important role during and after the process of family breakdown (Perry et al., 2000).

The impact of parental problems

The capacity of parents to meet the developmental needs of their children can be affected by a wide range of problems (DH/DfEE/HO, 2000). These include parental mental health problems, a history of childhood abuse, learning disability, substance misuse and domestic violence, some of which may co-exist (Rutter, 1989; Falkov, 2002). The mechanisms by which these problems affect a parent's capacity to meet their child's needs include difficulties in organizing their own lives, controlling their emotions, interacting appropriately with the child and neglecting their own needs (Cleaver et al., 2011). Parental behaviour which is characterised by chronic insensitivity, unresponsiveness, anger or criticism is likely to affect adversely the development and maintenance of the attachment processes (discussed in the next three chapters) which are a central component of children's development and well-being. Parental depression (Stroud, 1997) or substance misuse (Kroll and Taylor, 2003), for example, may render parents incapable of consistently providing the sort of warm, responsive and age-appropriate behaviours which are the foundation of secure attachments.

However, as ecological theory would suggest, the existence of parental problems does not inevitably lead to negative outcomes for children. Rather, children's well-being depends on the interactions between the risk *and* protective factors which exist at individual, family and community levels of influence. In the context of significant parental problems, potential protective factors include the presence of a caring and dependable adult who is not experiencing significant problems, support provided by siblings and other relatives, friends and neighbours, and the availability of effective parenting and family support services. There is a considerable body of evidence which demonstrates the benefits that families, especially those living in disadvantaged circumstances, can derive from protective factors of this nature (for reviews see Jack, 1997b, 2000; Jack and Gill, 2010a).

Legislation and social policies affecting children and families

All developed countries around the world now recognise 'childhood' as a distinct phase in human development, typically defined as the period from birth to 18 years of age (as it is in the UK), and requiring specific legislation and social policies. However, debates persist in relation to the appropriate balance to strike between, for example, children's rights to self-determination on the one hand, and the need for adults to decide what is in children's best interests on the other.

The most significant development in the international recognition of children's rights is the European Convention on Human Rights, incorporated into UK legislation by the Human Rights Act 1998, and the United Nations Convention on the Rights of the Child (UNCRC), ratified by the UK in 1990. The UNCRC is based on a set of fundamental principles which include the rights to life, protection from abuse and neglect, education, and to have a say in decisions that affect you. Whilst it is not part of UK law, as such, many of the principles on which it is based *have* been incorporated into UK legislation, primarily through the Children Acts of 1989 and 2004 in England and Wales, the Children (Scotland) Act 1995, and the Children (Northern Ireland) Order 1995.

Practitioners obviously need to be well informed about the full range of child welfare legislation, regulations and statutory guidance in force in the country in which they are working. Whilst it is beyond the scope of this book to examine these in detail for each of the four countries that make up the UK, information about their application in practice, with different groups of children, is provided in Part II of the book.

Although there are some significant differences between the legislative frameworks operating in different parts of the UK, such as the children's hearing system in Scotland, the emphasis on children's rights in Wales, and the joint health and social services boards which operate in Northern Ireland, there are also many similarities. For example, the child's welfare is the paramount consideration in court proceedings involving children across the UK, with courts (and local authorities) required to take into consideration the wishes and feelings of children before making any decisions which affect their lives. Furthermore, the legislation in all four countries is based on the principle that children are generally best looked after within their families, using the concept of 'parental responsibility' to ensure that both parents have the opportunity to play a full part in the child's upbringing, with legal proceedings only used if this is better for the child.

There are also some common areas of inconsistency in the way that the law relating to children across the UK is implemented. This is particularly evident in relation to the rights of 16- and 17-year-olds, who are often denied the full range of support available to younger children whilst being ineligible for many of the benefits available to adults (Fortin, 2009). This highlights the fact that legislation is only as good as the way it is implemented, and that many outcomes for children and families depend on the resources provided by the state to support them. Practitioners therefore need to be aware of the wider social policy context within which they are working, particularly the way that social and economic conditions affect the lives of children and families.

The impact of poverty and inequality

When the Conservative government led by Margaret Thatcher first came to power in 1979 the UK had historically low levels of child poverty and income inequality. However, as a result of the social policies implemented by successive governments during the 1980s and early 1990s, both of these measures climbed steeply. By the time that New Labour came to power in 1997 the UK was top of the European child poverty league, with a third of its children (4.2 million) living below the poverty line, as defined by the European standard, i.e. living in a household with an income of less than 60 per cent of the country's median, after housing costs. Income inequality in the UK had also reached historically unprecedented levels (ONS, 2004) – even after tax and benefits had been taken into account, the richest tenth of households took home more than nine times as much income as the poorest tenth of households at that time (DWP, 2005). It is also important to recognise that wealth in the UK, consisting of assets such as property, shares and savings, is distributed even more unequally than income. In 2001, for example, the richest 1 per cent of the population owned nearly a quarter of the UK's overall wealth, whilst the poorer 50 per cent of the population only held one-twentieth of these assets between them (ONS, 2004).

Despite introducing policies specifically designed to reduce child poverty, the Labour governments in power between 1997 and 2010 only managed to take a relatively small proportion of children out of poverty, and income inequality remained relatively unaffected, leaving the UK near the top of the international inequality league table (OECD, 2008; Joyce et al., 2010). More recently, the global financial crisis, combined with the huge cuts in public spending implemented by the Coalition Government elected in 2010, have further increased child and family poverty and income inequality.

In developed countries such as the UK, it might be argued that high levels of relative poverty and income inequality are not particularly significant. If a combination of paid employment and welfare benefits ensures that all households have enough money to at least meet their basic needs, why does it matter if some people have higher levels of income (and wealth) than others? However, this would be to ignore the evidence that has been accumulating around the developed world for many years now, which clearly shows that child poverty has adverse effects on children's development and future life chances (e.g. Jack and Gill, 2010b). Furthermore, many health and social problems are worse in more unequal societies (Wilkinson, 2005). The most significant factor which explains these findings is the chronic sense of unfairness experienced by disadvantaged individuals and groups within unequal societies. Persistent feelings of anger, frustration, helplessness, low self-esteem, anxiety and vulnerability seriously undermine personal health and well-being, resulting in higher levels of premature death (including suicide), infant mortality, drug and alcohol abuse, crime (and imprisonment), poor educational achievement, and child abuse and neglect (Wilkinson and Pickett, 2009).

Social and economic divisions on the scale found within the UK at the present time also have damaging consequences for the whole of society. Not only do they hugely increase the costs of providing sufficient health and social care to meet the high levels of need which exist, but they also reduce the effectiveness of those services because of the barriers of fear and mistrust which exist between the potential users of services and the organisations and practitioners providing them. This is the context within which social work in the UK has to operate, with the children and families in the greatest need more often than not also those who are most reluctant to seek or accept the services intended to help them (Jack and Stepney, 1995; Jack, 1997a).

Whilst social workers and other child welfare professionals, on their own, cannot be expected to make any significant impact on the levels of child poverty and income inequality found in the UK, nonetheless it is important that practitioners recognise the underlying cause of many of the health and social problems confronting them on a daily basis. It is also important that practitioners are aware that some social groups are more likely than others to be living on low incomes because of the way that the society in which they live is structured. The groups most likely to experience poverty in the UK include lone parent families, households with one or more disabled members, those who are unemployed, children in workless or large families, people from minority ethnic groups (particularly those of Pakistani, Bangladeshi or black non-Caribbean ethnic origin), and asylum-seeking and refugee families (Scottish Refugee Council, 2006; DWP, 2010). Although individual households move in and out of poverty from year to year, income mobility in the UK is actually very limited, which means that the families most at risk of experiencing poverty remain largely the same from year to year (Hills, 2004).

Geographical variations in disadvantage and child well-being

Besides varying according to the characteristics of different groups within society, child poverty and income inequality are also geographically distributed across the UK, with some areas experiencing much higher levels of disadvantage than others. Each of the four countries of the UK periodically compiles a geographical 'index of multiple deprivation' (IMD), which integrates data from a large number of indicators into domains typically including income, employment, health, education, housing, crime and the environment (Statistics for Wales, 2008; Scottish Government, 2009; DCLG, 2010; NISRA, 2010). The latest version of the IMD for England, for example, reveals that most urban centres, including in particular the conurbations of Manchester, Liverpool and Newcastle and their surrounding metropolitan areas, as well as those in Yorkshire and Humberside, the West Midlands and the north-east quarter of London (particularly Newham, Hackney and Tower Hamlets), contain areas with very high levels of deprivation. However, there are also pockets of deprivation in more affluent areas of the country as well, with over half of the 326 local authority districts in England, for example, containing at least one area which is amongst the 10 per cent most deprived (DCLG, 2010).

Similar patterns in the geographical distribution of deprivation are found in Scotland, Wales and Northern Ireland. Despite regional and neighbourhood policies designed to reduce the gap between the most and least deprived areas in each of the four countries of the UK over recent years, these patterns have remained relatively stable. For example, seven out of eight of the most deprived areas in England on the 2010 IMD were in the same category on the 2007 index, while more than eight out of ten of the most deprived areas in Scotland were in the same category on the *two* previous indices.

The same approach to collecting and analysing area-based data has also been used over recent years to construct indices of child well-being that allow comparisons to be made between the circumstances and development of children at national and local levels. The domains on which these indices are typically based include children's health, material circumstances, education, family and peer relationships, behaviour and risks, subjective well-being, and housing and environment. On these indices, child well-being in the UK is currently very poor compared with that in other developed countries around the world, being ranked 24 out of 29 countries in Europe, and bottom of 21 developed countries around the world (UNICEF, 2007; Bradshaw and Richardson, 2009). Although analysis of these results reveals that there is some relationship between a country's overall level of wealth (or average household income) and the well-being of its children, this does not explain the appearance of poorer countries like Spain and Slovenia near the top of the European index, or the lowly position of the UK on both the UN and European indices. The main factor which does explain the UK's poor performance is its high levels of income inequality (Pickett and Wilkinson, 2008). The combination of a large gap between rich and poor, together with selective welfare state provision for families and poor quality interpersonal relationships, produces a particularly toxic environment for children's development in the UK at the present time. The quality of life experienced by children across the UK is demonstrably poorer than that of children in more equal societies, especially where they either have better universal welfare state provision for families, as in the Netherlands and the Scandinavian countries, or better quality interpersonal relationships between children and within extended family networks, such as in Spain and Slovenia (Bradshaw and Richardson, 2009).

A child well-being index has also been developed at local area level within England (DCLG, 2009). As with multiple deprivation, many of the local authority districts with the lowest child well-being scores are found in the major urban areas and their associated conurbations and, as a general rule, the more deprived an area the lower its level of child well-being, although there are some notable exceptions, where well-being is much better (or worse) than predicted by the level of deprivation in the area. This clearly indicates that other factors, including the social and cultural 'climate' of different areas, also plays an important role in child and family well-being (Jack, 2011). Some of the implications of this conclusion for social work practice with families living in impoverished circumstances are explored in Part II of the book, especially in Chapter 4, which focuses on work with 'children in need'.

CHAPTER 1

Child development: the foundation years

CHAPTER OVERVIEW

In this chapter we use an ecological lens to examine the way that the development of children is influenced from birth by their characteristics and those of their parents, as well as the wider family and environmental circumstances in which they are living. The changes related to the child's own 'contribution' are subdivided into three broad areas of development – physical; cognitive and language; and personal, social and emotional. This chapter takes what we refer to as the 'foundation years' as its focus, covering the period from birth to the age of five, which are marked by major changes in all areas of children's development as they make the transition from dependent infant to increasingly independent school-aged child.

Introduction

As outlined in more detail in the Introduction to this first part of the book, the ecology of human development (Bronfenbrenner, 1979) conceptualises individuals, families and communities as social systems, within which different elements are in a constant process of interaction. At the individual level, for example, the social and emotional aspects of childrens' development are likely to influence their physical development, because children who feel safe and secure will have the confidence to test their physical capacities as well. However, it is also important to understand that the systems interact with one another as well. So, childrens' social and emotional development is also dependent on the characteristics of their parents, wider family members and peers, all of whom are also influenced by the wider environments within which they live.

The child's contribution

Physical development

0–12 months

The first year of life is a time of immense physical change and growth, with most babies, for example, doubling their birth weight. From being able to move through involuntary reflexes only, at birth, infants gain increasing control, developing motor skills in two broad patterns, from the head to the feet, and from the torso outwards. Babies gain control over their heads before they can sit, and move their arms to swipe at objects before they can use their hands to grasp them (Gesell, 1952). As infants master the motor sequence, they also learn that they have more control over their world and are no longer totally dependent on others to meet some of their needs.

Although it is important to keep in mind that each child is an individual and will develop at their own pace, there is growing evidence to support the existence of a common pattern, including sensitive or critical periods when learning from particular experiences is optimum. Opportunities lost or inappropriate experiences during sensitive periods may lead to difficulties in the future. Advances in neuroscience are making increasing links between these sensitive periods and 'surges' in particular areas of brain activity, which are followed by periods of stability in which innate processes and experience are integrated and consolidated into the architecture of the brain. For example, babies are born with the potential to speak any language, but between six and twelve months their ability to differentiate sounds not used in their native language begins to decline, indicating that unused connections in the brain are replaced by others which support more specialised functioning. Sensitive periods also influence emotional development in ways that it is often important for social workers to recognise. For instance, although children who experience a very emotionally deprived environment in their first year of life, and are subsequently separated from their birth families, should still be capable of forming close relationships with new carers, the attachments they form may never be as secure as they would have been if they had not suffered an initial period of emotional deprivation (Robinson, 2008).

1–5 years

After the first 12 months, although children's physical development proceeds at a slower pace than in the first year of life, major changes are still taking place. Growth charts, which typically plot height, weight and head circumference at different ages, are routinely used by health professionals to monitor physical development, with measurements significantly outside the normal range frequently used as markers, either of a failure to thrive, where growth is significantly below the average for children of a similar age, or where excess weight or obesity is a concern. There are many versions (e.g. WHO 2009), but it is important to remember that there are wide variations in 'normal' attainments, and average values do not take account of particular cultural, biological and environmental factors.

Besides overall growth, body *proportions* also change significantly during the foundation years. The torso and limbs lengthen, lowering the body's centre of gravity, which enhances balance, coordination and control of movements involving the large muscles of the arms and legs. This is known as 'gross motor development', with the first tentative attempts at walking unaided, that usually occur between ten and eighteen months, progressively extending to incorporate running, jumping, changing speed and direction, and catching and throwing objects with growing accuracy. Increasing mobility places greater responsibility on parents to ensure the safety of pre-school children, particularly as the single major avoidable cause of death in under fives in England is accidents in the home. Although overall death rates have declined over the last two decades, this is not the case for children in more disadvantaged families, for example where no adult is in paid employment (Edwards et al., 2006; Dyson et al., 2010).

Smaller movements of the arms, hands and fingers, known as 'fine motor development', also become more refined, with self-care skills such as independent feeding and dressing progressing alongside the ability to grasp a writing implement using the thumb and fingers rather than a fist. Making marks on paper, initially involving random scribbling but progressing to more controlled drawing, is perhaps the most universal form of fine motor play, and even in the early foundation years children understand that art can be used symbolically to represent ideas. Young children are able to tell stories about their scribbles, although at this stage the ideas may be generated after the drawing is finished and change in the retelling. Children of around three or four years, with a concept already in mind, begin to produce simple representations of the people and things that are important to them, and the stories attached now tend to be more consistent. Drawing, painting, sculpting and singing are all important ways in which children reinforce their learning (Trawick-Smith, 2010).

Cognitive and language development

0–2 years

Babies are innately social beings, ready to interact with those around them from birth. Hearing is the most highly developed sense at this early stage, and we know that, even before birth, the sound of the mother's heartbeat and voice are transmitted to the foetus, so that newborns are already familiar with some of the sounds they encounter outside the womb. They respond to voices and turn towards sounds to investigate them, as well as using movement to communicate, for example by kicking and using their arms to reach for people and things of interest. A great deal of initial communication, however, is through crying, which begins as a generalised way of drawing attention to their basic needs, but gradually evolves to signal more specific needs and wants, alongside the early stages of language, such as cooing and babbling, with monosyllables later put together into single words, as the precursor to the development of meaningful sentences. All this activity leads to the important discovery that their actions can cause others to respond in certain ways.

The development of independent movement during the first year allows infants to locate objects within a three-dimensional world, making reference to landmarks other than themselves, possibly contributing to their understanding of themselves as objects in space (Bee and Boyd, 2010). This is what Piaget, one of the leading theorists about children's cognitive development, referred to as the 'sensori-motor stage', when infants first develop a sense of 'object permanence' through touching and handling objects, understanding that things are solid, permanent and continue to exist, even when out of sight (Piaget and Inhelder, 1969). At this age, infants will actively search, albeit for a very short time, for something that they have seen but which is now out of sight.

2–5 years

In the years from two to five children develop their abilities to think beyond the objects that are immediately present to imagining future events and recalling past ones. According to Piaget (2001), the thinking adopted by most young children at first relies on the senses and environmental cues. Children at this stage tend to have difficulty coordinating more than one idea or activity, so that giving pre-school children more than one instruction at a time is likely to be pointless. Understanding that properties and amounts stay the same, even when physical appearances change, and the ability to group similar objects together, first based on one characteristic and later using two or more traits, also develops at this time. Very young children will focus on a variety of different aspects of a situation or problem at random, but by the end of the foundation years children are more able to pay attention for an extended period of time, and to select those things that are critical for either solving a problem or gaining the approval of adults. In a clear demonstration of ecological theory, these early cognitive developments are integrally connected to children's social behaviour, and they become eager to carry out responsibilities, help with familiar tasks and take pride in their accomplishments.

Cognitive developments also promote the ability to link and interpret cause and effect, which Piaget called 'transductive reasoning'. Pre-school children tend to put two immediate events together and assume, sometimes erroneously, that one caused the other. For example, if a child is disciplined for noisy behaviour and is then immediately told about the illness of a parent, she or he is likely to feel guilty for 'causing' the illness.

Practice pointer 1.1

Given this rudimentary understanding of 'cause and effect', it is important for social workers to ensure that parents and other professionals working with pre-school children are careful to explain the true nature of any relationship between concurrently occurring events.

This is also an important time for developing 'theories of mind', or what Rutter and Rutter (1992) refer to as 'everyday mind reading', in which children establish beliefs about what the mind is, how it works, and how it might be controlled. Having a theory of mind allows children to attribute thoughts and desires to others, predict or explain their actions, and distinguish between positive and negative motives and intentions. A growing awareness of their own thought processes, and an understanding that emotions come from within, are important in helping children to develop the ability to control their emotions, modify their behaviour and interact more effectively with those around them. Children who display aggressive behaviour, for example, are frequently less able to describe accurately the intentions of their peers, more often interpreting accidental events as intentional or malicious acts. Between two to three years of age children begin to move away from rigid thinking tied to their own perspective ('egocentrism'), towards a more general understanding that others see or experience things differently. At around four to five years of age, they understand that the mind can represent objects or events accurately or inaccurately ('false belief reasoning'), and that people will act on the basis of their representations, even if those representations are inaccurate. The development of false belief reasoning strengthens children's sensitivity to the perspectives of others and helps to foster their burgeoning attempts to 'put themselves in others' shoes', marking a genuine perceptual change which has a consistent 'step like' trajectory, common across different cultures. Interestingly, children with one or more siblings appear to attain false belief understanding at an earlier age, and it is this ability, amongst others, that appears to be impaired in individuals with an autistic spectrum disorder (Wellman and Hickling, 1994; Wellman et al., 2000).

The development of communication and the use of language is at the heart of young children's learning (Roulstone et al., 2011). Early experiences are crucial, and children thrive in relationships in which adults respond to their initiation, often called 'contingent responding'. Even before they can speak, children use gesture to communicate, and it has been shown that there is a positive impact on later vocabulary where mothers themselves use gestures and 'translate' their children's early gestures into words. Day-to-day verbal interactions need to be frequent, using a wide vocabulary and sentences of increasing length to encourage conversation, rather than simply using language to direct, discourage or prohibit behaviour. Questions framed to require more than a 'yes/no' answer, or that test children's knowledge, understanding or feelings, encourage them to become confident oral communicators (Herrenkohl et al., 1984; Rowe, 2008). Children quickly discover the power of language as they attempt to influence others around them, and bargaining may begin to replace some of the earlier physical aggression, defiant behaviour or tantrums often associated with thwarted toddlers.

The development of symbolic thought is another crucial milestone in children's cognitive development at this age, and play, involving imagination and enactment of make-believe roles, comes to dominate much pre-school activity. Children readily use every-day objects to represent something completely different, and in their play with peers transform themselves into imaginary characters in which they try out a variety of roles. Skill at this sort of play is closely linked to false belief understanding, and the joint planning and negotiation involved in increasingly complex themes and plots encourages the development of children's positive social and verbal interactions, providing the foundation for later social and emotional competence.

Personal, social and emotional development

0–12 months
At birth, infants show a limited range of emotions, with cooing noises used to signal comfort, and crying to signal discomfort that needs attention, although they are unable to distinguish between different kinds of discomfort to begin with. Gradually, however, different needs become associated with particular responses from their carers, enabling babies to differentiate between types of discomfort, and marking the beginnings of a rudimentary under-standing of cause and effect. This process of consistent and repeated nurturing, known as 'operant conditioning' within social learning theory, results in ever strengthening feelings of trust and security (Skinner, 1948). However, infants who have been repeat-edly neglected or rejected by their carers do not develop feelings of security and have difficulty developing the skills needed to socialise with others.

It is crucial that infants have the opportunity to develop a secure emotional bond or attachment to at least one person, which provides the foundations for the 'safe base' needed to extend their development in the social world beyond the immediate family. The concept of 'attachment' was first used by John Bowlby (1969) to refer to a particular form of relationship between children and their mothers. He viewed attachment as a biologically driven form of behaviour designed to ensure the infant received comfort, love and attention from their mother. The child's behaviour, particularly when they experience anxiety, ensures close contact with an adult who can provide both protection and stimulation (Howe, 1995). Subsequent work by Mary Ainsworth and colleagues (1978), which involved exposing children to brief periods of separation from their mothers, identified the features of a secure pattern of attachment, as well as three forms of insecure attachment – 'avoidant', 'ambivalent/resistant' and 'disorganised'.

In Ainsworth's 'strange situation' test, infants classified as having a secure attachment played happily in the presence of their mothers, showed distress at separation, but were easily comforted on their return. They also showed some wariness of strangers and a strong preference for their mothers when fearful, anxious or ill. Securely attached infants first began to show a fear of strangers and anxiety when separated from their mothers between the ages of six and nine months. However, infants classified as having insecure (avoidant) attachments tended to display a general sense of wariness and more inhibited play, and were not distressed on separation from their mothers, either ignoring or avoiding them on their return. In sharp contrast, insecure (ambivalent/resistant) infants were highly distressed at the point of separation and very difficult to pacify on reunion with their mothers, often both demanding and resisting parental attention, as well as being reluctant to return to independent play. Infants identified as insecure (disorganised) showed elements of both of the other categories of insecure attachment, displaying either confusion or a total lack of emotions when separated and reunited with their mothers. As we will consider in the next section on parents' contributions to children's development, these different patterns of attachment behaviour represent strategies adopted by the child to cope with different forms of parental insensitivity to meeting their needs.

The proportions of children who display each type of attachment behaviour has been found to be similar in cross-cultural and intercountry comparisons, with over half (55–60 per cent) typically demonstrating secure attachments to their mothers, followed by nearly one in four (23 per cent) showing insecure (avoidant) patterns of behaviour, one in seven (15 per cent) insecure (disorganised) patterns, and one in every 12 to 13 children (8 per cent) being classified as having insecure (ambivalent/resistant) attachments (van Ijzendoorn et al., 1992).

More recent research (Boushel et al., 2000) has demonstrated that secure attachments are:

• Multiple: attachments can be made to more than one person.
• Adaptable: attachments are not limited to mothers, with the quality of the relationship being more important than the gender or other characteristics of the carer.

- Flexible: attachment patterns may vary between different carers, and they may also change across the life course.
- Influenced by culture: attachment patterns are also influenced by culturally determined ideas about children and parenting.

Emotional attachment is an important concept in many areas of social work practice, and we consider its influence on later development in Chapters 2 and 3, together with more specific implications for practice with different groups of children in Part II of the book.

Some of the behaviour that babies use to express their needs and wants is innate and can be related to three broad categories of temperament – 'easy', 'slow to warm up' and 'difficult'. Most babies have an easy temperament, adjusting readily to new situations and settling into a regular schedule of feeding and sleeping. Babies with a 'slow to warm up' temperament approach life more cautiously and are more likely to become overwhelmed or overstimulated by activity around them, and tend to respond slowly or quietly to hunger and other discomforts, making it more difficult for their parents to know when their babies have such feelings. Babies with a 'difficult' temperament engage in almost constant physical activity and are generally restless and easily distracted. They can be very hard to soothe as well as finding it more difficult to soothe themselves, potentially leading to parental stress, anxiety and doubts about their parenting skills and abilities (Bee and Boyd, 2010).

Practice pointer 1.2

The temperament of parents can be quite different to that of their infants. If this causes significant problems, practitioners may need to help parents understand what is happening and to adapt their parenting style to fit with that of the baby (rather than the other way around).

1–5 years
Early childhood is a crucial period for the formation of positive feelings about oneself, about others, and about the world beyond the immediate family. The warmth and contingency of relationships are of central significance in a young child's emotional development, alongside the need for structure which brings predictability and control to his or her everyday experiences

(Laible and Thompson, 1998). Children who are nurtured, encouraged to experiment and take risks, and who are accepted by adults and peers are likely to be emotionally well adjusted (Erikson, 1995). Supporting the creative processes of young children, rather than focusing on a perfect end-product, is more likely to promote their feelings of success and 'self-efficacy'. Conversely, when children are repeatedly neglected, discouraged and led to believe that their efforts are wrong, a sense of worthlessness and guilt is likely to develop. Although feelings of guilt are necessary, to some extent, in helping children to assume responsibility for their own actions, where there is continual or harsh criticism and punishment, overwhelming guilt leads children gradually to cease their efforts and to construct an understanding of themselves as 'naughty' or 'bad'. Children immobilised by guilt are likely to be less confident and remain on the fringes of groups, either ignored or rejected by peers, setting up a negative cycle which further restricts the development of their imagination and play skills, resulting in yet more isolation from peers and greater dependency on adults.

Making relationships and understanding others are two key developmental challenges during the foundation years. Historically, it was thought that very young children were too egocentric to show empathy or altruism (e.g. Piaget, 1932), but research now suggests that many pre-school children are capable of showing these traits. Empathy, for example, can be fostered in the early years by parents who are warm, responsive and nurturing, and who model sharing and cooperation (Rah and Parke, 2008), whilst children who fail to develop empathy may display negative social behaviours, particularly aggression, which can lead to rejection by peers and low social participation. However, it is important for parents and professionals to be able to distinguish between aggression, on the one hand, and appropriate assertiveness and rough and tumble play, on the other. Whilst acts of aggression are likely to require an immediate response, conflicts or displays of assertiveness may not require adult intervention, which can deprive children of opportunities to solve social problems for themselves (Trawick-Smith, 2010). The ability to cope with and manage feelings, using 'effortful control' to both inhibit and activate responses to instruction, or to delay gratification, is therefore important (Rothbart et al., 2007).

Perhaps because these 'unseen' abilities are developing at the same time as more visible skills, such as mobility and language, the personal, social and emotional aspects of development can receive less recognition than they deserve. Well regulated emotions support higher cognitive functions, such as planning and decision-making, but when poorly controlled they can interfere with attention and attainment. From a social learning perspective, Vygotsky (1986) posited that children move from regulation by others to self-regulation through a process of internalisation. He ascribed a pivotal role to the externally audible 'self-talk' of toddlers as a bridge towards the creation of internal speech, later transformed into thought, which children (and adults) use to regulate their behaviour. Differences in how children understand and regulate their emotions are closely associated with acceptance by peers, successful friendships and the positive perceptions of carers and teachers in pre-school and nursery settings (Ladd, 2006; DCSF, 2010a). Children's ability to regulate their emotions is enhanced where parents and caregivers explicitly discuss feelings, helping them to frame in words their growing awareness of themselves in relation to others (Evangelou et al., 2009).

The parents' contribution

Children's developmental needs must be met in a timely, consistent and responsive way if they are to become caring, cooperative, creative and contributing young citizens (Ramey and Ramey, 2004). Parents' own attachment histories are an important element in the development of attachment relationships with their children. Where parents have experienced an abusive or neglectful childhood, it is the ability to talk about, reflect on and make sense of those experiences that will enhance their own sense of security and enable them to be available and sensitive to their infant's needs (Fonargy et al., 1994).

Lending support to the ecological approach taken throughout this book, Michael Rutter, perhaps the leading child development researcher in the UK over the past 50 years, suggests that insecure attachments tend to develop 'when parents are depressed or exhibit personality difficulties, when the marital relationship is strained, when there are external stresses, and when there is a lack of social support (Rutter, 1991, p. 358). More specifically, insecure (avoidant) children can be seen to be attempting to 'parent themselves' (Fahlberg, 1991) to avoid being rejected by their parents, whereas insecure (ambivalent/resistant) children, who can be clingy, nervous, angry and resentful, are responding to insensitive, inconsistent and even chaotic parenting. Insecure (disorganised) children, by way of contrast, who can appear to lack any defensive strategy in the face of overwhelming anxiety, have often been abused or severely neglected (Howe, 1995). The ways in which these different forms of attachment behaviour, which emerge during the foundation years, are consolidated during later stages of children's development are discussed in the next two chapters, with the implications for social work practice with different groups of children considered in Part II of the book.

Research has identified the main contributions parents can make to their children's development, across different cultures (Ramey and Ramey, 2004):

- Providing a 'safe base', whilst also encouraging exploration: widening the child's experiences but remaining available to offer comfort when needed.
- Mentoring in basic skills: including the provision of appropriate opportunities for making independent choices.
- Celebrating developmental advances: supporting effort and praising attempts at new skills, regardless of achievement, and encouraging persistence.
- Rehearsing and extending new skills: supporting play but allowing children to take the lead, offering hints and tips to promote independent problem-solving.
- Protecting from inappropriate disapproval, teasing and punishment: creating a nurturing and supportive environment in which children feel successful.
- Communicating richly and responsively: using child-centred speech that goes beyond just prohibiting or limiting behaviour, to elicit two-way conversations.
- Guiding and limiting behaviour: providing consistent boundaries, talking about emotions and seeking children's own explanations of actions and reactions, modelling and demonstrating emotional control and acceptable behaviour.

Meeting children's needs in the first year

The first year of life is characterised by complete dependency, during which parents are responsible for meeting all of an infant's basic needs, including food of the right kind and quantity, sleep, nappy changing, and sufficient clean clothing and bedding to maintain an appropriate body temperature. However, as has already been noted, the task of parenting is also dependent, to some extent, on the temperament of the child. Where babies have an easy temperament and do not fuss, it is possible for parents to overlook some of their needs; whilst infants who are slow to warm up may not provide sufficiently strident messages to galvanise parents into action; and parents of babies with difficult temperaments are often made to feel inadequate, mistakenly believing that they are to blame for their baby's mood.

Physical and emotional availability

Parents need to be both physically and emotionally available to their children in the early stages of their development. There is evidence to suggest that parents who respond promptly and with warmth to their infants' demands at three months of age, for example, will have babies who are more content at nine months (Robinson, 2008). Conversely, mothers affected by severe depression may present their children with an enduringly 'blank' expression that lacks movement and smiles and which has a damaging impact on the early development of their infants (Dawson et al., 1997). Chronic depression may result in hostile and intrusive or disengaged and withdrawn parenting, possibly resulting in lasting effects on infants' brain development and stress response systems (Iwaneic et al., 2007). Where maternal depression occurs alongside other adversities, the symptoms are less amenable to standard treatments, placing children at even greater risk of poor outcomes (DCSF, 2010a; Horwath, 2011).

Practice pointer 1.3

What protective factors (in the wider family and environment) might help to ameliorate the potentially damaging consequences of parental depression on a child's development? How could you, as a social worker, help to promote some of these protective factors?

Reliability and consistency

In the first year of life, through babbling, facial expressions and gestures, babies and their parents continually engage in what has been likened to the 'serve and return' process in a game of tennis

(Shonkoff and Phillips, 2000). A sensitive parent's response to the signals from their infant about readiness for interaction or, equally important, the need for disengagement is sometimes referred to as 'attunement' (Harrist and Waugh, 2002). Where parents do not actively observe their babies carefully, taking note of their expressions, body movement and mood, and tailoring their responses accordingly, there is a risk that they will misinterpret signals or miss them altogether, leaving the infant unsure and confused about their carers' reliability and their own self-worth. Erikson's (1995) psychosocial theory of child development suggests that the first major task facing infants is the need to establish trust in their carers, with failure to achieve this potentially resulting in an enduring sense of fear, anxiety and insecurity. However, where parents are attuned and responsive, providing reliable and consistent care, their interactions will contribute to orderly neural development in the brain and the infant's growing sense of security in knowing his or her needs will be met and the world is a safe and predictable place.

Practice pointer 1.4

Where adult–child relationships need strengthening:

- How might you help parents to understand their own patterns of interaction and develop attuned parenting, particularly with babies and infants?
- Do you know what parenting programmes are available in your area, including any specifically aimed at fathers or parents from particular ethnic minorities? If not, try to find out.
- Which other professionals might help to support the families you are working with?

Support for learning

The experiences of being held, returning a gaze and hearing a parent's vocalisations not only enhance an infant's developing senses, but are likely to engender the flow of positive emotions which promote important early learning. In the early weeks and months, social interactions may include stimulation of any of the senses, later moving on to reciprocal play, for example involving clapping, singing or 'peek-a-boo' games. The more lively the social interaction with their parents, the more likely babies are to feel lovable and worthwhile, which are important building-blocks for cognitive development (Fahlberg, 1991). Babies are not able to perform tasks for which they are not developmentally ready, and as already noted, the level, timing and duration of activities needs to match carefully the infant's stage of readiness, individual preferences and temperament. Sensitively planned and appropriate activities will help to 'scaffold' infants' learning (Vygotsky, 1978) as they watch, absorb and imitate the actions of their parents, preparing the way for the start of formal schooling. This is one of the most important transitions in a child's life, and much activity in the foundation years should help children to attain 'school readiness'. Overall, the home learning environment has a greater influence on a child's intellectual and social development than factors such as parental occupation, education or income – what parents *do* is more important than who they *are* (Raikes et al., 2006; Hansen, 2010). The types of parent-led activities most associated with a positive home learning environment include:

- Reading to children and listening to them reading.
- Playing with letters and numbers.
- Painting, drawing and creative play.
- Taking children to the library.
- Teaching nursery rhymes, songs and poems.
- Taking children out on visits and providing opportunities for play with other children and family members. (Sammons et al., 2004; DCSF, 2008)

Practice pointer 1.5

What resources might help parents to provide a good home learning environment? In what ways could you support, advise or signpost families to services or resources to help them enrich the home learning environment for their children?

Wider family and environmental contributions

Risk and protective factors

The ecological theory which underpins our approach in this book reminds us that parent–child relationships are always located in a wider context, within which there are both risk and protective factors. Whilst a variety of experiences is needed for healthy development, dangerous or impoverished environments can be very harmful. For instance, the impact on the foetus of the mother smoking, drinking alcohol or taking illegal drugs during pregnancy is linked to low birth weight, which in turn has enduring negative implications for children's future health and well-being, lasting well into adulthood (C4EO, 2010a). Risks may also reside in the nature of the social environment encountered by the infant, with family composition and birth order, for example, being important if parents' availability is significantly restricted by responsibilities for other children. Infants exposed to parental conflict and domestic violence are also at greater developmental risk, and family poverty concentrates and amplifies all other risk factors. In fact, the greatest threat to healthy development lies in an accumulation of adversities, rather than any single factor alone (Balbernie, 2009; Flouri et al., 2010).

Child care and pre-school

Early care may not always be provided exclusively by parents. Policies encouraging particularly lone mothers to work outside the home highlight the importance of alternative forms of early child care. Pre-school provision, especially where the setting includes children from a mix of social backgrounds, can play an important role in combating social exclusion by offering disadvantaged children, in particular, a better start to primary school. There is increasing evidence that part-time attendance generally enhances children's development, with an earlier start (before age three) establishing benefits that persist at least to the age of seven (Sammons et al., 2004; Belsky et al., 2007). Children at risk of learning or behavioural difficulties have been found to be helped by pre-school experiences that are also linked to a range of support, training and welfare services for their families (Roberts et al., 2010). However, the quality of the provision is important, with indicators of good quality including: warm, interactive relationships between staff and children; a trained teacher as manager; a high proportion of trained staff engaging in 'sustained shared thinking' with children; and an equal focus on social and educational development (Smith et al., 2009; Melhuish et al., 2010). Early intervention, likely to be more effective than remediation in later life, is promoted in universal services such as Sure Start children's centres and Nurse Family Partnerships (see Chapter 4), and full participation should be encouraged, particularly for the most disadvantaged families who may not be willing to use services if they are perceived to be stigmatising or intrusive (Speight et al., 2010; DfE/DH, 2011).

Practice pointer 1.6

Practitioners need to ensure that the parents they are working with are aware of the child care options available to them, and encourage their use where this would benefit the children and parents concerned.

Local neighbourhoods and outdoor play

Beyond meeting their children's basic needs and developing a sense of being loved and belonging, parents must also ensure their children's physical safety, both inside and outside the home. This presents an increasing challenge as infants become more mobile during their first year and beyond, and parents need to remain alert to their child's changing capabilities.

The neighbourhoods in which children grow up can also have a profound effect on their development. From an early age, the opportunity to use and enjoy safe play areas, leisure facilities and green spaces is crucial for children's development and well-being, as they explore and discover the world about them. Parents frequently voice fears that their neighbourhood is unsafe, with the result that access to the outdoors for many children is restricted, or curtailed altogether, placing increased reliance on less active play and undermining the variety of experiences needed for optimum development (4Children, 2007). This is where the development of what are often referred to as 'child-friendly communities' (discussed in Chapter 5) can play a significant role in promoting children's well-being.

Practice pointer 1.7

How can you encourage parents to build positive and supportive social networks, in their local areas or communities of interest, which help to promote their use of leisure and outdoor recreation facilities?

Key messages for practice

1. The total dependence of infants on their parents means that practitioners must do everything in their power to support parents who are experiencing difficulties in meeting their children's needs, for as long as it remains in the child's best interests.

2. The rapidity and complexity of early child development makes it vital that action is taken speedily, in collaboration with other professionals (e.g. health visitors, paediatricians, early years workers), whenever there are indications that a child's welfare is threatened by inadequate or harmful parental care.

3. Practitioners need to have a good understanding of child development, including knowledge about attachment theory and the existence of sensitive or critical periods, when they are involved in assessing the suitability of parents and home environments for children of different ages.

4. The importance of the quality of the home learning environment for children's future life chances makes this an obvious target for prevention and early intervention, focusing on, for example, the benefits of early language development by talking and reading to children throughout the foundation stage of their development.

5. Practitioners should ensure that they play their part, alongside other professionals and child welfare agencies, in efforts to develop 'child-friendly communities' and to ensure that children have access to the safe and stimulating local environments that promote their health and well-being.

Additional resources

N. Williams, S. Mughal and M. Blair (2008) Is my child developing normally? A critical review of web-based resources for parents, *Developmental Medicine and Child Neurology*, 50: 893–7.

Center on the Developing Child, Harvard University, www.developingchild.net.
Early childhood development, brain architecture and the impacts of neglect and abuse.

The Effective Provision of Pre-School Education Project, www.education.gov.uk/publications/eOrderingDownload/SSU-SF-2004-01.pdf.
Data on children's developmental profiles at three, four/five, six and seven years, and findings and implications for practice.

National Childbirth Trust, www.nct.org.uk/professional.
Support for parents; specific pages for professionals.

Reviewing attachment styles, www.teachingexpertise.com/articles/attachment-supporting-young-childrens-emotional-wellbeing-2358.

CHAPTER 2

Child development: middle childhood

CHAPTER OVERVIEW
In this chapter we look at the changes in middle childhood, broadly covering the years from 5–11, during which children begin formal schooling, and enter a much broader social sphere in which parents and other family members are joined by peers and members of the community at large, all of whom make important contributions in different ways to children's growing competence, personal identity and sense of self-worth. The enduring importance of a secure base, the development of pro-social behaviour to support satisfying and successful friendships and developing a positive attitude to learning are all explored. As in the previous chapter, we consider the key influences on development in middle childhood under three broad headings covering the contribution of the child, the parents, and the wider family and environment, as well as the interactions between them.

Introduction

The development of children in middle childhood has historically been presented as a relatively quiet period, sandwiched between the rapid changes which occur in the foundation years and the turbulence normally associated with adolescence. Until recently this interpretation of child development was also reflected in child welfare services, with far more investment in early years and youth offending services, for example, than those directed at children in their primary school years. However, recent research has highlighted the importance of providing a continuum of support throughout the whole of childhood in order to achieve optimum outcomes (Feinstein and Bynner, 2004; 4Children, 2007).

The child's contribution

Physical development

Appropriate nutrition and adequate medical care are just as important during middle childhood as they were during the foundation years, even though the rate of physical growth slows considerably. Average yearly increases of around 5 cm in height and 2 kg in weight can normally be expected. However, in developed economies around the world excessive weight gain during middle childhood is becoming an increasingly serious problem. A recent study in the UK found that over one in five 7-year-olds were classified as overweight or obese, with girls more likely than boys to be found in this group, as were children with a sedentary lifestyle, or who were large at birth, or who had high risk family health behaviours (e.g. overweight mothers, smoking near the child and missing breakfast) or were from a family with low income or low educational attainment (CLS, 2005).

The gross and fine motor skills acquired in the foundation years become more refined in middle childhood, and research has demonstrated that there are important connections between the development of motor skills, brain growth and learning, with exercise promoting brain organisation, which in turn enhances children's abilities to attend to learning tasks, so that far from being just a time to 'let off steam', opportunities for physical activity and play are crucial elements in children's development (Warren, 2006).

> **Practice pointer 2.1**
>
> Childhood obesity tracks into adulthood and is associated with risks of chronic disease. What opportunities are there to promote children's health through links with other professionals or organisations (e.g. school breakfast clubs, sports classes or after school clubs)?

Cognitive and language development

Formal education

The time between five and seven years is a period of significant psychological growth, and it therefore comes as no surprise that formal education begins at this age in most developed countries (Trawick-Smith, 2010). At this age children enter a new stage of cognitive growth (Piaget's 'concrete operations'), becoming less egocentric and using logic to think about the properties of objects, make inferences and come to conclusions. Children adapt and organise their thought processes by taking in a new idea and comparing it with their existing way of thinking (assimilation), subsequently making adjustments to fit the new information (accommodation). Thinking processes can become disorganised if children are unable to assimilate, or become rigid and unchanging if they have problems with accommodation. By the age of seven children are typically more able to concentrate, screening out distractions and beginning to construct a more sophisticated understanding of space, number and time. They also become able to link direction, location and distance to create a more coherent mental picture of their home territory. The ability to reverse steps mentally or physically, to retrace a path and return to a starting point, also emerges. This is crucial for understanding that it is possible, for instance, to reverse the process of addition by subtracting the same amount. Children also develop a better understanding of time, including concepts such as the past, present and future. By the age of nine or ten, most children are able to understand something of themselves as babies and toddlers, integrating reflections on the past into the present and the future as part of their evolving sense of personal identity. However, although children's understanding of cause and effect, including the relationship between their actions and possible outcomes, continues to develop, the many 'why' questions they continue to ask still require appropriate responses if errors and misunderstandings are to be avoided.

Interactions between cognition and language

It is during the early primary school years that children also begin to internalise the audible 'self-talk' characteristic of pre-school children, learning to manipulate silently this internal language in their minds as part of a complex interaction between the maturation of cognition and language. According to Vygotsky (1978), children acquire the tools necessary for thinking and learning through social interaction with 'more knowledgeable others' in mutual activities in which experimenting, instruction, demonstrating and modelling, pitched just beyond the child's current level of mastery (known as the 'zone of proximal development'), are all used to support or 'scaffold' the child's learning. Viewed in this way, cognitive development becomes an essentially interpersonal activity, with learning influenced by the wider family and cultural context in which it is taking place. The same sensitive stimulation that supports secure emotional attachments in the foundation years – by someone familiar with the child's level of functioning, and with an interest and investment in the child – also enhances cognitive development in middle childhood. This is particularly important where children are cared for away from home, a theme which is explored in more detail in Chapter 6.

Practice pointer 2.2

Can you think of ways that you could use an understanding of the 'zone of proximal development' to promote the development of a child with whom you are currently working (or have known in the past)?

Conscious awareness of language

Whereas most pre-school children learn to speak competently, in middle childhood children become consciously aware of language itself, are able to define words and can contemplate their meanings. They understand and use language to express themselves and are beginning to understand metaphor, ambiguity and verbal jokes. By the age of eight, for example, most children understand that language can have multiple meanings, and they enjoy puns, riddles and word games. In parallel, an understanding of narrative, telling stories and relating feelings and motives is also developing, although even in adolescence children may not have all the vocabulary necessary to describe the full range of their emotions and may sometimes find it easier to act out their feelings rather than talk about them (Fahlberg, 1991). In the wider social world that opens up at primary school, children need not only to use words and sentences to express themselves, but they must also learn the basic 'social rules' of language; for example, being polite when addressing an adult, making requests rather than demands, using a pleasant tone with those in authority, taking turns in two-way conversations, and using simpler language with younger children. Children also have to learn to move back and forth between the formal language and turn-taking expected in the classroom and the more informal language, including slang, which is acceptable in interactions with their peers (Trawick-Smith, 2010).

Reading and writing

Reading and writing are highly interrelated skills that are the main focus of teaching and learning in middle childhood. Reading systematises language, developing logic and reasoning; and when they look at books children construct an understanding of print, letters as making sounds, and stories that have been written down. They begin to follow the narrative, initially with the help of illustrations, then using their increasing memory to learn the story by heart, matching their retelling to the text. Memory is an important element of school success, and the ability to attend to the important features of a problem, as well as processing, storing and retrieving information, all improve during the primary school years. For young children, memory appears to be greater when information is linked to specific interests, and it can be enhanced by a number of processing strategies, including encouraging rehearsal or verbal repetition when storing important information and persistence with efforts to remember or retrieve stored facts (Flavell, 1985). Understanding stories in this way is an important precursor to later reading ability. Whilst the skill of reading should not be used as an indication of overall intelligence, problems with reading can be disabling to children and have a negative impact on their overall adjustment to school, so prompt attention to literacy difficulties is important.

Personal, social and emotional development

Friends
School presents children with a wider social environment, within which relationships outside those established with parents and family become increasingly important. Through the wider range of daily social interactions, children start to appreciate that others have a view of them which they use to develop their own view about themselves. Children also begin to define themselves, not only in terms of visible external characteristics, but also by using a range of internal traits and abilities to analyse their strengths and weaknesses by close comparison with others. Children at primary school become increasingly concerned about having and keeping friends with whom to share enjoyable activities (Schneider et al., 1994). They expect material assistance and tangible support from their friends and place importance on trust, including keeping secrets and fulfilling promises. 'Best friends' become important, with the children concerned tending to take turns in the different roles they adopt in play. The expectation of reciprocity and equal treatment increases as children grow older (Hartup, 1996). However, there are marked gender differences in both the form and

style of relationships. Boys' relationships tend to be more 'extensive', forming larger groups which are generally accepting of newcomers, often playing outside, with high value placed on competition, dominance and displays of emotion. By way of contrast, girls' relationships tend to be more 'intensive', forming smaller groups built around agreement, compliance and self-disclosure, often playing indoors. Skill in emotional regulation tends to increase the friendship networks of girls and potentially decreases those of boys (Bee and Boyd, 2010).

Identity

Through their social interactions, children develop views about their identity in relation to both gender and ethnicity. For example, by around the age of seven, play becomes almost entirely segregated by gender. Children express notions of both male and female characteristics, not just in terms of physical appearance, but also in relation to a set of expected behaviours. Those who exhibit fewer rigid, gender-stereotyped traits tend to demonstrate higher self-esteem, with boys expressing emotion, social perception and nurturance, and girls who are independent and autonomous, appearing to be more resilient, popular and successful. Support and encouragement to take part in activities or develop skills outside rigidly gendered expectations can therefore be beneficial during middle childhood. Ethnic identity also contributes to a growing sense of self, with children who understand they are part of a group, and who hold positive opinions of that group, more likely to have high self-esteem. Children with a strong ethnic identity, who are encouraged and supported by the positive attitudes of their parents and family, are less likely to suffer harm from the experience of prejudice (Daniel et al., 1999).

Play

Children's play now becomes more organised and rule-governed. Many games increasingly come to resemble real-life situations, with the focus moving from more imaginative forms of play to impersonating 'grown up' behaviour and language, with children assigning one another roles, announcing actions and taking turns. Other organised games, involving rules, strategy and competition, also come to the fore, influenced by the histories and values of the society in which children are growing up. Rituals, frequently incorporating predictable, rhythmic routines, are another important element of play in middle childhood, reflecting the need at this age for order as well as opportunities to enhance memory skills and functioning, thereby socialising children into their own playground culture and establishing membership of a peer group through ways of interacting that are exclusive to the children concerned (Trawick-Smith, 2010).

Social status

Acceptance by teachers and peer groups becomes a major focus of most children's social and emotional well-being at this time. For both boys and girls, social status within their peer group can have a profound impact on their personal development. While popular children tend to have more reciprocal or mutual close friends than their less accepted classmates, those who experience social rejection may often have only one close friend from whom they can enjoy mutual support and companionship. Chronic rejection by peers in primary school is associated with school failure, truanting, depression and emotional problems which may persist into adulthood (Ladd, 2006). Such children frequently develop a 'reputation', or cluster of negative characteristics assigned to them by peers, that may or may not be justified, but which determines their social status. Once established, a negative reputation may endure in spite of improved social behaviour. Rejected children may externalise their feelings, hitting out at other children and adults, in outward displays of emotion, or internalise them, becoming anxious, depressed and socially withdrawn, perhaps refusing to go to school or developing recurring complaints about physical ailments. Importantly social support derived from good peer relationships can compensate for poor attachment experiences, maltreatment and adversity, but it appears that secure attachment predicts more positive peer interactions, so that those most in need of social support may be the least likely to find it (Bee and Boyd, 2010).

Self-efficacy

Children of this age also begin to understand that success comes from a combination of intrinsic abilities, individual effort and a variety of external factors. Developing a belief in their own ability to achieve success, or self-efficacy, is crucial for long-term well-being, but it can be undermined by expectations of failure from important adults, especially parents and teachers. Where children believe that success is due to chance, and failure to immutable factors such as a lack of ability or intelligence, helplessness, self-defeating behaviour and the expectation of failure is likely to ensue. However, ecological theory suggests that positive experiences in one area of a child's life can have benefits in another, so that seeking out even small 'islands of competence' for each child, where they feel in control of positive outcomes, can be extremely important (Brooks, 1994).

Practice pointer 2.3

Can you think of any occasions when you have identified 'islands of competence' with a particular child? What were they and what were the ways in which they were used to promote the child's sense of success, autonomy and control?

Moral development

Moral reasoning is another important area of development during middle childhood, involving a complex interaction of cognitive, emotional and behavioural maturation. Piaget (1932) first systematised understanding of the development of moral reasoning, with later refinements added by Kohlberg (1969). According to these theorists, school-aged children understand the need to live up to the expectations of family and important others, and by the age of nine or ten they begin to understand that rules are not immutably derived from a higher authority, usually parents or teachers (moral realism), but can be changed by agreement within groups (moral subjectivism). An appreciation of intention, as an important factor in making judgements about actions, is also beginning to inform children's reasoning. They know that the reactions of others may be different from their own and show an increasing awareness of and consideration for the needs, interests and feelings of others. In parallel with developing empathy, which encourages children to 'do the right thing', they are also developing a conscience that will inhibit them from 'doing the wrong thing'. They focus on trying to please the adults important in their lives, gradually internalising these adult 'voices' as the basis of conscience (Daniel and Wassell, 2002).

Children are described as 'well-behaved' according to their compliance with the expected social norms of behaviour in the family, in school and in the local neighbourhood. At the start of middle childhood their self-control is limited, and adult supervision will be needed to prevent misbehaviour; but by the end of this stage of development children are starting to consider alternative actions for themselves which, alongside their developing sense of right and wrong, leads to increasingly self-controlled behaviour, with a decreasing need for adult supervision. Problems arise where children appear unable to feel guilt or remorse or to exert control over their own actions. However, it should also be borne in mind that moral reasoning and moral action do not necessarily develop in tandem.

Practice pointer 2.4

What risk and protective factors might influence the ways in which children in middle childhood deal with moral dilemmas? What part do the interactions amongst children, their parents and the wider family and environment play in influencing their behaviour?

The parents' contribution

Parents' contributions to the home environment during middle childhood is significant and may take many forms, including: the continuing provision of a secure and stable base built on good parent–child relationships; encouragement of pro-social behaviours that enhance peer friendships; support for educational values and high aspirations for personal fulfilment; and participation in school events and sharing of appropriate information about the child with the school. Differences in levels of parental involvement with their children's education are associated not only with social class, poverty and health, but also with parents' perceptions of their role and levels of confidence in fulfilling it (Desforges with Abouchaar, 2003; DCSF, 2008).

Providing a secure base

School-aged children may not demonstrate attachment behaviour in quite the same way that is observable in early infancy, but their need for a secure base from which to explore their widening world is still just as great. Research (Baumrind, 1972; Maccoby and Martin, 1983) has identified specific aspects of parenting that can help to provide the security needed. 'Authoritative parenting', which is warm but firm, is generally accepted as being the most helpful in developing a child's full potential. Authoritative parents:

- Set standards and expectations for behaviour which are appropriate for the capabilities of the child and his or her level of development.
- Encourage and value increasing independence and autonomy, but accept responsibility for their child's behaviour.
- Use discipline that is rational, incorporating discussion and appropriate explanation.
- Avoid expressing dissatisfaction with a child's performance through constant criticism, rebuke and withdrawal of affection, warmth and treats. (Iwaniec et al., 2007)

However, parents experiencing significant problems of their own, such as mental illness, drug and alcohol abuse, domestic violence or learning disability, may not have the capacity to meet their children's needs satisfactorily. Neglect is the most common form of maltreatment (NSPCC, 2000), and neglected children are likely to experience more severe delays in cognitive and social development than those who have been physically abused (Hildyard and Wolfe, 2002). School-aged children who have experienced neglect may exhibit problems in their language development, in poor behaviour and in social withdrawal (Ventress, 2009). If allowed to accumulate, the negative impact of neglect can be long-lasting, even if the child is subsequently removed from the neglectful environment. The implications of neglect for social work practice are explored in more depth in Chapter 5.

Supporting peer relationships

The establishment of satisfying peer relationships is an essential component of well-being during middle childhood, and parents can support positive relationships by allowing and encouraging their children to spend increasing amounts of time with peers, not only at home, but also in the neighbourhood. This can involve either free play or participation in more structured activities in non-academic settings such as youth groups, sports and music clubs, thereby helping to build a sense of social connectedness and belonging in the local community. Wherever possible children should be free to choose their own friends, but parents may need to be more directive if children want to spend time with anti-social peers who are having a negative influence on their child's behaviour and attitudes. Parents can also broaden children's social networks by providing opportunities for them to explore as wide a range of interests and activities as possible, helping children to become aware of their own likes and dislikes, talents and interests, strengths and weaknesses (Sylva et al., 2004).

Enhancing self-esteem

Problems with self-esteem can become apparent during middle childhood, but parents can play an important role in helping their children to feel good about themselves by identifying, supporting and nurturing talents, interests or skills, and facilitating experiences that reinforce their probability of success and feelings of mastery, where achievement is due to the child's abilities and efforts, rather than luck or innate characteristics. Parents can also promote their child's coping capacity by encouraging him or her to attempt a task rather than avoiding it, creating an environment in which mistakes and failure are a natural part of the learning process (Siraj-Blatchford, 2009). It is also important that parents provide emotional support, positive feedback and approval, to boost confidence and encourage the development of discipline and self-control.

Promoting pro-social behaviour

The term 'pro-social' has come to represent all aspects of caring and helpful behaviour or empathy towards others, which forms an important part of self-esteem, and underpins peer acceptance and successful relationships (O'Connor and Scott, 2007). Parental behaviour closely linked with the development of pro-social behaviour includes:

- Providing clear and consistent rules and expectations for behaviour, alongside clear explanations of consequences.
- Delivering important messages with a strong emotional component, as opposed to calm detachment.
- Attributing good intentions to actions and offering praise so that children are more likely to live up to the attribution and incorporate it into their self-definition.
- Acting as a positive role model when involved in moral reasoning and decision-making with children.
- Maintaining warmth and acceptance within the parent–child relationship.

Support for education

Recent research has shown that educational deficits tend to emerge early in children's lives, and the gap between the attainment of children from the poorest and the most affluent backgrounds widens as they move through the education system. Important factors which appear to explain these differences include parental attitudes and aspirations for higher education while their children are still in primary school and the extent to which parents (and their children) believe that their own actions can affect their lives. Behavioural problems, conduct issues and problems relating to their peers also exert their influence (Goodman and Gregg, 2010). Research has shown that parents who take an active interest in their children's education at the age of ten, for example, help them to achieve better educational and economic outcomes later in life (Blanden and Gibbons, 2006). It is interesting to note that fathers' interest in schooling appears to have a significant impact on the educational achievement of their daughters, but not on that of their sons (CLS, 2005; Flouri, 2006; Siraj-Blatchford and Siraj-Blatchford, 2010). In fact, boys and girls tend to experience significant differences in the home learning environment, with boys generally offered less rich learning opportunities.

Practice pointer 2.5

What factors could inhibit parental involvement in their children's education, and what is the likely impact on their development? How can parents from all backgrounds and cultures be supported to feel motivated, confident and competent to take a full part in school activities?

Wider family and environmental contributions

Whilst parents obviously play a central role in promoting their children's resilience, when asked what helps them 'succeed against the odds', children also frequently refer to their extended family, neighbours and friends (Newman et al., 2004). When children lack a close bond with at least one of their parents, affectionate ties with another member of their wider family, often a grandparent, can protect them from harm and promote their well-being and sense of personal identity and belonging. School can also act as an effective refuge and protective environment, particularly for children under stress, such as those who have experienced abuse or are living in very disadvantaged circumstances. However, whilst mutually trusting relationships with teachers, for example, can support academic attainment and positive self-esteem, for children struggling to adapt school may also be a source of stress. There is more about promoting resilience with older children in Chapter 3 and in working with children looked after away from home in Chapter 6.

Sibling relationships

Where they exist, sibling relationships are likely to represent the most enduring relationships in a person's life. Siblings play a very important role in many children's lives, providing companionship, support and protection, as well as contributing to their sense of personal and family identity. Talking together tends to be particularly important to girls in their relationships with their sisters, while doing things together usually matters more for boys (Edwards et al., 2005). Conversely, however, sibling relationships can be a source of unhelpful competition, rivalry and even bullying, particularly where unequal treatment or scapegoating by other family members occurs.

Practice pointer 2.6

When making decisions about out-of-home placements, social workers in the UK are required to keep siblings together wherever possible. Do you think this is always the best policy? What factors might lead to a decision to separate siblings?

Pets and companion animals

While relationships with siblings may be important, children often develop strong attachments to key animals in their lives. Even those who do not have a pet in their own home may feel that they have ownership of an animal, for example at the home of grandparents or a separated parent. Children frequently regard their pets as important family members and special friends who can be safe recipients of secrets and private thoughts as well as providers of companionship, social interaction, non-judgemental affection and emotional support (Triebenbacher, 1998). When stressed, sad, angry or afraid, when facing a temporary change, separation or significant transition, children often turn to their pets as a source of first comfort, and promoting a pet relationship may be a valuable way to reduce feelings of threat or loneliness for some children (Black, 2012). It has been suggested that involvement with a pet, particularly during the ages of 9–13 years, can help to develop a child's sense of responsibility, offering an opportunity to engage in nurturing and caring behaviour, promoting the development of confidence, building empathy toward others and a sense of self-worth (Daly and Morton, 2006; Williams et al., 2010). Animals may also provide children with insights into other aspects of life, including reproduction, illness and accidents as well as experiences of loss and grief if a pet is lost or dies. However, children are unlikely to be able to take full responsibility for all the needs of a particular animal and parents must be prepared to provide ongoing guidance and monitoring to oversee the welfare of any pets in the household. It is also important to keep in mind that children's relationships with pets should always be complementary to, rather than a substitute for, meaningful relationships with other caring adults. Taking a wider perspective, pet ownership has been shown to be positively associated with some levels of social interaction and with perceptions of neighbourhood friendliness so that the promotion of social capital in this way is a potential mechanism through which pets may contribute to overall family health and well-being (Wood et al., 2005).

Neighbourhoods

The local community is likely to exert significant influences on children during this stage of their development. For example, there are fairly stark contrasts in the ways that children from different socio-economic backgrounds tend to spend their free time and make use of their local environment. Those from more affluent backgrounds, who tend to be 'chaperoned' by adults to friends' houses, clubs and other organised activities, are thereby protected from any neighbourhood threats, such as traffic accidents and 'stranger danger'. At the same time, however, they are being allowed less freedom than they might if they wished to go out unaccompanied, particularly as they near the end of middle childhood. On the other hand, children from disadvantaged backgrounds are more likely to spend their free time socialising and playing games in the streets and open spaces around their homes, usually unaccompanied by adults but open to sanctions from neighbours and others in authority. For children growing up in households with fewer resources, restricted inside space and limited opportunities to attend organised activities, open space which facilitates social interactions, especially with their peers, is vitally important (Sutton et al., 2007).

Key messages for practice

1. Optimum cognitive development during middle childhood crucially depends upon social interactions between the child and others who know them well but have more knowledge and can provide learning opportunities just beyond the child's current level of mastery, effectively 'scaffolding' the child's learning. It is imperative that these relationships are maintained and supported (or replaced) during this stage of a child's development.

2. The quality of the home learning environment also has a major impact on children's development during middle childhood. Parents have key responsibilities, including providing a secure base, encouraging pro-social behaviour, supporting children's friendships, and creating a positive attitude to learning. Practitioners need to recognise the impact of parents' own educational experiences, their background and current circumstances on their capacity to support their child's education, and to provide additional support where this is needed.

3. Middle childhood is an important period for the development of children's self-esteem and self-efficacy, and parents and other adults involved in children's lives can play an important role in promoting these attributes by identifying, supporting and nurturing talents, interests and skills, encouraging effort rather than just achievement, and identifying 'islands of competence' for each child.

4. Friendships, particularly at school, assume an increasingly important role in children's lives during middle childhood. Parents should therefore encourage and support positive friendships, as far as possible allowing the child to select their own friends but being more directive when anti-social friendships develop.

5. Sibling relationships, where they exist, are likely to play an important (and enduring) role in children's lives, potentially providing companionship, support and protection, as well as contributing to the child's personal identity. However, sibling relationships can also be sources of rivalry and bullying, and practitioners need to be alert to all of these possibilities when they are assessing the needs of children.

Additional resources

Equality and Human Rights Commission: Research Report Series
P. Johnson and Y. Kossykh (2008) *Early Years, Life Chances and Equality: A Literature Review*, available on line at: www.equalityhumanrights.com/uploaded_files/research/ 7_earlyyears_lifechances.pdf

Barnardo's Research Reviews
R. Smith (2002) *Promoting Children's Emotional Health: Findings and Implications for Practice*, available on line at: www.barnardos.org.uk/promoting_children_s_emotional_ health_a_research_review.pdf

Centre for Longitudinal Studies, Institute of Education, London (CLS)
CLS houses three of Britain's birth cohort studies, including the Millennium Cohort Study, following the lives of around 19,000 children born in 2000–01, and contains a wealth of briefings highlighting outcomes for children and families www.cls.ioe.ac.uk/ page.aspx?andsitesectionid=939andsitesectiontitle=Recent+ working+papers

Joseph Rowntree Foundation: Findings Informing Change (February 2006)
Parenting and children's resilience in disadvantaged communities www.jrf.org.uk/sites/files/jrf/0096.pdf

Sibling Relationship Checklist
www.proceduresonline.com/wandsworth/childcare/pdfs/ Perm%20Plan%20Sib%20Attach.pdf

CHAPTER 3

Child development: adolescence

CHAPTER OVERVIEW

As in the previous two chapters, we consider this final stage in children's development in relation to the contributions made by the child, the parents and the wider family and environment, as well as the interactions between them. The impact of puberty, close relationships and developing sexual identity are explored as well as the importance of establishing a sense of autonomy and independence as part of the process of psychological, social and physical separation from parents. The responsibilities of parents in developing a new parent–child relationship and the need for adjustments in parenting style in order to maintain a secure base promoting resilience and self-efficacy are considered. We examine key issues in the wider community, including risky behaviour and decision-making, truancy, bullying, the impact of drugs and alcohol as well as teenage parenthood and some of the issues raised for young carers.

Introduction

Adolescence, which covers the period in human development between the beginning of puberty and adulthood, is usually broken down into three phases: *early adolescence* (11–13 years), which signals fundamental change in virtually every aspect of a young person's development; *middle adolescence* (14–17 years), which is essentially a period of consolidation as new roles, relationships, goals and values are beginning to be established; and *late adolescence* (18–21+ years), which is a period involving the formation of emotionally intimate sexual partnerships and a firmer sense of personal identity (Sugarman, 2001). Adulthood is achieved through a series of transitions that unfold at different rates, times and intensity, in a mix which is unique to each individual. Despite these variations, three fundamental changes normally occur during adolescence: the onset of puberty; the development of more advanced thinking skills; and the move to new roles in society.

The child's contribution

Although typically something of a stop-start process, adolescence is not necessarily the time of 'storm and stresses' represented in much advertising and popular fiction. Such pervasive images undoubtedly influence the expectations and meanings that become associated with adolescence, yet the majority of children manage to navigate this period of their development without major problems (Hall, 1904; Spear, 2000). Having said that, adolescence is undoubtedly a period during which significant changes occur in all aspects of children's development.

Physical development

Puberty
Puberty is the key biological change of adolescence, normally commencing for girls between the ages of 10 and 14 years, and for boys at any time between 12 and 16. The onset of puberty is linked to changes in the ratio of muscle to body fat, and may be accelerated by mild obesity or delayed by excessive physical exercise. There is also a link between social factors and the onset of puberty, which tends to occur earlier for girls growing up in families experiencing conflict, or where there is either no father or a step-father is present (Ellis, 2004), with a certain amount of stress apparently accelerating maturation, but high levels impeding it (Steinberg, 2011).

Strictly, puberty refers to the period during which an individual becomes capable of sexual reproduction, although the term is often applied more generally to include all the physical changes of adolescence, signalled initially by a dramatic growth spurt and the development of mature sex characteristics. Although pubertal development occurs in a highly consistent sequence, there is wide variation in its onset and duration. 'Tanner Stages' is a system of categorisation that is widely used by child health professionals that provides a helpful guide to the sequence of physical changes which take place during puberty (Tanner, 1990). Development during puberty is frequently rapid and uneven, and the way that adolescents respond to these changes is strongly influenced by their peers, families, schools and communities. However, behaviour appears to be related more strongly to perceptions of maturity than actual age or stage of physical development. There are both positive and negative consequences for those whose development is out of step with the majority of their peers, and the timing and tempo of puberty may be of considerable psycho-social significance. Those maturing early or late often see themselves as different, are treated differently by others, and may behave differently as a result (Daniel et al., 1999; Steinberg, 2011).

Early maturity

The onset of menstruation for girls, which usually occurs between the ages of 11 and 13 years in the UK, is typically accompanied by increases in social maturity, peer prestige and self-esteem, although early maturing girls tend to hold more negative attitudes about it. Girls gain more body fat than boys over the course of puberty, and for early maturing girls this, along with the development of breasts and the social taboos of menstrual periods, may result in feelings of ambivalence about the physical changes of puberty which can set them apart from their peers in highly visible and socially less desirable ways at a time when they would often prefer to be like everyone else.

Adolescent girls who mature early are more likely than later maturing girls to develop dissatisfaction with their body image, sometimes leading to eating problems or self-harm. Food preferences in adolescence are frequently based on feelings of peer acceptance, with 'junk' food strongly associated with fun and independence from parents and family (Stang and Story, 2005). However, a diet consisting mainly of junk food increases the risk of obesity, which in turn is associated with depression, particularly in middle adolescence. Early maturing girls are also generally at higher risk of developing conduct and emotional problems, and achieving less academic success. Conversely, for boys, early puberty often bestows a culturally admired lean and muscular body shape which typically increases their popularity, confidence and self-esteem, although it may also expose them to increased risk-taking and involvement in anti-social behaviour, truancy and school problems (Spear, 2000). Based on appearance, early maturing adolescents of either sex are often invited to join groups of older teenagers in environments where risk-taking, including higher levels of sexual activity, smoking, alcohol and substance use, as well as reinforcements for delinquent behaviour, may already be more prevalent and accepted.

Brain development and sleep patterns

Brain maturation plays a critical role in biological and behavioural development during adolescence. The pre-frontal cortex, which regulates judgement, caution and appropriate behaviour, does not mature completely until late adolescence or early adulthood, in contrast to those areas, notably the limbic system, which make adolescents more responsive to emotional arousal and stress, and more likely to engage in immediate gratification and sensation-seeking behaviour (McAnarney, 2008). This may help to explain the heightened levels of experimentation and risky behaviour that tend to occur during adolescence (Spear, 2010), as well as increasing individual vulnerability to the onset of a range of psychiatric problems which often first manifest themselves at this age, such as anxiety, depression and schizophrenia (Paus et al., 2008). Chapter 9 provides further information about the development of childhood mental disorders.

Another noticeable physical change triggered by puberty is a disturbance in sleep patterns, with adolescents typically showing a preference for going to sleep later and waking later. Evidence suggests that many adolescents do not get enough sleep (approximately nine hours per night), increasing the risk of poorer outcomes in terms of mental health (Fuligni and Hardway, 2006), obesity (Fredriksen et al., 2004) and school performance (Snell et al., 2007).

Cognitive and language development

Hypothetical thinking and 'formal operations'

Unlike children in the earlier stages of cognitive development, adolescents are able to think beyond what is concrete to contemplate more abstract ideas, through a process of hypothetical thinking, in the stage of development that Piaget (1932) called 'formal operations'. Hypothetical thinking is linked to decision-making, and most adolescents become increasingly able to plan ahead and weigh the consequences of different options and life choices.

In general, adolescents are more likely to see things as relative rather than absolute, and no longer accept the views of others without question, creating arguments and counter-arguments in addressing everyday decisions. Adolescents are also able to deal more efficiently with multiple perspectives, processing information systematically and methodically to arrive at more comprehensive conclusions. Understanding of language and the enjoyment of metaphors, analogies, satire and sarcasm all depend on the increasing facility of adolescents to think in multiple dimensions. These developments allow adolescents to describe themselves and others in more complex terms, referring to factors such as beliefs, relationship quality and personality traits. Understanding that personalities have more than one facet, and that social situations can have different interpretations depending on an individual's standpoint, supports the development of more sophisticated and complex relationships with others (Bee and Boyd, 2010; Steinberg, 2011).

Although much research supports Piaget, formal operational thinking is most often found in industrialised societies, which not only demand more complex thinking but also provide more opportunities in which to rehearse the necessary skills (Kuhn, 2008). However, not all adolescents (or adults) achieve the stage of 'formal operations' or use hypothetical thinking in their daily problem-solving, so the development of thinking in abstract terms during adolescence needs to be nurtured, encouraged and supported.

Meta-cognition

Another striking advance at this stage of children's development, related to the maturation of the pre-frontal cortex of the brain, is the ability to think about thinking itself, a process referred to as 'meta-cognition'. This ability heightens adolescents' self-consciousness, as thinking about how others think about them develops. Adolescents also become capable of greater intellectualisation as they develop their own ideas and internal reflections. These processes contribute to the exploration and self-examination that is an important precursor to the formation of a more coherent personal identity. Increased capacity for introspection can lead to intense self-absorption, which may lead some teenagers to believe that their peers are an 'imaginary audience', constantly watching and evaluating them, with the adolescent perhaps privately rehearsing different attitudes, styles and behaviours designed to gain favour. Others may create a 'personal fable', a mentally constructed autobiography in which their experiences are interpreted uniquely, for example: 'this behaviour may be risky for others, but not for me' (Elkind, 1967). However, while an imaginary audience and personal fable may provide some protective benefits where other supports are lacking, enhancing feelings of self-importance and bolstering self-esteem, both types of thinking can lead adolescents to poor decision-making and risky behaviour.

Moral reasoning

Moral reasoning also progresses significantly during adolescence, allowing beliefs about justice, rights, equality and human welfare, for example, to become more nuanced. The major theories of moral development (Piaget, 1932; Kohlberg, 1969; Turiel, 1983) emphasise the changes in reasoning that individuals use in their decision-making, with Kohlberg identifying a universal, stage sequence in which adolescents move from earlier modes of thinking, based on tangible rewards and punishments, to 'conventional moral reasoning', in which individual behaviour is guided by respect for authority and a willingness to follow rules in order to maintain the accepted social order. Kohlberg suggested that the majority of adolescents (and adults) use this type of moral reasoning in dealing with daily dilemmas and that, although diminishing egocentrism and increasing role-taking in adolescence are necessary cognitive changes to support more advanced forms of moral reasoning, they are not in themselves sufficient. Optimum development of moral reasoning during adolescence (and beyond) requires a social environment which provides frequent opportunities to engage in discussion of moral issues and dilemmas (Eisenberg et al., 2009). However, these potential advances in moral reasoning are likely to come into conflict with some of the personal, social and emotional aspects of development that are also taking place during adolescence, which are considered next.

Personal, social and emotional development

Increasing cognitive resources provide new ways of thinking about identity, relationships and values, whilst the desire for greater control over their own lives, balancing autonomy and independence with new responsibilities and consequences, can become an enduring struggle during adolescence (Settersten, 2011).

Self-esteem

It is often assumed that adolescents have low self-esteem, although this is not necessarily the case. In general, all-round self-esteem becomes more stable with age, and actually increases slightly throughout adolescence (Harter, 1998). However, there is frequently a marked decline in self-esteem during early adolescence, coinciding with the transfer from primary to secondary school when young people are faced with increased demands for new social skills and more complex tasks at school. Where these demands are combined with other stressful life events, such as moving house, bereavement or parental separation, there is the greatest potential for loss of self-esteem, as well as a rise in problem behaviour and a drop in academic performance.

Practice pointer 3.1

What life events and experiences have had a negative impact on an adolescent that you know, and how might an understanding of ecological theory, which looks at the interactions between risk and protective factors, help to identify ways of promoting the young person's development?

Personal identity

According to Erikson (1968), adolescence is essentially a time of self-exploration and identity formation. Although much subsequent research has supported Erikson's understanding of adolescent development, it now appears that a coherent sense of identity is not established until early adulthood and continues to be revised throughout the life span. Marcia (1980) introduced the idea of a 'psychosocial moratorium', an extended period of time for active self-exploration, free from the need to commit to any particular role, value system or goal. The increasing participation of middle and late adolescents around the developed world in further and higher education and training certainly offers them this opportunity, although self-conceptions necessarily become more established as adolescents encounter a broadening range of social roles, including those of employee, partner and parent.

Adolescents tend to make global evaluations of themselves, as well as those based on specific domains such as appearance, academic abilities and athleticism, which are of varying importance for different individuals. Typically, appearance is most important for overall self-esteem, especially for girls, but context also influences self-conceptions, and adolescents often view themselves differently when with friends, parents and teachers. They may also act in ways that do not reflect their true self, demonstrating what is referred to as 'false self-behaviour', particularly when they are with friends or romantic partners. Although this is not usually harmful, where adolescents engage in false self-behaviour because they do not value their true self it may lead to feelings of low self-worth and even depression (Harter et al., 1996).

Culture also exerts important influences on identity formation, with adolescents growing up in immigrant or refugee families, for example, sometimes experiencing a crisis in identity when continuity with their history and traditions becomes difficult to maintain. If parents and families from minority communities fear or resent their children's assimilation into the dominant culture, adolescents may be faced with the difficult task of respecting their culture of origin at the same time as wanting to share the same experiences as their peers from other cultural backgrounds. Whilst sometimes difficult to achieve, adolescents from minority backgrounds who are able to establish a secure and positive ethnic identity tend to have higher self-esteem, which can serve as a protective factor in adverse circumstances (Bee and Boyd, 2010).

Mood

Although adolescent moods are often attributed to 'raging hormones', it appears more likely that daily fluctuations, or 'mood swings', result from the interaction between hormones and environmental influences (Buchanan et al., 1992). Mood is strongly influenced by the immediate social environment, generally being more positive with friends, and more negative in school or when alone. Within the family environment mood tends to be most negative in early adolescence, making this the peak time for strains in parent–child relationships (Steinberg, 2011). The highest levels of positive mood, including high levels of concentration, motivation and engagement, tend to occur during self-chosen and structured leisure activities, for example whilst attending sports or youth clubs, so spending free time in this way offers some of the best opportunities for adolescent psychological development (McHale et al., 2001; Zaff et al., 2003).

Autonomy and independence

For most adolescents, establishing a sense of autonomy and independence is as important as establishing a sense of identity. Some theorists explain the drive for independence as part of a process of psychological, social and physical separation from parents, or 'individuation', beginning in adolescence and involving a gradual and progressive shaping of a sense of self as an autonomous, competent and separate person able to accept responsibility for choices and actions (Blos, 1967). Whilst the balance between dependence and independence varies across cultures, all adolescents need to move away from the total dependence typical of earlier childhood, to attain a more mature interdependence with their family, which recognises their individuality but retains their emotional connectedness. Indeed, healthy functioning throughout the life course typically depends on supportive family networks, as well as relationships with friends and partners (Sugarman, 2001; Armsden and Greenberg, 1987).

New cognitive skills allow adolescents to see their parents no longer as all-knowing and all-powerful, and adolescents typically become more critical of their parents' behaviour, opinions and family functioning, countering parents' arguments with increased facility and adopting opinions and tastes, for example in clothes and music, that emphasise their separate identity. Developing autonomy need not necessarily be a stressful and turmoil-laden process, although day-to-day bickering and occasional confrontations with parents, sometimes reflecting larger underlying issues of control, may increase, particularly during early adolescence when young people tend to be at their most rebellious. As adolescents acquire a new status within the family, involving more equal relationships, they begin to interact in different ways with their parents, as people rather than just parents, with control depending on the quality of relationships rather than physical strength or cognitive superiority (Greenberg et al., 1983; Markiewicz et al., 2006).

Close relationships, social status and social groupings

Adolescents continue to need the secure base and approval provided by parents from which to meet the more complex demands of their changing social and emotional environments. In fact, the idea of a yawning 'generation gap' appears to be something of a myth, as the views of young people on important matters tend to be remarkably similar to those of their parents, and less variation is found between than within generations (Brown, 1990). However, as children move through adolescence, friendships become increasingly important to them, with most transferring some of their dependency needs from parents to peers. The friendships of early adolescence are typically based on a deepening need for intimacy, in which self-disclosure, mutual trust, commitment and loyalty become increasingly important. For girls, intimacy is fostered primarily through talking together, while for boys it depends more on shared activities. It has been estimated that, during an average week, adolescents spend one-third of their normal waking hours talking with peers, compared with less than one-tenth in conversation with adults, including their parents (Spear, 2000). The increasing importance of peers can have both positive and negative influences on children's behaviour, particularly during early adolescence when the pressure to conform is at its height (Steinberg and Morris, 2001).

Adolescent social groupings tend to move through a number of different stages, characterised by Brown and colleagues (1994) as 'cliques', 'crowds' and 'couples'. 'Cliques' are usually relatively small same-sex groups, based on mutual interests and activities, in which members are generally of similar age, ethnicity and socio-economic background. These are the social groups in which adolescents often 'hang out', learning the skills for effective communication and often forming close friendships. Whilst adolescents may gather in cliques for purely social reasons, or because of the 'safety in numbers' protection that they offer, such groups are often rather loosely identified as 'gangs' by others living in the local area, with groups of teenagers typically perceived to be a threatening presence. However, especially for adolescents living in more disadvantaged circumstances and communities, groups that are more appropriately identified as gangs, which typically engage in anti-social and criminal behaviour, can provide some of the social status and sense of belonging, order and security that may otherwise be lacking in their lives. Many adolescents caught up in gangs of this nature require specialist interventions and alternative sources of support to extricate themselves from the web of obligations and threats which may characterise such groups.

By way of contrast, 'crowds' are larger collections of peers, who are not necessarily close friends but who identify with one another and are readily recognisable to others, often under collective labels such as 'goths', 'chavs', 'musos' and 'townies'. They contribute to adolescents' self-conceptions by locating them within networks which establish socially desirable 'norms' for their members and through which many adolescents increasingly come to view themselves and identify with one another. Over time the structure of the adolescent peer group changes again, in a way that reflects their increasing desire for intimacy within romantic relationships, so that crowds diminish in importance by the end of middle adolescence to be replaced in late adolescence by looser associations of 'couples'.

Sexual identity

For many adolescents, concerns over the presence, absence and quality of romance in their lives is of paramount importance (Steinberg, 2011). Developing skills in personal intimacy and self-disclosure, as well as understanding and interpreting the social cues used by others, are crucial precursors to establishing a fully adult sexual identity, and the shift from friendships to sexual partnerships is an important transition for the majority of adolescents. While all adolescents explore their developing sexuality, with experimentation possibly involving members of both sexes, their sexual orientation is not a matter of choice. Changing social attitudes in the UK over the last 20 years have helped gay and lesbian adolescents to feel more comfortable with their sexual orientation (BSA, 2010), but where family conflicts over sexuality emerge adolescents are likely to need support and advice from their friends, and possibly professionals.

Risky behaviour and decision-making

Whilst hazardous, some risk-taking is an essential element of healthy development during adolescence, with the potential benefits including exploration of adult behaviour, the acquisition of self-knowledge through experience, and respect from peers. Undue avoidance of risk may therefore be developmentally harmful (Johnson and Jones, 2011).

As a result of maturational changes in the structure and function of the brain following puberty, adolescents become temporarily more reactive to stress. Decision-making capabilities are impaired in situations where there are high levels of stress, arousal or conflict, and most especially in the presence of peers. In general, risk judgements reflect experience, so that risky behaviour which doesn't result in negative consequences tends to be repeated. Awareness of risk does not necessarily deter participation because adolescents judge risks and benefits differently from adults. For example, the benefits of smoking and drinking, in terms of peer approval and social acceptance, outweigh the risks for many adolescents, who tend to weigh the *proximal* (near or short-term) consequences of behaviour more heavily than *distal* (distant or long-term) ones. Prevention strategies based on the idea that understanding the negative consequences of behaviour will provide the motivation for adolescents to behave differently are therefore likely to be ineffective, and bringing young people together who are at risk of, for example, delinquent behaviour may serve more to reinforce their identity as 'delinquents' than to bring home the potential risk of future problems such as loss of liberty (Petrosino et al., 2002). These issues are explored in more detail in Chapter 8.

The parents' contribution

Adolescence can be a confusing time, not only for the children going through it, but also for their parents. In many families, the adolescent phase of development coincides with parents' own transition into mid-life, which may represent something of a challenge in its own right. Parents' own vulnerabilities may be brought to the fore as they observe the increasing opportunities available to their children at the same time as feeling that their own opportunities may be shrinking.

Developing a new parent–child relationship

As their children move through adolescence, parents have to adjust to the child's new status within the family. Those parents who accept the need for 'individuation' will be best placed to establish more equal relationships with their adolescent children that provide a mutually beneficial alliance, rather than one centred on a struggle for control. Occasional disagreement and conflict is to be expected, but regular and chronic negative communication to achieve compliance, including nagging, harsh criticism and shouting, is likely to be harmful to all concerned. Where parents have difficulties in managing their own emotions and actions they are more likely to become involved in damaging confrontations with their children. However, this does not mean that parents should habitually give in to the demands of their adolescent children, which can often be completely unreasonable. A combination of discussion, resistance and willingness to compromise, which allows the adolescent to express his or her views without the need to resort to direct confrontation, is likely to be effective in many situations (Steinberg and Morris, 2001).

Providing a secure base

The perception that the family continues to provide a secure base is linked to well-being, support-seeking and resilience throughout adolescence (Armsden and Greenberg, 1987). In times of trouble the existence of a secure base allows adolescent problems to be discussed and resolved together, increasing everyone's satisfaction with family relationships. In a recent study (Markiewicz et al., 2006), adolescents consistently reported that they continued to use their families (particularly their mothers) as a secure base, regardless of whether or not they had a romantic partner. It is therefore important for parents to understand the enduring importance of these relationships for adolescents and that the quality of attachment to parents during this stage in children's development is significantly more powerful than peer relationships in predicting their future well-being (Greenberg et al., 1983).

Parenting style

Above all, perhaps, parents of adolescents need to be flexible, adjusting their parenting style to meet the changing needs of their children, striking an appropriate balance between offering increasing privacy and independence, on the one hand, while remaining involved, concerned and available to offer support, guidance and feedback, on the other. An authoritative, democratic parenting style is likely to be most effective in promoting positive outcomes (Baumrind, 2005) and parents of adolescents should strive to:

- **Be warm and involved, but firm and consistent** in setting and implementing appropriate limits, boundaries and expectations, balancing protection and control, whilst encouraging exploration of things that are unfamiliar or do not meet with their approval. Openness to change and a sense of humour are also important traits in regulating behaviour, rather than enforcing punishments, particularly if these result from angry or emotional encounters.
- **Model tolerance and acceptance** (distinct from approval), alongside clearly expressed personal beliefs and values (especially if they can demonstrate that these have worked well for them in their own lives) and tolerating that of which they disapprove.
- **Use communication styles** appropriate to the situation, including dialogue, discussion and debate, to create a nurturing environment in which pleasure in, and support for, the child is tangible.
- **Maintain a proactive interest** in the whereabouts and everyday events in their adolescents' lives, so that remaining connected

and the monitoring of activities is based on freely offered adolescent disclosure, rather than adult 'prying'.

Maintaining the parent–parent relationship

The ways in which parents either support or undermine each other, in terms of recognising, respecting and valuing the distinct contribution of each to the roles and tasks of parenting, is particularly pertinent during adolescence when parental values and standards may be increasingly challenged. Parents need to be aware that the nature of their parent–parent interactions influences the functioning of the rest of the family, with consequences for the quality of parent–child and sibling interactions, which are ultimately reflected in the adolescent's relationships with peers outside the home (Woodhouse et al., 2009). For some parents, 'latent relational strengths' which serve to underpin their parenting alliance will emerge, while for others a 'battleground' may develop in which competing self-interests dominate. Evidence suggests that disharmony poses sufficient risk to focus attention on maintaining a positive parenting alliance throughout adolescence (Gable et al., 1992).

Nurturing goals

The transition from 'controller' to 'mentor' is a key development for parents at this stage. Adolescents tend to have difficulty making realistic estimates of their own abilities, so parents often need to identify and nurture their children's ideas and interests, helping them to make appropriate links to aims and goals for the future. Problems in delaying gratification may also influence early adolescent decision-making, leading some to prioritise the present over longer-term goal setting. In these circumstances, parental guidance, helping adolescents to balance periods of expanding horizons with periods of consolidation and reflection, is likely to be most successful in building realistic and achievable long-term plans (Settersten, 2011).

Support for developing sexuality

Parents' (and schools') responsibilities in relation to children's sexual development begin long before the onset of puberty, and difficulties during adolescence are likely to be minimised if younger children know what changes to expect and are helped to develop a positive attitude towards them. Unfortunately, UK surveys (e.g. Natsal, 2000) repeatedly reveal a high level of self-perceived ignorance about sexual matters amongst children. Whilst parents and schools are identified as the sources from which they would prefer to receive more information, adolescents typically rate sex and relationship education at school as poor, partly because there is no clear consensus about 'what works' in sex education and who should be responsible for providing it, but also because adolescents often fail to see its relevance until a particular issue touches them individually. It is important, therefore, for parents and teachers of adolescents not only to support one another, and ensure the availability of good quality information, but also to understand that sex education is not a one-off event; opportunities need to be provided to revisit issues, questions and concerns throughout adolescence. Parents should also be aware that adolescents are likely to use their same sex parent as a role model and their opposite sex parent for affirmation and approval of their emerging sexuality. Both parents, whether they live together or not, therefore have a role to play in modelling mutuality, consideration and respect in their relationship (Fahlberg, 1991).

Wider family and environmental contributions

In addition to the personal characteristics of children and parents, there are also elements of the wider family and environmental context within which they live which influence adolescent development.

Resilience

The level of resilience displayed by children of all ages depends on the balance between risk and protective factors in their lives. These may be derived from children's personal characteristics such as their competence, coping skills and self-efficacy, or external factors such as parental support and community resources. As all of these influences are content and context specific, it is important to recognise that adolescents may be resilient in the face of one type of threat to their development, whilst being unable to overcome others successfully. A resilience framework focuses attention on the importance of facilitating change by enhancing protective factors and minimising risk factors in children's lives. Whilst many protective factors operate at the individual level (e.g. social competence, decision-making skills, self-efficacy, self-control and academic achievement), there are also a number of resilience factors external to the adolescent that may help to support their optimum development, including:

• Family connectedness and the continued provision of a 'secure base'.
• Parenting skills, including open communication and monitoring.
• Opportunities to build relationships with trusted adults outside the family and to establish adult mentorship.
• Links with faith groups, where appropriate.
• Participation in extra-curricular activities.
• Involvement in community activities. (Fergus and Zimmerman, 2005)

Practice pointer 3.2

Thinking about an adolescent that you know or work with, what strengths can you identify in their extended family and wider community? How might these strengths be supported and extended?

Schools, truancy and bullying

Educational attainment is associated with positive outcomes that endure across the lifespan, so experiences at school are of central importance for adolescents. Regular attendance is crucial because, even with the same qualifications at the age of 16, employment outcomes and later educational attainment are poorer for those who have been truants (NAO, 2005). For some, school may be a haven of safety and achievement, while for others it may be the site of more unhappy experiences. Parents and teachers therefore need to be aware of the importance of the culture and ethos of the school, in which a favourable disciplinary climate, good relationships between teachers and pupils, and strong parental involvement all serve to enhance children's experiences. Factors that make adolescents vulnerable to truancy include low socio-economic status, a lack of homework monitoring, and negative attitudes towards teachers and education, although truancy can also be linked to more specific events such as a change of school or bullying (Attwood and Croll, 2006).

Bullying, which involves aggression, anger and malice intended to inflict misery, isolation and fear on the victim, can be both emotionally and psychologically abusive. The people who bully children are most frequently other children, either at school or in the wider community, but they can also be adults, including parents and other family members, and school staff, including teachers. Bullying is the biggest single reason for calls to Child Line, and it has been estimated that as many as 16 young people in the UK commit suicide each year as a direct result of bullying. Friendship is a key protective factor against bullying as it promotes self-esteem and provides a source of potential help and support (Beatbullying, 2006).

Increasingly, however, cyber-bullying using mobile phones and the internet means that bullying is no longer confined to a known perpetrator or location, and widespread access to email, chat rooms and social networking sites means that greater numbers of children are involved, in one way or another, than ever before. Posting abusive messages (flaming), personal information (outing) or embarrassing pictures (sexting) are all ways in which adolescents can be made to feel uncomfortable or threatened. Adolescents need to be made aware of the potential for such communications to escalate out of control and the distress that they may cause. Attempting to prevent cyber-bullying through censorship is not likely to be effective, as denying adolescents access to information technologies can actually put them at greater risk, by virtue of inexperience and lack of knowledge about the on-line environment (Cross et al., 2009). Schools and parents therefore have key roles to play in helping young people to understand and manage the risks of cyberspace, at the same time as enjoying the undoubted benefits. Despite its ubiquity in their lives, a recent study revealed a widespread inability amongst young people to discriminate between 'good' and 'bad' information on-line. New knowledge about how search engines function, for example, will be needed if young people are to be able to make informed judgements about their use of the internet (Bartlett and Miller, 2011).

Practice pointer 3.3

What can you do to raise the aspirations and expectations of education for young people and their parents? Who else can be relied upon to help? What support, if any, might they need from you or other services or professionals?

Delinquency, drugs and alcohol

Delinquency shows marked continuity with increasing age, but its prevalence changes dramatically, increasing almost ten-fold during adolescence (Moffitt, 1993). Evidence shows that there is a small group of persistent young offenders whose anti-social behaviour from an early age distinguishes them from adolescents whose anti-social or criminal activities start later, end sooner, and tend to be less serious (Sutton et al., 2004). Ironically, whilst being responsible for committing a significant number of criminal acts themselves, adolescents are also most likely to be the victims of many crimes, including theft, robbery, rape and assault. There is more about working with young offenders in Chapter 8.

Although substance use amongst adolescents has declined in recent years, it remains a significant problem, with alcohol generally more of a problem than illicit drugs (Chamberlain et al., 2010). High sensation-seeking adolescents are more likely to use drugs and alcohol in company with friends who adopt the same behaviour, but 'loners' may also be at risk. Because disinhibition is higher during adolescence than adulthood, larger doses of drugs and alcohol are often required to achieve the desired effects, increasing the risk of serious damage and addiction. Adolescents may also lack the ability to judge 'non-drug rewards', such as educational achievements, with the result that drug and alcohol use can represent a substantial threat to their overall development (Bee and Boyd, 2010). Evidence suggests that parental abstinence or moderation, clear 'family rules' and the monitoring of peer groups are all powerful tools for limiting tobacco and substance use by adolescents (Beinart et al., 2002).

Teenage parenthood

Despite national initiatives in different parts of the UK (e.g. DCSF, 2010b), and a conception rate that has fallen steadily over the last decade, the UK still has the highest teenage birth and abortion rates in Western Europe (FPA, 2010). Evidence suggests that the average age of first heterosexual intercourse in England is 16, for both sexes (Natsal, 2000), yet according to a recent ONS survey (Lader, 2009), over 40 per cent of 16- to 19-year-olds do not use contraception, leaving much to do in communicating sexual health messages.

The groups most vulnerable to becoming teenage parents include adolescents with experience of the local authority care system, as well as those who are homeless, under-achieving at school, involved in crime, or living in areas of higher social deprivation. There is considerable diversity in outcomes, with some mothers less affected by early childbearing than others, and research suggests that age at motherhood is an important pathway through which intergenerational disadvantage is transmitted, with negative consequences for mothers and fathers as well as their children (RIP, 2009).

Young carers

Of the estimated 200,000 young carers in the UK, those who look after a family member with a physical illness or disability tend to be more widely recognised than those caring for a relative with a mental health or substance misuse problem, who are more likely to remain 'hidden' (NSPCC, 2006; MHF, 2010). Where positive relationships and support exist, young carers can experience increased resilience, personal growth, confidence and maturity as a result of their caring role (Joseph et al., 2009). However, where these are absent the damaging consequences for a young person's development may include a lack of friends, poor engagement with school and educational under-achievement, and social exclusion including, for girls, reinforcement of gender inequalities. These negative outcomes rarely exist in isolation but become interrelated in cumulative, mutually reinforcing pathways (NSPCC, 2006).

A recent study carried out by one of the authors (Helen Donnellan) illustrated the high level of caring undertaken by children at the threshold of adolescence, particularly those making the transition from primary to secondary school, with its attendant loss of familiar peers and adults as sources of support. However, most stress is likely to be experienced by young carers in middle adolescence, when developing independence from parents. Opportunities for peer group friendships may present complex challenges in the context of caring roles and tasks which draw them back repeatedly to the confines of home and family. Young carers need to be able to consider different options, particularly at times of change, and to ask questions about the condition, diagnosis and prognosis of those for whom they are caring, as well as about their own well-being. Unfortunately they frequently report feeling ignored or excluded by a range of professionals. Further information about support services for young carers is included in Chapter 7.

Key messages for practice

1. Whilst adolescence is not necessarily the time of perpetual turbulence often portrayed in popular media, it does involve major changes in all areas of children's development, and those who mature early are at increased risk of a range of emotional and behavioural problems, including eating problems and obesity, poorer educational performance and increased risk-taking, including earlier sexual activity, tobacco, alcohol and drug use, and delinquency.

2. Brain development during adolescence is largely responsible for significant advances in cognitive and language skills, including the capacity for meta-cognition (thinking about thinking) and moral reasoning. Whilst these developments require some major adjustments in their relationships with parents and teachers, in particular, it is important to remember that they still have significant limitations in their thinking skills, including a strong tendency to focus only on short-term goals, largely ignoring longer-term consequences.

3. Significant advances in children's social and emotional development during adolescence demand that adults responsible for their care and education adjust their expectations and relationships with them. Parenting, for example, may need to be more flexible, allowing adolescents to become progressively more autonomous and independent whilst continuing to provide the secure base and clear boundaries that all children need for optimal development.

4. Much social work intervention with adolescents and their families who are experiencing significant problems can benefit from an understanding of the concept of resilience, with interventions designed to reduce the risk factors and promote the protective factors at individual, family, school and community levels.

5. Bullying, increasingly involving communications via mobile phones and the internet, is a significant problem for many children, especially during adolescence. Parents and schools need to be aware of both the potential benefits and dangers of cyberspace and alert to any signs that children's well-being and development is being harmed by its use.

Additional resources

Beatbullying
> Beatbullying works across the UK to stop bullying, using online and face to face peer mentoring, counselling and support
> www.beatbullying.org/index.html

Royal College of Psychiatrists (RCPSYCH)
> Readable information on a wide range of issues affecting the emotional and mental health of young people
> http://www.rcpsych.ac.uk/expertadvice/youthinfo/parentscarers.aspx

L. Steinberg (2005) Cognitive and Affective Development in Adolescence, *Trends in Cognitive Sciences*, 9(2), available online at www.scribd.com/doc/2074118/Cognitive-and-Affective-Development-in-Adolescence-Laurence-Steinberg

Barnardo's Research Briefing: 'Bouncing back'
> This promotes resilience in vulnerable children and young people
> www.barnardos.org.uk/bouncing_back_resilience_march09.pdf

PART II

Professional Practice

Introduction: social work as a professional activity

In Part II we explore a range of issues involved in contemporary social work practice by applying ecological theory and knowledge of child development (covered in Part I) to social work with specific groups of children. However, before doing so it is important to recognize that social work is a professional activity, governed by particular expectations and requirements that have profound influences on practice.

The professional identity of social work

Throughout its history social work has been a contested activity, shaped by the conditions and requirements of the times in which it has been practised. However, Thompson (2009) has identified five key aspects that mark social work out as a unique activity, distinctive from any other profession:

1. **The central role of statutory duties,** with social workers often acting as representatives of a local authority (as well as being personally accountable for their actions). The limits of a social worker's powers and actions are often misunderstood by the wider public and other professionals, and practitioners have a responsibility to ensure that their role (and its constraints) is at least understood by those with whom they are working.
2. **Managing care and control,** with social workers typically bearing a dual responsibility for promoting and protecting the wishes, needs and rights of their service users, at the same time as protecting the interests and welfare of others, including the wider community.
3. **Working for change in individuals and in society,** often at the point where 'personal troubles' become intertwined with 'public ills', which means that action designed to safeguard and promote the well-being of individuals must always be

taken within the context of an understanding of wider social problems such as poverty, deprivation, social exclusion, exploitation and abuse.

4. **Dealing with the failures of social policy, systems and structures**, where social workers can often feel blamed or used as scapegoats as they set about 'doing society's dirty work', especially in areas of practice that are sensitive to public opinion, such as child abuse or domestic violence.

5. **A commitment to social justice**, with social workers required to challenge injustices, including individual, institutional and structural discrimination.

It is clear, therefore, that whatever the social, political or organisational contexts within which they are required to operate, social workers are often called upon to manage conflicting demands and tensions, balancing issues of care and control, empowerment and protection, support and surveillance, prevention and crisis intervention, and statutory duties and available resources. This requires a high level of professional integrity and expertise, as well as an understanding of issues related to the boundaries of professional relationships and the process of professional decision-making.

Professional integrity

In its everyday use, the term 'integrity' typically refers to people who behave in an honest, fair or truthful way, upholding conventionally accepted moral standards, especially in the face of adversity. However, it can also be used more specifically in a professional context to signify actions based on codes of conduct drawn up by professional associations and regulatory bodies to guide practitioners in what they should do and how they should do it. Professional integrity also involves the capacity continually to review and reconcile the tension between personal and professional values, a process which is likely to include consideration of over-arching issues such as human rights, social justice, inclusion, equality and anti-discrimination, as well as more specific issues such as protecting vulnerable people from harm, promoting their independence, and respecting their privacy (providing that this does not threaten their welfare).

Whilst a combination of legislation, statutory guidance, agency procedures and professional codes of conduct lay the foundations for professional practice, individual workers also need to use reflexive skills to make sense of their practice in the context of their own values, and vice versa, enabling professional integrity to be maintained even if the organisational climate is less than ideal (Banks, 2010). Many of the issues that crop up in every day practice are explored in relation to work with the different groups of children in Chapters 4 to 9.

Professional expertise

In contrast to the emphasis on the values which underpin the development of professional integrity, the issue of professional expertise casts the spotlight first on the use of occupational power, and then on the knowledge and skills of social work.

Although professions may vary in important ways, professional identity usually involves laying claim to a particular area of expertise, based on a minimum of degree-level specialist training, formal processes of registration and regulation, and a shared identity between members (McSweeney, 2012). All of this means that professionals can exercise occupational power in ways that do not necessarily benefit the people who use their services. However, this should not deter social workers from aspiring to develop the sort of knowledge and skills that give rise to legitimate claims to professional expertise, as long as this is always done with the clear intention of promoting the well-being of service users, rather than serving the self-interests of a particular professional group (Burt and Worsley, 2008).

Thompson and West (2012) have identified five aspects of knowledge essential for all forms of social work practice:

- **Background knowledge** is based on everyday experiences and includes the common sense that everybody possesses.
- **Procedural knowledge** is concerned with how to get things done within particular roles, organisational settings and national contexts.
- **Theoretical knowledge** covers the principles and concepts that underpin social work practice.
- **Empirical knowledge** refers to the factual knowledge based on evidence from research.
- **Self-knowledge**, which includes awareness of personal capabilities and, importantly, limitations.

However, whilst these different forms of knowledge provide the foundations for the development of professional expertise, it is the way they are integrated with more experiential forms of knowledge, and used in practice, that ultimately determines the quality of service provided. This is where social work skills come to the fore, as they determine how effectively practitioners are able to use their knowledge in interactions with a wide range of individuals, groups and communities. Social work skills can be grouped under the following broad headings:

- **Communication skills:** appropriate for working with a wide range of service users, involving verbal, non-verbal and written forms of communication, and utilising specific skills such as listening, reflecting, summarising, influencing and negotiating, as well as advocacy and mediation.
- **Relationship-building skills:** which enable practitioners to engage effectively with people of all backgrounds, including the ability to develop, maintain and (ultimately) end relationships based on principles of partnership and a focus on strengths, demonstrating respect, empathy and authenticity.
- **Interprofessional working:** based on an understanding of the roles and responsibilities of different professionals and organisations, sharing information when appropriate, and taking a partnership approach.
- **Personal skills and qualities:** including the capacity for critical reflection, empathy, reliability and honesty, skills in assessment and analysis (including the use of imagination, creativity and curiosity), and awareness of the impact of self.

Whilst all social workers are required to demonstrate the use of these skills during their qualifying training, they should aim to enhance them further throughout their careers, as part of their continuing professional development.

Professional relationships

Social work practice also involves the ability to establish and maintain appropriate boundaries within the relationships that practitioners form, especially with service users. Elsewhere in the book we will highlight the central importance of relationships in social work, but in an analysis of professional conduct cases undertaken by the General Social Care Council in England (before it was dissolved in 2012) inappropriate relationships between social workers and service users were identified in 20 per cent of the referrals they had received. Some of the most serious breaches of the professional codes of conduct in place at the time involved inappropriate sexual relationships; and other transgressions included social workers allowing service users to visit their homes or failing to declare other contacts outside of work, as well as exchanging personal telephone numbers and buying presents (GSCC, 2011).

Although the professional codes of conduct governing social work practice in different parts of the UK provide general guidelines about professional relationships, they cannot specify the behaviour appropriate in every situation, so individual practitioners will need to work these out for themselves in the particular circumstances of each case. However, it should always be borne in mind that, because of their prior experiences and disadvantages, many people involved with social workers will be particularly vulnerable to exploitation by others, especially those in positions of greater power and influence. It is therefore essential that practitioners understand the responsibilities they carry for setting appropriate boundaries in these relationships, ensuring that service users have a clear understanding of the worker's role in their lives. Whilst close and confiding relationships will inevitably (and appropriately) develop with some service users, it must always be made clear by the social worker that the basis of all such relationships is professional rather than personal. Practitioners are more likely to overstep appropriate relationship boundaries with service users when they are feeling emotionally vulnerable or unsupported themselves, so it is important to develop self-awareness and to attend to self-care, as well as talking about relationships with service users within supervision, maintaining personal support networks, and having an identity outside of the professional role.

Professional decision-making

Two modes of thought – *intuition* and *analysis* – are typically involved in making professional decisions. Although they are frequently cast as opposites, in practice each contributes distinctive but complementary ways of helping to order information and knowledge to assist deliberation in the contexts of complexity and uncertainty which typically characterise social work with children. Although intuition is related to the 'background' knowledge already discussed, it is based more on perceptions and emotions than conscious cognitive processes, and is most likely to come to the fore where there is a need for rapid decision-making. It is a significant component of professional practice, without which social workers would probably be unable to deal with many of the situations they face on a daily basis. However, because intuition typically operates in advance of more conscious deliberation and analysis, it is often difficult to explain. Practitioners therefore also need to use their capacity for critical reflection and analysis to identify the various sources of knowledge informing their intuitive judgements. Schön (1995) has proposed a series of questions that can be used to promote critical reflection and analysis in relation to intuition, including:

- What features of the situation am I noticing and why?
- How am I framing the situation?
- What previous experience am I drawing upon?
- What knowledge and skills am I using?

The key task for a professional social worker often lies in identifying the salient features of a situation amongst the infinite amount of information potentially available and piecing them together to form an accurate and coherent 'picture' and hypotheses for different courses of action. This is where ecological theory can be of great help, providing a logical, systemic, organizing framework. Where there are ambiguities about what is happening, choices will have to be made on the basis of deliberation, understanding and judgement about the balance of probabilities at the time, and the nature of the services or interventions that are considered to have the best chance of being effective according to the available evidence. Professional social workers must develop the ability to formulate reasoned arguments and sound judgements in the face of uncertainty, while continuing to question their hypotheses and fostering a willingness to adjust or abandon an approach in the light of fresh evidence. This last point is particularly important when it is realised that, for example, serious case reviews of children who have suffered abuse and neglect frequently highlight the tendency for social workers to make an initial decision which they then stick to, even in the face of subsequent contradictory evidence (Brandon et al., 2005).

CHAPTER 4

Working with children in need

CHAPTER OVERVIEW

In this chapter we begin by considering variations in the way that the concept of 'children in need' is used across the UK and the close links between family poverty and children in need. We then go on to examine critically assessment and planning processes for children in need, as well as prevention and early intervention services, including evidence about the effectiveness of family and children's centres and home visiting services, and conclude by giving some consideration to a number of parenting programmes.

Introduction

The legislation in force in each of the four countries of the United Kingdom places similar duties on local authorities to safeguard and promote the welfare of 'children in need' within their area. Children are considered to be in need if they require services in order to achieve or maintain a reasonable standard of health and development, to prevent significant or further impairment of their health and development, or if they are disabled. So far as is consistent with these duties, local authorities are required to promote the upbringing of children in need by their families and to provide a range and level of services appropriate to the needs of children in their area. As well as social work activities (including assessments, care planning and casework involving advice, guidance and counselling), the services provided can include financial assistance, family centres, day care, out of school activities, accommodation, groupwork, therapeutic interventions, domiciliary support and welfare rights advice. Local authorities are required to publish information about the services they provide, as well as facilitating the provision of services by voluntary, private and independent organisations.

Children in need across the UK

Despite this apparent uniformity in approach across the UK, there are inevitably variations in the way that different jurisdictions, as well as individual local authorities and practitioners interpret and use the concept of 'children in need'. England and Wales, for example, publish information based on an annual census of local authority involvement with children in need, but no similar information is gathered under this heading in Scotland and Northern Ireland. The annual census conducted in England and Wales indicates that somewhere between 3 and 3.5 per cent of children in the general population are considered to be 'in need' at any one time (DfE, 2010; Statistics for Wales, 2011). However, this figure represents a considerable underestimate of the real level of need amongst children across the UK, with over 7 per cent estimated to be disabled, for example, and 10 per cent to have a mental disorder (Green et al., 2005; Blackburn et al., 2010). National statistics about children in need also mask considerable variations between local authorities, largely as a result of differences in their socio-economic characteristics. For example, the 2010 children in need census in England revealed variations from less than 1.5 per cent of children coming under this heading in Herefordshire, one of the least deprived local authorities in the country, to nearly 9 per cent in Haringey, one of the most deprived.

In both England and Wales, the main reason for children being assessed as 'in need' is abuse or neglect (including domestic violence), followed by childhood disability or illness, family dysfunction, acute family stress, parental disability or illness (including substance misuse), absent parenting, socially unacceptable behaviour, and low income, normally in that order. However, the appearance of 'low income' at the bottom of this list, as the primary reason for a child being in need, is rather misleading as relative poverty and other aspects of inequality provide the context within which the vast majority of child welfare concerns arise in the UK (Little et al., 2003).

Families living in poverty

The negative effects of living in poverty on the health and well-being of parents and children have been well documented in a large number of research studies. For example, it has been found that children growing up in poor households have more negative attitudes towards their school and teachers, more difficult home lives, lower self-esteem, and engage in more risky behaviour, including truancy, smoking and drug use (Tomlinson et al., 2008). Some of the early causes of childhood disadvantage are revealed in the longitudinal *Growing Up in Scotland* study, which found that young motherhood (under 25 years) and lone parenting are particular risk factors for social and economic disadvantages, which in turn are associated with poorer health-related behaviour, such as lower levels of breastfeeding and attendance at antenatal classes, and higher levels of smoking (Bradshaw and Martin, 2008). The health inequalities literature also makes it clear that children from disadvantaged homes are much more likely to have poor physical and mental health and lower incomes throughout their adult lives (e.g. Graham, 2000; Davey Smith, 2003).

One of the most detailed ecological studies of the effects on families of living in disadvantaged circumstances investigated the stress, support and coping strategies of parents living in areas characterised by high levels of poverty, unemployment, overcrowding, residential instability and lone parent households (Ghate and Hazel, 2002). The parents who lived in these environments reported much poorer physical and mental health than the general population, with similar but smaller trends reported for the well-being and behaviour of their children. The study also demonstrated that the poorer the area in which families lived the greater the likelihood that parents would experience more stress factors and the less positive they would be about the area.

Despite their increased levels of problems compared with the general population, most parents living in what were classified as 'poor parenting environments' made limited use of the family support services provided by statutory agencies, voluntary organisations and community groups. Such services were often considered to involve stigma and professional interference, with the risk of losing control over one's life and children. The reputation of some services, as agents of control rather than sources of support, often preceded them, and even informal support from family and friends was considered to present a risk of loss of privacy, as well as potentially imposing reciprocal obligations, thereby causing more stress. As the researchers noted 'support, viewed from this perspective, looks distinctly disempowering' (ibid., p. 179).

A number of factors were identified that were linked to increased risks of parents feeling that they were not coping successfully, including parenting alone, large family size, having a difficult child, being in poor emotional health, and having a lot of current problems. The parents who considered that they were coping tended to *feel* well supported, although this perception was not dependent on the size of their social support networks or their actual use of support. In fact, the parents who rated themselves as coping least well also tended to be the greatest 'consumers' of both informal and formal support.

The lessons that emerge from this and other studies are that many parents living in disadvantaged circumstances are reluctant to accept help, even when they have significant problems; and when support is accepted it does not necessarily increase parents' ability to cope. Besides resolution of some of the underlying disadvantages which they are experiencing, such as poverty and poor housing, what these families require, therefore, is the availability of family support services which do not stigmatise and disempower them, and which openly acknowledge and aim to address the full range of difficulties that they are facing.

Practice pointer 4.1

Think about an example from your own experience where poverty or other aspects of disadvantage had a significant impact on the family. How did this affect the parent(s) and child(ren), and what was or could have been done to improve their lives?

Assessment and planning processes

In order to establish whether or not a child has unmet needs affecting their health or development, social workers and other professionals are often required to undertake assessments, usually in partnership with the child and family concerned. Practice tools, such as *The Framework for the Assessment of Children in Need and their Families* used in England and Wales (DH/DfEE/HO, 2000; NAW/HO, 2001), and similar frameworks used in Scotland and Northern Ireland (Scottish Government, 2008; DHSSPS, 2008), have been developed to help practitioners determine whether or not a child is 'in need' (or is suffering or likely to suffer significant harm), and whether any action needs to be taken to promote the child's welfare, including the provision of services. Whilst frameworks of this nature have been criticised for their limitations in addressing such things as the explicit assessment of risk, the impact of the wider socio-economic and political environment on children and families, and the needs of particular groups (e.g. disabled children), nonetheless they represent the best tools currently available to assist practitioners in what is often a complex task (Calder and Hackett, 2003; Jack and Gill, 2003).

Practice pointer 4.2

If you have used one of these assessment frameworks (and associated forms), how helpful was it in promoting the welfare of the children and families concerned? How did you try to encourage the full participation of the children and families involved?

Based on ecological theory (Bronfenbrenner, 1979), these frameworks present the factors to be considered as a triangle, with three interrelated domains covering the child's developmental needs, the parents' capacity to meet those needs, and the impact of wider family and environmental factors (see Figure 4.1). They are

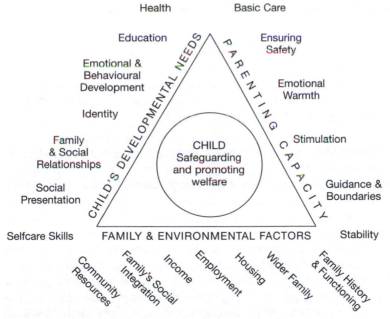

Figure 4.1 Assessment Framework (Department of Health, (DH/DfEE/HO), 2000)

intended to help practitioners not only to gather information about all of the relevant factors in a child's life, which is recorded on standard forms, but also to consider the influences that they have on one another. The capacity of parents to ensure their child's safety, for instance, will be influenced not only by their own personal characteristics and behaviour, but also by other factors, such as the child's health and education (e.g. long-term illness and attitude towards bullying within the child's school) and the family's social integration and access to community resources (e.g. local play and youth facilities, and parenting support services).

However, it is important to stress that any approach to assessing children's needs is not simply a paper exercise. It requires that social workers engage directly and attempt to work in partnership with the children and family members they are assessing, using appropriate communication skills to make it clear why and how the assessment is being undertaken, who it will be shared with and what will happen next (Rose, 2010). By getting to know the child and other family members in this way, as well as taking a systematic, ecological, evidence-based approach to recording and *analysing* all of the relevant information, practitioners should be able to develop a detailed, holistic picture of their lives.

Practice pointer 4.3

Think about the range of communication skills you have either used or might need to use when undertaking assessments with children and families. How confident do you feel in each area, and in what ways do you need to develop your skills?

Unfortunately, research into social work decision-making suggests that practitioners are generally better at collecting information than they are at analysing it (Horwath, 2002; Cleaver et al., 2004; Turney, 2009). As already discussed, decision-making can be understood as occurring along a continuum, from analytical at one end to intuitive at the other. Although there is movement backwards and forwards along this continuum, according to factors such as the circumstances and complexity of the case and the level of expertise of the worker, most practitioners rely more on intuition, which is primarily based on their own (subjective) experience, than on analytical strategies, which are primarily based on (objective) evidence (Taylor, 2007). Whilst both forms of decision-making have their place in social work, and often co-exist to a greater or lesser extent, it is especially important that student social workers and newly qualified staff, who are likely to lack the depth of professional experience necessary for reliable intuitive decision-making, are able to formulate their decisions primarily on the basis of systematic analysis of the evidence.

This requires that practitioners in the early stages of their careers develop their analytical skills, including the ability to break issues down into their component parts, exploring the relationships between them in a rigorous, systematic and methodical way. The capacity for critical thinking is also important, taking a questioning approach to issues and evaluating different claims and arguments in a way that enables reasoned, logical and justifiable conclusions to be reached. Reflexivity, which involves the capacity both to reflect back on things that have happened ('thinking-*on*-action') and to think on one's feet ('thinking-*in*-action') is also important, always recognizing the historical, socio-cultural and political contexts within which these thoughts are taking place. It is only by questioning oneself in this way, and making appropriate use of supervision, that inexperienced practitioners will learn to cope successfully with the uncertainty, complexity and conflict with others often involved in social work with children and families, enabling them to come to truly independent professional judgements (Fook, 2002; Turney, 2009; Donnellan and Jack, 2010).

Practice pointer 4.4

Think about the various approaches to decision-making that you have used in different cases and situations. What were the reasons for using either a more intuitive or a more analytical approach? How effective do you think your approach was? How well are you able to explain the basis of your intuitive responses to others?

Family group conferences

In order to ensure that the rhetoric of partnership with children and their families is translated into practice, many local authorities across the UK (and other countries around the world) use what are known as 'family group conferences' (FGC) to ensure that parents, children and extended family members are all given the opportunity to be involved in making plans for children's welfare. Although the details of different FGC schemes vary, the majority share several features (Marsh and Crow, 1998; Jackson and Nixon, 1999;

Thomas, 2000; Nixon et al., 2005). For example, after the family and the agency concerned have agreed that an FGC would be helpful, an independent coordinator with the necessary mediation, listening and organisational skills for the role, but no direct responsibility for the case, is normally appointed. After identifying the relevant members of the family network to involve, the coordinator will then discuss the reasons for the meeting with them and invite their participation. At the conference, agency staff and other interested parties are typically asked to provide relevant information and all who are present discuss the situation, including the reasons for concern and possible ways forward. The family members then usually meet together as a group, along with any advocates acting for vulnerable participants (e.g. children or abused women), to formulate a plan. The other members of the FGC then rejoin the meeting to discuss and, if necessary, amend the plan before it is agreed to by all present. Depending on where the FGC sits in the overall decision-making processes of the agency concerned, the plan may have to be forwarded to another forum (e.g. child protection case conference or looked-after children review) for final ratification. The plan normally consists of agreed aims, actions and timescales, with a date identified to review its operation, at which point the full FGC may be reconvened and the plan revised, as necessary.

Whilst evidence about the effectiveness of FGCs is relatively limited, a survey of stakeholders interviewed in Scotland revealed that the whole process was widely valued as a means of 'empowering' families and ensuring that children were given the opportunity to participate in decisions affecting their lives. Overall, those consulted viewed FGCs as an effective means of producing comprehensive and realistic plans for children which were 'owned' by the whole family (Scottish Executive, 2007).

Whether or not FGCs are used, all child welfare agencies will have clear processes for planning and reviewing the services they provide for children in need. Whilst the specific procedures and recording formats used vary between countries and individual agencies, practitioners should be aware that legislation across the UK requires that the wishes and feelings of the child and the views of parents are taken into account in any decisions that are reached. The procedures to be followed also vary in relation to work with specific groups of children, with those relating to safeguarding, looked after children, disabled children, young offenders and children with mental health problems each being covered in more detail in the following chapters.

> ## Practice pointer 4.5
>
> Think about your experience of a decision-making forum about a child in need. How helpful was it for the child and any family members involved? Is there anything about the process that could have been better and, if so, what?

Prevention and early intervention

It has already been acknowledged that, on their own, social workers are unlikely to be in a position to *prevent* many of the underlying causes of children's needs, such as poverty and inadequate housing. Nevertheless, it is imperative that the effects of disadvantages like these are fully recognised and openly acknowledged, and that concerted efforts are made to address them, often in collaboration with other professionals and agencies. Unfortunately, several studies in the UK (e.g. Dowling, 1999) have revealed that social workers often display what is referred to in the literature as 'poverty blindness', failing to identify the central role that poverty and other social and economic disadvantages play in the lives of the majority of people with whom they are working. If practitioners are not to add to these disadvantages they need to be alert to the factors in society that underpin different forms of inequality and, at the very least, to acknowledge the effects that they are having on the well-being of the children and families with whom they are working.

In order to work effectively with people from a range of backgrounds, practitioners need to recognise the values, norms and traditions that influence the way that different individuals and groups think and behave (Korbin, 2002; Laird, 2008; BASW, 2009). Despite the diversity of cultures with which practitioners need to be familiar, the majority of those in contact with child welfare services are likely to have many problems in common with one another, particularly their experience of living in disadvantaged circumstances. Whatever their background, families with limited financial resources, for example, are likely to be heavily dependent on their local neighbourhood and kinship networks for their day-to-day survival and sense of belonging (Mumford and Power, 2003), to share feelings of stigma, guilt and shame, and to experience high levels of stress and social isolation (Attree, 2004; Seaman et al., 2006; Green, 2007; Hooper et al., 2007; Ridge, 2009).

Culturally competent social work practice with families living in poverty therefore needs to recognise and attempt to address these issues (Jack and Gill, 2012).

Besides being familiar with the literature, the best way for practitioners to develop the knowledge which underpins cultural competence is to listen closely to the children and adults they work with when talking about their lives. The communication and listening skills used in these encounters need to be allied to empathy for the particular difficulties faced by different family members as they attempt to cope with living in disadvantaged circumstances on a daily basis. Practitioners need to be able to communicate an understanding both of the way that economic opportunities are structured within society and of the impact that economic inequalities can have on family functioning and child well-being (Jack and Gill, 2010a, 2010b).

Beyond these communication skills, practitioners (and their employing agencies) need to be willing and able to advocate on behalf of disadvantaged families in order to help them maximise their level of income and address any other significant problems that they are experiencing, as well as supporting efforts to improve the resources available in their neighbourhoods. This might involve supporting the establishment or maintenance of anti-poverty community organisations, such as food cooperatives or credit unions, as well as informal child and family support services, such as pre-school play groups for younger children and sports and youth clubs for older children.

Where prevention of a family's problems is not possible, at least in the short term, child and family social workers also need to be aware of the benefits of early intervention. International reviews of the evidence demonstrate that the most effective forms of intervention often involve a combination of early years development for children alongside support for their parents (C4EO, 2010a; Sylva et al., 2010). As a result of evidence of this nature, early intervention services, including family and children's centres, home visiting schemes and parenting support programmes, have received government support across all parts of the UK over recent years (e.g. Allen, 2011). Evidence about the effectiveness of each of these approaches to early intervention is reviewed below, with the emphasis on services for pre-school children and their families, as information about services for older children and their families is included in later chapters.

Family and children's centres

Integrated family centres, which provide combinations of day care, early years education, parenting support and community development, typically run by local authorities or voluntary organisations, have been in existence across the UK for many years (e.g. Gill, 1988; Southwell, 1994; Tisdall et al., 2005; Warren-Adamson and Lightburn, 2010). The comprehensive range of interprofessional services provided by these centres has been identified as the best way of delivering a continuum of support for young children, families and communities with additional needs, in particular helping children to develop the language and communication skills vital for the 'school-readiness' discussed in Chapter 1 and making opportunities for peer and professional support available to parents (C4EO, 2010a).

Evidence about the effectiveness of family centres in supporting children and families experiencing significant difficulties has tended to rely heavily on parents' (usually mothers') self-report studies. However, an evaluation that involved more objective outcome measures and a comparison group, carried out in South Wales, found that families referred to a centre because of child protection concerns did notably better than similar families supported only by the local social work team. Although the sample sizes were small (only ten in each group), none of the children referred to the family centre was on the child protection register or in local authority care after 12 months, while the number of children on these measures in the families receiving only field social work services had actually risen (Pithouse and Lindsell, 1996).

More recently, a particular model of family centre services, designed to provide improved access to childcare, health, early education and family support, was developed under the Sure Start programme established in England in 1999. Based largely on evidence of the long-term benefits of early intervention programmes for disadvantaged families in the USA (Weikart and Schweinhart, 1997; Garces et al., 2002), Sure Start Local Programmes (SSLPs) were initially located in some of the most disadvantaged areas of the country, but with their services available to all who lived there to avoid stigmatising their users. SSLPs initially used a community development approach, with services shaped to meet the particular needs and wishes of local people and managed through partnerships involving all relevant agencies, parents and community representatives (Glass, 1999). Although this resulted in some variation between the services offered by different local programmes, the core services available always involved a combination of home visiting and centre-based support for children and parents, including day care, play and learning, access to health care, advice about children's health and development, and additional support for those with special needs.

From 2005/06 SSLPs came under local authority control and began to operate as 'children's centres', with ring-fenced funding phased out. By April 2010 there were over 3,500 Sure Start children's centres across England, but major reductions in central government funding and changes to the governance arrangements meant that, in the words of one of the original architects of the programme, 'only the brand name survived' (Glass, 2005). In 2012 the national evaluation programme reported the findings of a longitudinal study, comparing outcomes in over 5,000 families with 7-year-old children from 150 SSLP areas with those for children and families living in similarly disadvantaged areas without an SSLP. The researchers found that the Sure Start families had benefitted in a number of ways, with mothers engaging in less harsh discipline and providing more stimulating home learning environments for their children, as well as providing less chaotic home environments for boys. Although lone parents and those in workless households in SSLPs also displayed better life satisfaction, no consistent SSLP effects were found for children's development at the age of seven, possibly because *all* children would have benefitted from pre-school and primary school experiences by this age.

From the evidence available it is possible to conclude, therefore, that whilst the services provided by integrated family centres and Sure Start children's centres have the potential to improve outcomes for children and parents, the size of any beneficial effects is dependent on the quality and availability of the services provided (Statham, 2000).

Home visiting services

Whilst many family centres provide outreach or home visiting services alongside their centre-based activities, another category of early intervention services focuses on providing support to families either exclusively or primarily within their own homes. Most of the home visiting schemes in operation in the UK today have their origins in the work of David Olds, a paediatrician who began a nurse home visiting scheme for low income first-time mothers in the USA in 1977. Since then this approach has grown to become an established model, serving over 20,000 mothers in 20 states across the USA. Strongly influenced by the work of Uri Bronfenbrenner (1979) on the social ecology of families, these programmes:

- Work with disadvantaged first-time parents.
- Take place in the home.
- Use specially trained nurses.
- Start during pregnancy and last for up to two years after the child's birth.

Old's model is the basis of the Family Nurse Partnership (FNP) programme, introduced in the UK in recent years, which aims to improve pregnancy outcomes, children's health and development, and the life course of the disadvantaged first-time mothers targeted. Evaluations of nurse home visiting services of this nature, including the FNP programme in the UK, demonstrate that they have the potential to reduce the incidence of childhood injury and improve maternal well-being and parent–child relationships (Oakley et al., 1990, 1996; Roberts, 1996; Olds et al., 1997; Bull et al., 2004; Barnes et al., 2011).

Other home visiting services for parents with pre-school children operating in the UK, of which Home-Start is probably the most well-known, involve a combination of home visiting by trained and supported volunteers (often other local parents) rather than professionals, as well as group support. The stated aims of Home-Start are to help parents develop better coping strategies and improved confidence, make better use of local services, feel less marginalised and isolated, and develop stronger relationships with and provide happier and safer homes for their children. In 2009–10 there were 240 Home-Start schemes operating in England, with a further 32 in Scotland, 26 in Northern Ireland, and 18 in Wales, with over 21,000 volunteers supporting more than 34,000 families across the UK (Home-Start, 2010). Most families who use Home-Start services are experiencing multiple stresses, including physical and mental health problems (particularly maternal depression), social isolation and problems with the social and emotional development of their children. Parents say that the voluntary nature of Home-Start and the use of local parent volunteers rather than professionals help to overcome their natural reluctance to accept support. However, the results of Home-Start evaluations have been rather mixed. For example, although the recipients of the services interviewed in one study stated that it had made a positive difference to their lives, no differences in actual outcomes were identified when they and their children were compared with a control group (McAuley et al., 2004). This suggests that, whilst the voluntary elements of Home-Start can make it more acceptable to parents than other home visiting programmes involving elements of compulsion or delivered by professionals, the support provided may need to be more intensive and comprehensive to be effective for families experiencing multiple problems.

Parenting programmes

Parenting programmes delivered by professionals offer one of the main ways in which more intensive support can be provided to families with multiple needs. Whilst the aims, content, modes of delivery and theoretical ideas underpinning different parenting programmes vary, reviews of the international literature (e.g. Moran and Ghate, 2005) indicate that effective schemes share a number of features, including:

- Clear aims, with an understanding of the mechanisms involved in achieving them.
- Multiple components, providing support for children as well as parents, and using a variety of methods, materials and approaches to learning.
- Professionally trained workers capable of building relationships with parents through partnership working.
- Non-stigmatising and culturally appropriate services, including specially designed activities for fathers, employing ethnic minority staff and using culturally appropriate materials.

Several programmes meet these criteria, including the Incredible Years, Parents Altogether Lending Support, and Mellow Parenting programmes. The Incredible Years (IY) Basic, for example, is a 12-week group-based parenting programme, with sessions lasting for approximately two hours. Leaders are trained to build on parents' strengths, helping them to develop their knowledge and confidence, as well as extending their support networks. The programme uses a range of strategies designed to bring about cognitive and behavioural change, which include showing parents video vignettes of families (from different cultural backgrounds) to develop understanding of effective approaches to parenting tasks. Parents also learn about child development, parent–child relationships, the development of predictable routines, how to teach their children problem-solving skills, and home safety-proofing and monitoring strategies (Webster-Stratton and Reid, 2010). It has been found to reduce harsh parenting and increase positive discipline and nurturing behaviour in parents, as well as reducing conduct problems in children and improving their social competence. Significant effects of this nature, for example, were identified six to eighteen months after the intervention in two UK evaluations (Hutchings et al., 2007; Bywaters et al., 2009).

Parents Altogether Lending Support (PALS) combines aspects of the IY programme with SPOKES (Supporting Parents on Kids Education), which focuses on enhancing parental support for children's reading. In a controlled trial with parents and primary school children living in a disadvantaged area, the researchers found that PALS improved several aspects of parenting, including increased sensitive responding to children and use of effective discipline approaches, and reduced levels of criticism. Child concentration was also observed to have improved, although parental reports of child behaviour problems did not show any improvement (Scott et al., 2006). The research team also noted that the majority of families in this highly disadvantaged area were actually coping satisfactorily, from which they concluded that area targeting of parenting support interventions was unlikely to be effective, on its own, and should be combined with individual assessments of need.

The final programme considered here is Mellow Parenting (MP), which is an intensive, 14-week, group-based programme for families with severe problems, including child protection concerns. Parents attend the programme one full day each week, with their children being cared for separately. The morning sessions for the parents focus on the links between their own experiences of childhood and their current parenting, whilst the afternoon sessions use videos of parent–child interactions to help parents identify positive strategies which they are encouraged to try out for themselves as 'homework'. Some of the video material involves recordings of the parents' interactions with their own children in the middle part of the day, when they have lunch and play with their children. The video feedback on these interactions, which is given by trained group leaders, has been identified as one of the key components of effective parenting programmes (Bakermans-Kranenburg et al., 2003). MP has been evaluated in a number of studies, including one conducted in three family centres and a community centre in Scotland, which involved comparisons between 54 mothers who received the intervention with 28 who did not (Puckering et al., 1999). By the end of the programme the researchers found that the majority of the intervention mothers had improved emotional health and better relationships with their children, and that the behaviour of the children had also improved. At follow-up a year later, the intervention parents who had initially benefitted from the programme tended to have maintained the benefits.

Information about other evidence-based parenting programmes, for specific groups of children, is provided in later chapters. However, evidence about the effectiveness of the programmes discussed so far indicates that most parents who attend derive some benefit, but that those with multiple problems, often involving combinations of poverty, poor housing, social isolation, marital conflict, poor physical and mental health, and children with severe emotional or behavioural problems, often drop out or do not have their personal difficulties satisfactorily resolved. These are, of course, the very families most likely to be involved with social workers, who may therefore require more intensive interventions. For example, where issues of anti-social behaviour and associated threats of eviction are present, the services provided by Family Intervention Projects (FIPs), set up in different parts of the UK in recent years, may be needed. Using 'assertive' and 'persistent' approaches, FIPs aim simultaneously to challenge and support families to address the roots of their antisocial behaviour, normally working in the families' own homes over periods ranging from six to twelve months. An evaluation of 53 FIPs established in England in 2006–07 found that the majority of the families who had completed programmes during the study period showed reduced antisocial behaviour, criminal activities and evictions, as well as improved outcomes for their children. The main features of FIPs associated with successful outcomes (which could equally be applied to any aspect of social work practice with children and families) were: the quality of the staff; small caseloads; a dedicated key worker; a whole family approach; involvement for as long as necessary; creative use of resources; sanctions only used in combination with support; and effective multi-agency relationships (White et al., 2008).

Practice pointer 4.6

What do you know about the early intervention and support services in your area? How can you find out about the availability and quality of what is available, and what can you do to ensure that appropriate families use them?

Key messages for practice

1. Ecological theory serves to remind us about the importance of assessing the contribution of factors at individual, family and community levels (including the interactions between them) to the well-being of children and families.
2. Most children and families involved with social workers will be living in disadvantaged circumstances, so it is important to recognise the effects this is having on their lives, which often includes a reluctance to accept help from professionals or other sources.
3. Family group conferences or other approaches, which give children and families a central role in making decisions which affect their lives, have the potential to improve their engagement in assessment and planning processes and to commit to achieving the agreed goals.
4. International evidence clearly indicates the benefits and features of successful early intervention services for children in need and their families, including integrated family/children's centres, home visiting schemes and parenting programmes.

Additional resources

Family Rights Group
  Advises families in England and Wales whose children are involved with or need children's services and promotes family engagement by professionals with a specific section about FGC processes for families.
  www.frg.org.uk/the-family-group-conference-process

Family and Parenting Institute
  Publications specifically for professionals in relation to parenting and early learning
  www.familyandparenting.org/All-Our-Publications/For-Practitioners

Joseph Rowntree Foundation: Education and Poverty Programme
A round-up of evidence from eight studies exploring children's different backgrounds and experiences of poverty and social differences in education
www.jrf.org.uk/sites/files/jrf/2123.pdf

CHAPTER 5

Working to safeguard and promote the welfare of children

CHAPTER OVERVIEW

In this chapter we begin by considering the extent of child abuse and neglect and the ways that official responses have developed in the UK, including the legislation, policy and procedures currently in place. This is followed by a critical examination of the causes and effects of child abuse and neglect and consideration of effective approaches to assessment and intervention, including relationship-based child protection practice.

Introduction

The mistreatment of children has occurred throughout history, and children growing up in the UK today are exposed to a wide range of risks, including accidents on the roads and at home, abuse and neglect by adults, and bullying by other children. Whilst some social workers are employed in specialist 'child protection' roles, such as initial response or assessment teams, it is important to stress that *every* practitioner working with children is engaged in safeguarding to a greater or lesser extent. All social workers in the UK carry professional responsibility for promoting the welfare of children and taking appropriate action when they have reasonable grounds to suspect that a child is at risk of significant harm (Jack, 2006).

The extent of child abuse and neglect

The extent of child abuse and neglect depends not only on the definitions used, but also whether the estimates are based on general population surveys or officially recognised cases. Only a small proportion of children who experience abuse or neglect are known to child protection agencies, and even those children who are known report far more episodes of abuse than appear in official records (Gilbert et al., 2009). For example, a study of children attending hospital accident and emergency departments in the UK estimated that only about one in thirty who were considered to have been physically abused by their parents were investigated by child protection agencies (Woodman et al., 2008).

The National Society for the Prevention of Cruelty to Children (NSPCC) have conducted two large-scale prevalence surveys, using a definition of 'severe maltreatment' which includes: serious emotional neglect or lack of physical care and supervision that would place a child at risk; physical abuse that results in an injury such as a broken bone or black eye; and rape or forced sexual contact with an adult or a child. Based on thousands of interviews with young people across the UK, the most recent survey estimated that nearly 20 per cent of 11- to 17-year-olds are likely to experience 'severe maltreatment' at some time (Radford et al., 2011). This figure is in stark contrast to the much lower proportion of children officially identified as being at risk at any one time by the child protection systems which currently operate across the UK, which are typically in the range 0.25–0.40 per cent, representing less than 50,000 children. Whilst this is likely to be only a fraction of the actual number of children suffering significant harm as a result of abuse and neglect at any one time, it is important to remember that the NSPCC estimate is based on children's experiences throughout their childhood, rather than on one particular day in the year.

After many years of steady decline, the number of children across the UK who are the subject of 'child protection plans' because of ongoing concerns about neglect or abuse has risen over recent years. However, this is likely to say more about changes in child welfare practice, in response to further child abuse tragedies and new research findings, than about the incidence of maltreatment *per se*. Neglect now accounts for up to half of all officially recognised child protection concerns, followed by physical and emotional abuse, with the smallest proportion falling under the heading of sexual abuse (Vincent, 2008).

> **Practice pointer 5.1**
>
> What do you think about the different approaches to estimating the prevalence of child abuse and neglect? Which approach most accurately captures the real scale of ill-treatment experienced by children in their own families across the UK?

Official responses to child abuse and neglect

Official concern and state action to protect children from abuse and neglect by their parents and carers is nothing new, as evidenced by the emergence in late Victorian times of national societies for the prevention of cruelty to children, and the passing of no fewer than four Acts of Parliament about the protection of children between 1889 and 1908. However, most commentators point to the emergence of 'battered baby syndrome', based on the work of Henry Kempe and his medical colleagues in the USA in the 1960s, as key to the 'rediscovery' of child abuse in modern times (Parton, 1979, 1985; Corby, 2000). This work was influential in the UK and elsewhere, helping to create an understanding of child abuse within a 'medical model' involving individual diagnosis and treatment, often with limited recognition of the social and economic factors involved. However, it was not until the official inquiry into the death of Maria Colwell (DHSS, 1974) that child abuse was brought to the attention of the wider public in the UK. Maria, who had been in foster care for five years following severe neglect within her birth family, was killed by her stepfather after being returned home under local authority supervision. Although the agencies involved in the case were criticised for failing to work effectively together, the inquiry report concluded that the ultimate failure rested with the system for dealing with child abuse and neglect itself, which they considered should still have been able to function adequately despite the individual errors which occurred.

In the wake of the Maria Colwell inquiry, new procedures for dealing with cases of child abuse and neglect were introduced across the UK, including case conferences, child abuse registers and multi-agency area review committees, all of which, in amended form, are still in existence today. However, despite these changes, in the years following Maria's death more child abuse inquiries were held into the deaths of children during the 1980s. To a greater or lesser extent, all of these inquiries started from the assumption that child abuse was predictable and therefore preventable. However, whilst this can appear to be true when looking back at what has gone wrong in an individual case, there is good evidence that knowledge about risk and protective factors cannot reliably be used to *predict* the families in which child mistreatment will occur. For example, in a cohort study involving over 14,000 children screened for potential child abuse and neglect, only one in nine children considered to be at high risk at birth had been the subject of a child protection case conference by the age of five. Overall, for every family correctly identified, more than 12 families were falsely identified (Browne, 1993).

Despite such evidence about the limitations of screening tools, the widespread belief that child abuse and neglect can be prevented still persists today, which means that social workers and other welfare professionals are often criticised for not acting quickly or decisively enough to protect children. However, this criticism was turned on its head following the events in Cleveland in the north-east of England in 1987, when over a hundred children were taken into local authority care in the space of a few weeks because of alleged sexual abuse within their families (Butler-Sloss, 1988). Many of them were subsequently returned to their families (like others taken into care as a result of similar allegations in the Orkneys, Rochdale and Nottingham at around the same time) because of the problems of proving allegations of child sexual abuse in the courts, where disputed medical evidence and the testimony of typically young and frightened children, as well as shortcomings in the practice of social workers and other welfare professionals at that time, came up against the vehement denials of adults who were often strongly supported by politicians and the media. The fact that the adults accused of child sexual abuse in many of these cases came from across the social spectrum, rather than being restricted to those from the disadvantaged backgrounds typically associated with parents accused of physical abuse and neglect, was also significant, often rendering the suspicions 'unthinkable' (Campbell, 1988, p. 6). In a reversal of previous attacks on social workers, they were now widely criticised for acting too hastily and without sufficient evidence, intervening inappropriately in the lives of 'innocent families', as they were often uncritically portrayed in the media.

> ## Practice pointer 5.2
>
> What effect do you think criticism of social workers, in relation to balancing the sometimes conflicting rights and needs of children and their parents, is likely to have on practice? Think about how you might try to ensure that you strike the right balance in individual cases.

The development of child protection legislation, policy and procedures

Whatever the rights and wrongs in cases of alleged child abuse and neglect in the UK in the 1980s, it was clear that the legislation and procedures governing the protection of children within their own homes needed to be redrawn, not only to balance the sometimes conflicting rights and needs of children and their parents, but also to refashion the relationships between families and welfare professionals. In England and Wales these considerations helped to shape the Children Act 1989 and the accompanying statutory guidance (DH, 1989). A greater emphasis was placed on professionals working closely together and in partnership with families, with parents given new rights to attend case conferences and challenge emergency interventions by local authorities. Children were also given more say in decisions which affected them, and local authorities were given powers to facilitate the accommodation of alleged abusers so that children could remain at home whilst inquiries were carried out.

Child protection inquiries in England and Wales are carried out under section 47 of the Children Act 1989, which requires local authorities to investigate if they have reasonable cause to suspect that a child in their area is suffering or is likely to suffer significant harm. Further legislation (section 175 of the Education Act 2002 and section 11 of the Children Act 2004) places duties on local authorities and their partner agencies (including schools, NHS bodies and the police) to ensure they discharge their functions with regard to the need to safeguard and promote the welfare of children. The procedures to be followed in carrying out these duties in England are detailed in the statutory guidance *Working Together to Safeguard Children* (DCSF, 2010a). Similar legislation and statutory guidance exists in the other parts of the UK, with practitioners and agencies in Wales required to follow the *All Wales Child Protection Procedures* (SSIA, 2008), whilst those in Northern

Ireland work to the *Standards for Child Protection Services* (DHSSPS, 2008). In Scotland, where the Social Work (Scotland) Act 1968 provides the overarching mandate for social work intervention, it is the Children (Scotland) Act 1995 which adds specific duties in relation to investigating the likelihood or risk of children suffering significant harm, with the legislation once again being supported by statutory guidance (Scottish Executive, 2010).

As a result of the legislation and statutory guidance in force in different parts of the UK, as well as other organisational and legal differences such as Northern Ireland's joint Health and Social Services Boards and Scotland's Children's Hearing system, there are inevitably some variations in child protection arrangements. However, despite these differences there are a number of common features, including multi-agency child protection case conferences, which use the same four categories of maltreatment ('neglect', 'physical abuse', 'emotional abuse', 'sexual abuse') to identify and register ongoing concerns via child protection plans, with similar processes for the review of plans and the deregistration of children where concerns no longer exist. All four countries also operate multi-agency strategic partnerships, at local levels, to develop, disseminate, monitor and review their child protection procedures and services.

Reviews of the child protection systems in Scotland and England

Despite the significant developments which have taken place in child protection legislation and procedures in the UK over the last four decades, it is an uncomfortable fact that children who are already known to child welfare agencies continue to suffer abuse and neglect, causing policy-makers periodically to re-examine the effectiveness of their safeguarding systems. In recent years, for example, the deaths of Kennedy MacFarlane in Scotland, and Victoria Climbié and Peter Connelly in England, have prompted wide ranging reviews of the respective child protection systems.

An audit of child protection services across Scotland identified that statutory child protection agencies were only dealing with a small proportion of the actual numbers of abused and neglected children, partly because many children and parents didn't trust them and therefore wouldn't approach them for help (Scottish Executive, 2002). This lack of trust is a serious problem which is found in all parts of the UK and is one of the main reasons for the development of confidential helplines for vulnerable children alongside formal child protection systems (Butler and Williamson, 1994; Jack, 1997a). Just as worrying, however, was the finding that less than half of the children who were referred for help were effectively protected or had their needs met, and that in one in five cases child protection services were judged to have made the situation *worse*. The outcomes for individual children were found to be highly dependent on the quality of social work practice, the key features of which were knowledge and skills in assessment, analysis and planning, and partnership work with parents and wider family members designed to achieve positive change. Unfortunately, the achievement of good quality practice was often not supported by the agencies involved, which characteristically were overloaded with information and used the child protection register as a gateway to resources, with no other benefits identified (Scottish Executive, 2002).

Following the audit, Scottish agencies providing services for children were initially given three years to reform their activities, with the focus on partnership approaches to improving outcomes for children. The aim, set out in *Getting it Right for Every Child* (Scottish Executive, 2008), was to ensure that all children in Scotland are safe, healthy, active, achieving, respected, responsible and included. A single, multi-agency assessment, planning and recording framework was introduced to facilitate the coordination of services, with a greater focus on early intervention. This was backed by a new multi-disciplinary child protection inspection regime, as well as additional resources to strengthen local children's services, including the creation of a 'child protection hub' to develop and disseminate knowledge. Evidence from inspections suggests that progress across Scotland was initially rather patchy, with only a small number of areas showing significant improvements, leaving many children and families who did not meet the thresholds for child protection services with little or no help (Perrott, 2009).

In many ways, the policies implemented in Scotland mirror those developed in England following publication of the Green Paper *Every Child Matters* (DfES, 2003), which also emphasised the importance of integrated, multi-agency working, a focus on outcomes for children, and the benefits of early intervention. The English reforms followed the public inquiry into the death of Victoria Climbié which concluded that, yet again, there had been a 'gross failure' of the child protection system, with several opportunities to protect Victoria missed by agencies that were 'under-funded, inadequately staffed and poorly led' (Laming, 2003, para. 1.18). Despite the major changes which followed this inquiry, the death of another child, Peter Connelly, as a result of abuse by his carers a few years later led to a further review of the system for safeguarding children in England (Laming, 2009). As in Scotland, the Laming Review recognised the central role of the quality of social work practice in outcomes for children and their families, but it also drew attention to the effects of long-standing difficulties in the recruitment, retention and support for social workers in children's services in England, which was linked to the effects of negative media reporting.

The Laming Review concluded that the safeguarding of children needed to be given greater priority and resources across all relevant government departments and policy areas, and also made recommendations for improvements in social work training, recruitment and retention as part of a wide-ranging reform programme to be led by a Social Work Task Force. Whilst all of the review's recommendations were accepted by the Labour Government of the day, they were soon to be replaced by the Conservative/Liberal Democrat Coalition Government elected in 2010, which immediately set up a child protection review of its own, headed by Professor Eileen Munro.

The Munro Review found that previous reforms in England had occurred in a piecemeal fashion in response to individual cases of abuse and neglect, without looking at the system as a whole. It identified four key 'driving forces' behind the child protection arrangements that had developed: reactions to child abuse tragedies; belief that the complexity and uncertainty of child protection work could be overcome; a focus on professional error in inquiry reports without sufficiently examining the reasons for such errors; and an emphasis on targets and performance indicators rather than the quality and effectiveness of the help given. Munro concluded that these factors had created a system which emphasised procedures and recording at the expense of the development and support of the professional expertise needed to work effectively with children and families (Munro, 2010). She therefore recommended that the child protection system in England needed to be based on less central prescription and more local discretion (Munro, 2011a, 2011b).

Although the coalition government accepted the recommendations of the Munro Review, and at the time of writing much reduced statutory guidance for child protection work is about to be published, it is not yet clear what impact the wider social work reform programme will have on child protection practice in England and other parts of the UK. However, the very difficult economic circumstances prevailing at this time, including major cuts in public spending, mean that any plans for developments in children's services requiring significant additional resources are unlikely to be implemented in the foreseeable future.

The causes and effects of child abuse and neglect

As already noted, the chances of children experiencing abuse or neglect depend on a wide range of interacting risk and protective factors operating at individual, family, community and society levels of influence (Belsky, 1993). For example, based on evidence from extensive reviews of the international literature (e.g. Cicchetti and Valentino, 2006), as well as general population surveys (e.g. Radford et al., 2011), we know that children born prematurely or of low birth weight are at increased risk of abuse and neglect, as are disabled children. The evidence also shows that parents' developmental histories, personal resources and family relationships can be major risk factors. For example, a history of maltreatment in a parent's own childhood has been found to be a significant factor in increasing the risk of child abuse and neglect, as has the presence of mental health problems, inability to cope with stress, drug and alcohol abuse, learning difficulties, parental conflict, and poor parent–child relationships, often characterised by a mixture of low warmth, high criticism and harsh discipline.

Moving out to wider community and society influences, the evidence indicates that culture can be an important factor, with social acceptance of violence towards children, for example, increasing the risk of physical abuse. Poverty, at both family and community levels, has also been found to increase the risk of different forms of child abuse and neglect. Not only does it tend to contribute to the stresses experienced by parents, but it can also have damaging effects on the social relationships which exist within impoverished areas, often referred to by the term 'social capital', with higher rates of abuse and neglect associated with both social isolation and community dysfunction (Jack, 2000).

Some of the best evidence about the particular risk and protective factors associated with child abuse and neglect in the UK is provided by a large cohort study of all children born in Avon (in the south-west of England) between April 1991 and December 1992. As part of this study, data on over 14,000 children and their families was analysed to identify the main factors associated with those either investigated for suspected abuse and neglect (293) or whose child's name was placed on the child protection register (115) before the child's sixth birthday. Reflecting national patterns across the UK, the majority of registrations fell under the headings of neglect, followed by physical and emotional abuse, with only about one in nine cases involving registration for sexual abuse (Sidebotham et al., 2001, 2002, 2006).

At the individual level, children of low birth weight were found to be at increased risk of registration, while at the family level the risk of registration was greater for children whose parents were young, had a record of low educational achievement, had a history of mental health problems or abuse as a child, or who had reported fewer positive attributes of their children when they were babies. Children in single parent and reconstituted families were also found to be at greater risk for registration, but the presence of domestic violence was not found to be a significant factor in this study, and maternal employment acted as a protective factor, being associated with a lower risk of investigation. However, the highest risks of being investigated and registered because of concerns about child abuse and neglect were associated with indicators of *economic deprivation* (paternal unemployment, occupancy of council housing, overcrowding and non-car use) and *social isolation* (number of meetings with friends during the previous month, perceptions of belonging to a close circle of friends, the number of people who could be confided in). The study found that there was a strong relationship between the number of indicators of deprivation and the risk of official concerns about child abuse and neglect, with children living in the poorest families 11 times more likely to have their names placed on the child protection register before their sixth birthday than those living in the most affluent households, after controlling for parental background factors. This latter finding indicates that the influence of parental background factors on rates of detected child abuse and neglect is largely explained by the way that these factors influence the family's socio-economic circumstances, rather than because of any direct effects of their own (Sidebotham et al., 2006, p. 498).

The evidence from many sources indicates that factors closest to the child, such as the parents' characteristics and behaviour, tend to have the most significant impact on the likelihood of child abuse and neglect occurring. However, the Avon study indicates that the socio-economic deprivation of families and communities exerts the most powerful influences on rates of officially recognised concern about these issues. Taken as a whole, this means that effective approaches to the prevention and reduction of child abuse and neglect must provide a combination of services and support that have the capacity simultaneously to address issues at individual, family, community and society levels of influence.

The effects of abuse and neglect on individual children depend on a large number of variables, including the nature, severity and frequency of the maltreatment, the individual characteristics of the child, the quality of their family and other relationships, and the wider environmental circumstances in which they are living. However, prospective longitudinal studies which take into account individual and family factors consistently show that child abuse and neglect are associated with long-term deficits in educational achievement as a child and in economic prosperity as an adult. Child maltreatment also increases the risks of children developing behaviour problems, anxiety and depression. For example, it has been found that between a quarter and a third of maltreated children meet the criteria for clinical depression by their late twenties, and there is also consistent evidence that both physical and sexual abuse are associated with a doubling of the risk of attempted suicide by this age. Prospective studies also reveal a strong association between all forms of maltreatment and negative effects on aspects of children's physical health, including higher rates of obesity, as well as increasing the risk that they will commit crimes, both as juveniles and as adults (Gilbert et al, 2009). The ways in which these issues influence social work practice with young offenders and children experiencing mental health problems are considered in Chapters 8 and 9, respectively.

Assessment and interventions

Whilst social workers usually have the lead responsibility for investigating cases of suspected child abuse and neglect, concerns about children's general welfare are often initially identified by professionals working in universal children's services. Health visitors and nursery staff, for example, are often the first to spot any problems amongst pre-school children, and teachers obviously play a key role in relation to school-aged children. However, many of these professionals face dilemmas about if and when to pass on any concerns that they might have, especially when they are based on a series of small worries, for example in relation to the early signs of neglect, rather than something more obvious and clear cut (Action for Children, 2012). This can be a particular issue within the safeguarding systems that operate across the UK, which are generally geared towards the formal investigation of higher-level concerns, but are not so good at responding in a more informal manner to the early signs of problems.

Practice pointer 5.3

In your role as a social worker, how might you ensure that you have good working relationships with the other professionals involved in safeguarding children?

Social workers (and their managers) are responsible for deciding what action to take in relation to any child protection referrals they receive, which can range from immediate action to safeguard the child to a decision that no further action is required, typically utilising the frameworks for assessing 'children in need' discussed in the previous chapter to guide their decision-making. In addressing questions of significant harm, for example in reports to child protection conferences or courts, social workers are expected to comment on the likely effects of any abuse or neglect on the child, both in the present and the future. This requires that decision-making is:

- **Child-centred:** which involves listening to the child and taking his or her wishes and feelings into account (along with factors such as racial heritage, religion, gender and any disability).
- **Rooted in child development:** recognizing the likely impact of any abuse or neglect given the child's current age and stage of development (as well as his or her future development).
- **Strengths-focused:** including identifying difficulties.
- **Multi-agency:** involving other professionals, particularly those responsible for the child's health and education. (HM Government, 2005)

Unfortunately research has revealed that, in their interactions with families when child protection issues are being investigated, social workers tend to be preoccupied with official concerns, rather than focusing on a family's strengths and resources. Typically, they also use a lot of closed questions rather than listening to the adults and children with whom they are engaged, providing few opportunities for reflection and demonstrating low levels of empathy. This latter finding is particularly important because the level of empathy shown was found to be a key factor in reducing parental resistance and increasing the amount of information they were willing to disclose, *without* reducing the attention also given to official concerns (Forrester et al., 2008).

If children talk to anyone about their problems, including abuse and neglect, it is most likely to be a friend, parent or sibling, although younger children may also talk to a teacher. However, children of all ages are generally reluctant to talk to *anybody* because of a mixture of: shame, embarrassment, self-blame and fear of loss of control; getting someone else into trouble; loyalty towards their alleged abuser; making things worse; not being believed; and stigma. On top of these feelings, many children also lack information and understanding about what constitutes abuse, who to speak to about it, and the possible outcomes of a disclosure. Research with children who have experience of safeguarding systems stresses the importance they place on feeling they are being listened to, understood and believed, as well as having some control over what happens (C4EO, 2010b).

There are clear messages here, not only for policy-makers in relation to providing information and education programmes for children about abuse and neglect, but also for practitioners. Social workers and other child welfare professionals need to ensure that they explain everything carefully to the children with whom they are working, drawing on knowledge about child development to ensure that they communicate in age-appropriate ways (e.g. regularly repeating important information and checking the child's understanding of the explanations provided), as well as reassuring the child that any questioning of his or her account does not imply disbelief. Practitioners also need to be aware of just how intimidating it can be for a child to talk about sensitive issues with strangers, especially authority figures such as social workers, and in formal settings such as case conferences. This requires that such settings are made as 'child-friendly' as possible, with the number of adults involved kept to a minimum, and good preparation and support provided for the children involved, possibly including the use of independent advocates and the opportunity to contribute to formal hearings via written testimonies, taped interviews and video-links.

Children with experience of safeguarding systems say they want social workers to be caring, understanding, knowledgeable and trustworthy. They particularly dislike frequent changes of social worker and any signs of disrespect towards themselves or their family. However, despite any concerns about the child protection system, most children ultimately express few regrets about disclosing their abuse and report that the support they received was beneficial in the long run (C4EO, 2010b).

As you would expect, the majority of parents with experience of child protection investigations report high levels of stress, with the impact of allegations on their family often being felt for a long time afterwards. Assessments are stressful, particularly if social workers do not strike a balance between recognizing their strengths and resources alongside their problems, and case conferences are experienced as particularly difficult, often because parents are given insufficient time to absorb what has been written about them in reports. Whilst many parents feel they are not able to influence decisions reached within case conferences, they appreciate being treated fairly, which reduces their feelings of disempowerment and facilitates subsequent engagement with professionals. Parents also value social workers and other professionals who listen to their point of view and display genuine empathy, take a partnership approach which involves them in decision-making, and are respectful, honest and consistent. Positive recognition of parents' *efforts* at all stages of the child protection process is also considered to be beneficial (Bell, 2003; Dale, 2004; Spratt and Callan, 2004; Buckley et al., 2008; Ghaffar et al., 2011).

Relationship-based child protection practice

The views of children and adults with experience of child protection systems underpin the 'Signs of Safety' approach to practice developed by Turnell and Edwards (1997, 1999). This approach, which draws heavily on ideas from the field of solution-focused brief therapy, is designed to help social workers build relationships with parents when child protection issues are involved by focusing on parents' strengths and the resources which exist within the family, rather than focusing only on problems and risks.

In practice this means:

- Listening to the story of each family member about the cause(s) of concern.

- Exploring exceptions (i.e. times when mistreatment could have happened but didn't, and why it didn't).
- Jointly assessing the family's strengths and resources and the likelihood of future maltreatment using scaling questions (e.g. where 0 = 'high risk' and 10 = 'complete safety').
- Establishing the goals of different family members in the context of the agency's concern that any abuse or neglect must stop: How will this be achieved? What will happen instead? How will changes be measured?
- Gaining the commitment of all family members to pursue the agreed goals.

Programmes for preventing or reducing child abuse and neglect

Many features of the family support programmes discussed in the previous chapter on working with children in need are also relevant when considering effective interventions in relation to families where there are child protection concerns. For example, there is good evidence of the effectiveness of the Family Nurse Partnership programmes in reducing physical abuse and neglect.

Other programmes which demonstrate effectiveness in reducing physical and emotional abuse and neglect include the Early Start parenting programme, which promotes collaborative problem-solving and the provision of support, advice and mentoring to help mobilise families' strengths and resources. In the first year, weekly home visits (of 60 to 90 minutes each) are made by specially trained nurses or social workers. Less frequent visits can continue to be made to individual families for up to five years, with the over-all aim of reducing child abuse and neglect by improving children's health, parenting skills, the stability of partnerships and the family's socio-economic circumstances. The Triple P programme also aims to enhance parental competence and address dysfunctional parenting by providing comprehensive, population-based services to parents with varying levels of problems. For parents with serious problems, often involving child protection concerns, a 'standard' or 'group' programme is provided, involving either ten sessions (of 90 minutes each), or an eight session programme consisting of five (two-hour) group sessions followed by three telephone follow-ups. Additional modules on partner communication, mood management, stress and coping skills can be added if required. Other interventions, such as Parent–Child Interaction

Therapy (PCIT), show benefits in preventing the recurrence of physical abuse. This is a behavioural approach which aims to increase parental skills and improve the parent–child relationship using direct coaching and skills practice in sessions led by PCIT trainers. Six group orientation sessions, focusing on increasing understanding of the negative consequences of physical abuse and the development of self-motivation, are followed by between 12 and 14 sessions involving individual parent–child pairs, and the programme ends with four follow-up group sessions for parents and children separately (Barlow et al., 2006; MacMillan et al., 2009).

However, evidence about the effectiveness of programmes for the prevention or reduction of child sexual abuse is more limited. Whilst a range of school-based education programmes have been shown to be capable of increasing children's knowledge and protective behaviours, their effect on the actual incidence of sexual abuse is unknown. There is evidence that cognitive behavioural therapy shows benefits for sexually abused children with symptoms of post-traumatic stress, and Treatment Foster Care (TFC) programmes also show benefits over remaining at or returning home for a range of maltreated children. TFC programmes typically involve extra training for foster carers in child behaviour management and parent–child interactions, as well as daily telephone support and supervision, weekly group meetings, and 24-hour on-call crisis interventions. Some also provide day treatment or weekly therapeutic playgroup sessions for the children concerned (ibid.).

The evidence about the causes of child abuse and neglect discussed earlier also points to the importance of ensuring that parents receive help to address their own problems, such as drug and alcohol abuse, mental illness and domestic violence. Unfortunately, research with parents who have been involved in child protection processes suggests that their experience of specialist services is variable. For example, the majority of the mothers involved in a study in three local authorities in the north of England reported satisfaction with the specialist drug and alcohol services they had received, but they were less happy with the domestic violence services on offer, and their experiences of mental health services were mixed, with most help coming from their own social workers because specialist services were difficult to access (Ghaffar et al., 2011).

Practice pointer 5.4

Not all programmes which aim to prevent or reduce child abuse and neglect exist in every area, so it might be helpful to gather information about what is currently available in the area where you work. Try to find out what each programme involves for the participants, what it aims to achieve, and how outcomes are measured.

Local authority accommodation

Many social work decisions about children considered to be at risk of significant harm, such as whether or not to recommend that they be removed from home in the first place, the placements provided for them if they are removed, and when (or if) to return them to their birth families, do not lend themselves well to the sort of controlled trials involved in developing the evidence of effectiveness reviewed so far. It is therefore necessary to draw on more 'real world' research to understand some of the outcomes of social work practice.

One such study involved tracking the progress of a group of 77 children referred into the child protection systems of four local authorities over an eight-year period (Brandon and Thoburn, 2008). Overall, there were good outcomes for many children who were removed from home permanently at the start of the study period, as well as for some who remained at home throughout, with outcomes generally less positive for children removed who later returned home. A common factor amongst the nine most successful cases at the end of the study was a long period of security and stability with family members or substitute carers who were committed to them, combined with good relationships with friends and at school. Of the children who demonstrated the worst outcomes, including significant behaviour and relationship problems, seven had never lived away from home and 13 had either returned home or were living independently at the end of the study period, with eight in placements away from home. A complex picture therefore emerges in which it is only possible to identify children who might have benefitted from earlier removal from home with the benefit of hindsight. In other cases it was clear that the quality and continuity of the services required, which included high levels of skill, fine judgements and good inter-agency working, was inadequate. The group with the worst outcomes had received episodic services, including frequent changes of social worker.

The role of communities and societies in safeguarding children

At various points throughout this chapter it has been pointed out that, because child abuse and neglect are determined by factors at individual, family, community and society levels of influence, services designed to prevent or reduce these problems have to be capable of addressing issues at all of these levels. Whilst it is therefore important for practitioners to be aware of the effectiveness of a range of interventions targeted at individual children and their families, it is equally important to consider the influence on children's well-being of factors outside of the family (Jack, 2006).

There is now considerable evidence, for example, of the way that the economic circumstances and social climate of local neighbourhoods influence outcomes for children and families (e.g. Ghate and Hazel, 2002). The umbrella term 'social capital' is used to refer to the qualities of the social environment, including the levels of trust, reciprocity, 'neighbourliness' and involvement in local activities and organisations which exist. The shared norms, values and understandings found where levels of social capital are high help to facilitate cooperation within and between different groups and are associated with a number of desirable outcomes, including lower levels of crime, better health and educational achievement, and improved child welfare, including lower rates of child abuse and neglect (Cote and Healy, 2001; Harper, 2001). Unfortunately, as you might expect, social capital tends to be lower in the disadvantaged areas in which social workers will most often find themselves working. This means that practitioners and organisations with responsibility for promoting the welfare of children and safeguarding them from harm need to be actively involved in supporting initiatives designed to promote the social capital of these areas. Amongst other things, this might involve supporting the safeguarding activities of local people and promoting partnership approaches to extending local community provision which facilitates opportunities for children and adults to interact in ways that break down barriers of mistrust and promote mutual support (Lloyd, 1993; Wilson, 2006; Jack, 2006, 2010; Gill and Jack, 2007, Jack and Gill, 2010c).

Practice pointer 5.5

How legitimate do you think it is for social workers to take the wider role suggested above, beyond the formal systems for assessing and managing risks in relation to individual children? What practical steps might you be able to take (in partnership with the children and families concerned) to improve the social environment in which they are living?

Key messages for practice

1. All practitioners working with children and families should recognise that they are involved in 'child protection' work, to a greater or lesser extent, not only preventing abuse and neglect from occurring in the first place by promoting children's welfare, but also carrying responsibility for taking appropriate action whenever they suspect that a child might be at risk of significant harm.

2. Many safeguarding outcomes are dependent on the quality of the relationships social workers are able to form with the children and families concerned. The level of empathy shown by the social worker has been found to be a key factor, for example, in reducing parental resistance and increasing the amount of information they are willing to disclose.

3. Children who have been involved in safeguarding systems stress the importance of being listened to, understood and believed, as well as having some control over what happens to them. They want social workers to be caring, understanding, knowledgeable and trustworthy, and particularly dislike frequent changes of social worker and any signs of disrespect towards themselves or their families.

4. Parents who have been involved in children's safeguarding systems find it particularly stressful if social workers do not acknowledge their strengths and resources, as well as their problems. They value professionals who take a partnership approach, listen to their point of view, involve them in decision-making, are able to meet their needs and are respectful, honest and consistent.

5. Because the risk that children will experience abuse and neglect is the product of a wide range of interacting factors operating at individual, family, community and society levels, services designed to prevent, reduce or ameliorate the effects of child

abuse and neglect must be capable of operating at all of these levels as well. This means that it is just as legitimate for social workers to engage in activities designed to build the capacity of local communities to safeguard their children, as to participate in the more formal aspects of the system for assessing and managing the risks faced by individual children.

Additional resources

Department for Education website
Provides on-line access to a wealth of policy and research material about safeguarding children. www.dfe.gov.uk

Centre for Excellence and Outcomes
Brings together information about best practice in local areas with national research and data about all aspects of services for children. www.c4eo.org.uk

K. Broadhurst, S. White, S. Fish, E. Munro, K. Fletcher and H. Lincoln (2010) *Ten Pitfalls and How to Avoid Them*. London: NSPCC
A summary of research relevant to the initial stages of assessment in children's services, available at: www.nspcc.org.uk/inform/publications/downloads/tenpitfalls_wdf48122.pdf

Working with children looked after away from home, placed for adoption or leaving care

CHAPTER OVERVIEW

In this chapter we begin by considering the characteristics of children who become looked after by local authorities and the issues of prevention and reunification. We then go on to examine what research can tell us about promoting the well-being and quality of care for looked after children, including consideration of the regulations governing visits, care planning and reviews. We conclude by critically examining social work practice with children in foster care, those placed for adoption or who are in residential care, and those leaving care.

Introduction

Local authorities in the UK are required to accommodate children who cannot be looked after at home, either through a voluntary agreement with their parents, a court order or, in Scotland, a supervision requirement. In all parts of the UK the relevant legislation is based on the principle that children are generally best looked after within the family, so if they cannot continue to live with their parents local authorities will initially explore whether they can live with a relative or friend. If this is not possible, a placement can be made with foster carers not connected to the child, or in a children's home or other form of accommodation, such as supported lodgings or a hostel, according to the needs of the child. Wherever 'reasonably practicable' placements should allow children to live near their homes, with their siblings, and not disrupt their education.

The balance of responsibilities for 'looked after children' (LAC) depends upon the route by which they become accommodated. When children are looked after under a voluntary arrangement, parental responsibility (PR) remains with the parents, but under court orders the local authority normally shares it with any other holders of PR for the child. In England, about a third of the children being looked after on any day are being cared for under voluntary arrangements, with the other two-thirds on court orders of one kind or another, mainly care orders. As 'corporate parents' for LAC, local authorities have a duty to safeguard and promote all aspects of the child's welfare.

Working with children looked after away from home

The characteristics of looked after children

Although the term 'looked after' covers a diverse range of children with different needs, most of them have experienced serious problems within very disadvantaged family circumstances. Abuse and neglect within families are the main reasons for children becoming looked after by local authorities, followed by other family problems. Children of mixed ethnic background and black children are over-represented amongst the looked after population, whilst children of Asian background are under-represented (Owen and Statham, 2009). Across the UK approximately 75,000 children are being looked after away from home at any one time, with a further 40,000 children entering or leaving care each year. The majority of children stay in local authority care for only a few weeks or months, with most returning to their families.

Whilst the number of LAC has been on the rise across the UK in recent years, it is important to point out that they still only represent a tiny proportion of all children in the general population. The majority of LAC (ranging from 72 per cent in Scotland to 88 per cent in Wales in 2010) are in foster care, with the proportion placed in residential establishments of one kind or another having dramatically declined over the past 30 years, although this has been less marked in Scotland than in other parts of the UK (DfE, 2011a; DHSSPS, 2011; Scottish Government, 2011; Statistics for Wales, 2011).

Looked after children tend to do worse than other children on a range of measures, with those in England who had been looked after continuously for a period of 12 months in 2010, for example, doing worse than children in the general population at each of the three main stages of educational assessment – Key Stages 1 & 2 and Year 11 (DfE, 2011b). Similar educational disadvantages, together with higher rates of special educational needs and mental health problems, are experienced by LAC in all parts of the UK (Maclean and Connelly, 2005). However, it is important to point out that statistics like these can be very misleading as research which compares outcomes for LAC with those of children from similarly disadvantaged backgrounds, rather than the general child population, tells a different story (Hannon et al., 2010). When the effects of pre-care experiences and circumstances are taken into account, UK research shows that children's welfare in local authority care generally *improves* over time (Forrester et al., 2009). The key, therefore, is good assessment of children's needs, identifying when some form of accommodation would help to promote their welfare, and when it would be more beneficial to continue to support them at home.

Practice pointer 6.1

Think of a case from your own practice experience in which a child's time in care clearly enhanced their development and welfare. What were the most important factors that contributed to this outcome?

Prevention and reunification

Many local authorities have established specialist services to prevent out-of-home care in cases where it is decided that it would be in children's best interests to remain with their families. In a survey of 11 English local authorities with these specialist services (Ofsted, 2011) the crucial factor identified in successful cases was the quality of the professional help provided, which was described by the children and families involved as persistent, reliable, open and honest, and involved listening to them and working from *their* starting point, helping them to recognise they had strengths and the capacity to address their problems, and balancing the needs of children with those of their parents. All of the children involved in this survey had remained at home or in the community and they and their families thought the outcomes had been positive, including improvements in their behaviour, school attendance and attainment, family and peer relationships, self-confidence and self-esteem, health and employability.

Where children do become looked after by local authorities, research consistently shows that the chances of them returning home decline sharply after about six months in care. In an effort to understand the reasons for this finding, Biehal (2006) reviewed the research in the UK and the USA and found that there was no evidence that contact with relatives per se increased the chances of children returning home, but that frequent parental visiting indicated the presence of other factors (e.g. a strong attachment, parental motivation, the absence of parental problems, positive social work activity) that did promote return home. The review also found that children placed in local authority care primarily because of their own behaviour, rather than as a result of abuse, neglect or parental problems, were more likely to return home. However, around half of children looked after by local authorities due to abuse or neglect are known to suffer further abuse if they return home, and between a third and a half of all children who return home come back into care at some future date (Biehal, 2006; Farmer et al., 2008), with some children going on to experience multiple failed attempts at reunification (Wade et al., 2010; Farmer et al., 2011).

Children who return home following a period of voluntary accommodation are deemed to be 'children in need' and a plan must be drawn up to identify the support and services required to ensure that reunification is successful. However, returns home subject to scrutiny by the courts (e.g. under care orders), which generally benefit from higher levels of assessment, monitoring and support, are more likely to be successful, as are those which benefit from skilled and purposeful social work (Farmer et al., 2008).

Promoting well-being and the quality of care

One of the best ways of promoting the well-being of LAC is for social workers and other child welfare professionals to help them to develop their resilience. This involves focusing on and developing children's strengths, ensuring, for example, that they maintain contact with family members when this is in their best interests and have the opportunity to develop secure attachments to their carers if they are looked after for any significant period of time. It also involves promoting children's self-esteem and self-efficacy through continuity of schooling and positive school experiences, enhancing their spare time experiences (e.g. culture, sport, caring for animals, volunteering and part-time work), helping them to develop a sense of purpose and involving them in making decisions about their own lives (Gilligan, 2000; Bostock, 2004).

Practice pointer 6.2

Factors that promote or undermine the development of resilience are located within children themselves, as well as in their families and the wider community. What ways can you think of that would help to develop the resilience of LAC in each of these domains?

In relation to enhancing LAC's experiences of education, for example, research in the UK indicates that schools with structures capable of meeting the individual needs of *all* pupils are best, but that additional support, for example through the advocacy role of designated teachers and good multi-agency working, are also important (Fletcher-Campbell et al., 2003). Social workers and local authorities also have key roles to play in promoting the education of LAC, not only by ensuring that they experience continuity of schooling through placement stability, but also in playing an active role in the educational progress of the children for whom they are responsible as corporate parents. This involves championing their educational needs (e.g. challenging negative attitudes and low expectations), celebrating their successes and ensuring they have access to the full range of educational opportunities (DfE/DH, 2000). This is important because research shows that 'parents' who provide a positive home learning environment and high aspirations promote children's self-concepts as learners, which in turn influences their educational achievement (Desforges, 2003).

In order to promote secure attachments between LAC and their carers the aims of any placement must also include the provision of continuity and stability. Factors which have been identified as important in promoting placement stability include:

- Good matching of the placement to the child's needs, with intensive social work support at the start of the placement.
- Arranging placements with relatives and friends (when appropriate) or experienced foster carers, and providing all carers with good support.
- Using a 'permanency planning' approach for all looked after children, including consideration of adoption (especially for younger children).
- Providing all substitute carers, including staff in residential settings, with training in behaviour management and access to

specialist support (e.g. child and adolescent mental health services).

- Avoiding changes of placement for administrative reasons, such as the child's age or the carers' approval status.
- Involving children in the design and delivery of services and listening to their views about where they want to live.
- Providing continuity in schooling, to promote educational achievement and enable children to maintain their friendship networks.
- Strong leadership from local authorities with a clear vision of their role as 'corporate parents'.
- Ensuring close collaboration between professionals and agencies, with a focus on outcomes for children. (Jackson and Thomas, 1999; Berridge, 2000; NICE/SCIE, 2010)

Visits, care plans and reviews for LAC

Each of the four countries of the UK has its own detailed regulations for LAC with which practitioners need to be familiar. However, whilst there are variations between these regulations, which take account of the different legislative contexts within which they are applied, they all have similar requirements for placement plans, visits, care plans and reviews. For example, children in the care of local authorities across the UK have to be visited at specified intervals by their social worker, typically within the first week of placement and six weekly thereafter. Social workers are required to record each visit, during which they are normally expected to see and speak to the child alone, to ensure that the placement is meeting their needs.

Care plans are also drawn up for all LAC, setting out the long-term plans for the child and arrangements for meeting their needs (including family contact, health and education), the wishes and feelings of the relevant people about the plan, and contingency arrangements in case it is not successful. Concurrent planning, in which the options of rehabilitation to the birth family and permanent placement options (e.g. adoption) are worked on simultaneously, is also common practice across the UK, especially for younger children (Monck et al., 2003). Care plans have to be reviewed within a specified number of days of the child becoming looked after and at regular intervals thereafter, with the expectation that children, their parents and carers will be fully consulted before a review, as well as attending the meeting, which aims to assess how far the care plan is working and agree any changes that are required. In England, reviews are chaired by independent reviewing officers, who are registered social workers with responsibility for monitoring the cases of LAC.

Working with children in foster care

The development of fostering in the UK

Foster care in the UK, which involves the placement of children by local authorities with approved families, originally provided a form of *permanent substitute parenting*, primarily for younger children, often with no intention that children would maintain contact with their birth families or return to live with them in the future. However, the Children Act 1948 signalled a significant shift towards the use of foster care for *temporary placements* as well, although foster parents still signed an agreement stating that they would bring the foster child up as they would a child of their own; and research at that time revealed that many foster parents continued effectively to exclude the foster child's birth family from their lives. Throughout this period, foster carers undertook the role on a voluntary basis, with payments only intended to cover the costs of caring for the foster child, without any element of financial reward.

Nowadays, however, fostering is probably best characterised as a *supplementary parenting service*, with carers (some of whom are relatives or friends of the child) normally providing placements in partnership with the child's family and working closely with social workers and other professionals. Foster care is also increasingly organised along professional lines, with foster carers being trained for the role and receiving a 'salary' in addition to reimbursement of the costs of caring for the children they are looking after. At the time of writing (2011–12) the recommended minimum weekly allowances paid to foster carers in England to cover the costs of looking after children ranged from £112 per week for a baby to £168 per week for 16- and 17-year-olds. The additional 'salary' payments made to foster carers at this time ranged from £300–700 per week, depending on the skills and experiences of the carers and the needs of the children placed with them (Fostering Network, 2011).

> ### Practice pointer 6.3
>
> What do you think about the 'professionalisation' of fostering? Do reward payments to foster carers undermine more altruistic motives or represent fair recognition for doing a very demanding job?

The modern fostering service which has developed in the UK is also much more diverse than in the past, offering care to children of all ages (over half are now aged ten years or older), and ranging in duration from only a few days through to permanent placements, but also including intermediate options (e.g. shared, part-time or respite arrangements). Many local authorities also run 'treatment' foster care programmes for children with acute and complex needs, paying the carers additional fees and providing them with specialist training and intensive support, in order to implement clearly defined plans. Research evidence indicates that programmes of this nature have the potential to increase the stability of placements, improve school attendance and reduce absconding, criminality and antisocial behaviour (Macdonald and Turner, 2007).

Private fostering

In addition to mainstream fostering services, social workers also need to be aware of the existence of private fostering, which occurs when a child under 16 years of age (18 if disabled) is looked after for over 28 days by a non-relative through a private arrangement with the child's parents. Private foster carers are required to inform the local authority about any such arrangements so that the suitability of the placement can be assessed and regular visits made to the child. However, many such placements are not notified to local authorities as a result of ignorance of the law or fear of involving social workers, and, historically, many local authorities have not provided the required levels of monitoring and supervision (DH, 2001a).

The training and assessment of foster carers

The process of recruiting, training and assessing prospective foster carers, which is governed by statutory regulations, usually takes several months. It typically requires the applicants to attend an information event, followed by an initial screening home visit, attendance on a programme of training and thorough assessment involving a series of home visits by a social worker, as well as information gathered from interviews with personal referees, reports about the applicants' health and criminal records, local authority references and a health and safety assessment of the home environment. All of the relevant information about the family is then collated and presented to the agency's fostering panel, which makes a recommendation to the agency for a final decision about the terms of any approval. Dissatisfied applicants have a right of appeal against agency decisions, and foster carers can only be approved by one agency at any one time.

According to their capabilities, successful applicants will be approved for particular types of placement (e.g. short-term or long-term/permanent) and categories of children (e.g. number, age range, special needs). Once approved, foster carers are allocated a supervising social worker who will visit them regularly to provide support and advice. Approved foster carers are required to undergo further training, as well as a process of annual review, following which their approval as foster carers is either confirmed, changed or withdrawn.

Practice pointer 6.4

What characteristics or circumstances do you think make somebody unsuitable to be approved as a foster carer, and why? Do you know the criteria used by your placement/employing agency? How do they compare with your own ideas?

Strains on the foster care system

The proportion of LAC placed in foster care has risen steadily in recent decades as awareness of the benefits of substitute family (as opposed to residential) care has developed. Foster carers currently provide placements for about three-quarters of the 75,000 children in the UK looked after away from home at any one time in approximately 45,000 foster homes. However, the pressures on fostering systems across the UK have probably never been greater, with one of the main foster care charities estimating that, in 2011, an extra 7,100 foster carers were needed in England, 1,000 in Scotland, 550 in Wales, and 100 in Northern Ireland (Fostering Network, 2011). This rising demand for foster carers is taking place at a time when the recruitment, assessment and retention of foster carers have probably never been more difficult. Not only are local authorities facing unprecedented cuts in their budgets as a result of central government policies, but other significant trends, such as growing awareness of accusations of abuse by LAC against foster carers (Biehal and Parry, 2010), and the later age at which couples tend to have their own children, hence the later that those children leave home, are limiting the supply of families willing and able to consider fostering. Pressures like these can place practitioners in an impossible situation, with limited (if any) scope to select the most suitable family to meet a child's needs, resulting in inappropriate placements having to be made. The social worker is then faced with the dilemma of whether to seek a more suitable placement for the child, necessitating further disruption, or to leave the child in a placement which may not be able to meet all of the child's needs.

Practice pointer 6.5

What factors do you think ought to be taken into account when deciding whether to leave a child in his or her current placement or to seek something better?

Family and friends placements

As noted at the beginning of this chapter, local authorities providing accommodation for children are required to consider placements with family and friends before any other options. Reviews of the research in the UK and elsewhere have found that placements with relatives, often referred to as 'kinship carers', produce similar outcomes for children as non-kinship placements, but tend to be more stable and better at facilitating contact with relatives. Looked after children also view kinship placements as more natural, and kinship carers generally show higher levels of commitment and provide better cultural matches for the children they look after. However, kinship placements can also place significant burdens on carers, who tend to be more disadvantaged, older and in poorer health than other foster carers, whilst also receiving less support and fewer services from local authorities (Nixon, 2007).

Many of the family and friends carers in one study, for example, which compared them with a similar number of unrelated foster carers, experienced strains on their relationships and a loss of earnings and pension entitlements as a result of having to give up work (Farmer and Moyers, 2005). Contact with family members was higher in family and friends placements, but, although difficulties over contact were more common, social workers were involved in supervising contact *less often* in these placements than in those with unrelated carers (27 and 45 per cent, respectively). Furthermore, when placements with family and friends were successful, the social workers involved (in line with their agencies' policies), tried to persuade the carers to apply for residence orders, which would have brought social work support to an end and a move to lower, discretionary payments. This is important because placements with family and friends were significantly more likely to survive if they received social work support, although virtually none of them had their own supervising social worker and few had access to any training or a support group. There appeared to be an assumption amongst the local authorities who took part in this study that family and friends carers ought to be able to manage without help. It is evidence like this which led Nixon (2007) to conclude that current fostering systems tend to discriminate against placements with family and friends in a way which is completely unjustified.

Practice pointer 6.6

How do you think you will manage any conflicts which arise between instructions from your manager (e.g. to persuade kinship carers to apply for residence orders to reduce costs for the local authority) and your responsibility as a professional social worker to promote the welfare of children? What actions could you take to challenge policies with which you fundamentally disagree?

Promoting successful long-term foster care placements

Reviews of the research literature indicate that the outcomes for many fostered children, particularly those who have experienced stable long-term placements, are better than those for similar children who remain at home. Despite initial difficulties on first leaving care, the majority of fostered children go on to lead happy, healthy and productive lives as adults. Whilst in foster care they value a normal family life, encouragement, respect, a good education, information about their entitlements and a say in what happens to them, including choice about family contact. Their level of satisfaction is dependent on a range of factors, including the reasons for being looked after, the balance between the care they receive in their foster families and their relationships with birth family members, and their experience of stability in care (SCIE, 2003; Sellick et al., 2004; Sinclair, 2005).

The research evidence also identifies the factors associated with successful long-term placements, which include good pre-placement assessment of children's needs, the active involvement of children in the planning process and careful matching between the needs of the child and the capabilities of well trained and supported foster carers who are provided with full information about the child. It may be important, for example, to ensure that there is a 'complementary fit' between the attachment styles of the foster carer(s) and the child (Walker, 2008). Increased risks are associated with the placements of older children and those with significant behaviour problems, or placing children close in age to, or older than, the foster carers' own children. Amongst other things, these factors should alert practitioners to the key role that the children of foster carers play in the success or otherwise of foster placements. Whilst the literature indicates that fostering has potential benefits for the children of foster carers, it also draws attention to some of the challenges involved in their relationships with fostered children (Twigg and Swan, 2007). They have to share their homes, families and possessions with children they don't know, often having to cope with difficult behaviour and upsetting issues. Success is therefore likely to depend on ensuring that their views are listened to and taken into account, and on the provision of support which helps them to anticipate and cope with any problems that might arise (Fostering Network, 2008).

Working with children placed for adoption

The first adoption legislation in the UK was introduced in 1926 in the wake of the First World War, which had resulted in a sudden increase in orphaned and illegitimate children. Up to the 1960s there were more children needing adoption than families willing to adopt, and half of the adoptions that took place were either arranged privately (by the birth mother's family) or through third parties (often doctors or members of the clergy). During this period, only 'healthy white babies' were normally considered for adoption, and the whole process was shrouded in secrecy, with no contact (or even information shared) between the child, the birth family and the adopters.

However, adoption practice began to change in the late 1960s when the number of babies available for adoption began to fall as a result of the wider availability of contraception and abortion and changing attitudes towards illegitimate children, as well as research which showed that thousands of older children were 'drifting' in care without any realistic prospect of the permanent family placements that they needed (Rowe and Lambert, 1973).

The Children Act 1975 and the Adoption Act 1976 revolutionised adoption practice by outlawing third party arrangements, enabling children in care to be 'freed for adoption' by the courts, introducing adoption allowances and post-adoption support, and giving adopted people in England and Wales the right to access their birth records (as had already been the case for many years in Scotland). These changes allowed adoption to be opened up to older children, those with special needs and children from minority ethnic backgrounds. New methods of finding families developed, and research began to demonstrate the success of adoption for this wider range of children, as well as the benefits of more openness, including greater sharing of information and on-going contact between the adopted child and members of their birth family.

Whilst the numbers of children in the UK adopted from care initially rose significantly as a result of these developments, by the mid-1990s they had begun to fall back, with wide variations also identified between local authorities. The problems at that time included many that will be familiar to practitioners today, including delays in the adoption process, difficulties in finding suitable families for the wider range of children requiring adoptive homes, the exclusion of some adoptive applicants on the grounds of, for example, smoking, weight and age, and inadequate post-placement support. As a result, new adoption targets and legislation were introduced in different parts of the UK, including the Adoption and Children Act 2002 in England and Wales and the Adoption and Children (Scotland) Act 2007, which amongst other things made provision for a permanence option (special guardianship), short of the complete and irrevocable transfer of parental rights involved in the making of an adoption order, and the development of contact and adoption registers (with strict conditions of access) to make it easier for adopted adults and birth family members to re-establish contact with one another if they wished to do so. The current legislation also makes it possible for unmarried couples (of any gender) to apply to adopt together in most parts of the UK, and ensures that the question of parental consent is dealt with before placements are made.

> ## Practice pointer 6.7
>
> What are you own views about adoption? How will you manage any tensions which arise between your personal views and beliefs (e.g. religious, cultural) and your professional responsibilities as a social worker?

The recruitment, training, assessment and approval processes for prospective adoptive parents are similar in many ways to those described earlier in relation to foster carers, but with the added complexity of planning for the whole of a child's life, requiring good knowledge of human development throughout the life course. Whilst the complexity of adoption work means that it is normally only undertaken by specialist social workers with a significant amount of relevant post-qualifying experience, all practitioners working with LAC need to know something about it. This is partly because it has to be considered as one of the options in the permanence plans drawn up for any child who has been looked after for more than a few months, and also because practitioners may be involved in preparing children for permanent placements (including adoption) through life-story work.

Life-story work

LAC separated from their birth families for any significant period of time may need help to make sense of past events in their lives. Life-story work, based on psychodynamic theory, recognises the influence of previous experiences on current feelings and behaviour, and therefore aims to provide LAC with information about their past and opportunities to talk about their experiences in a structured way, appropriate to their age and level of understanding, with someone that they know and trust. Linking children's current circumstances to their past experiences helps them to develop a more coherent narrative of their own lives, promoting the development of their identity and self-esteem, and enabling them to think about the future. Baynes (2008) identifies three main elements of life-story work: gathering together important objects, such as photographs, letters and important documents; creating a coherent narrative, often supplemented by drawings and diagrams; and communicating the story in a way that is meaningful for the child. Whilst children who are old enough are likely to be actively involved in these processes, through discussion, play, drawing and visits to previous carers and important places, they must always be given the option of not participating. Younger children may have life-story books (and memory boxes) provided for them, to use and add to as they get older.

Ryan and Walker (2007), the authors of the best known social work text on life-story work, stress the need for practitioners to have good communication and relationship-building skills and to undertake thorough preparation before they begin, as well as working at the child's pace and recognizing the need for sensitivity in handling difficult issues. It is therefore highly skilled work which should not be delegated to untrained or inexperienced staff, including students, unless they are very well supported and closely supervised.

Working with children in residential care

Background

The origins of residential care for children in the UK can be traced back to the large orphanages and reformatories, set up to care for children in need and to resocialise young offenders in the nineteenth century. Whilst the number of LAC accommodated in large institutions is now only a fraction of what it was in the past, and the proportion of all LAC placed in residential accommodation has been declining for many years, there are still children for whom it is the preferred placement option, often because a family placement is not able to meet their needs.

As a result of the greater use of foster care for LAC, the population in residential care these days tend to be older and to have more complex needs, including many who have experienced previous placement breakdowns. In a recent study in England, for example, the average age of residents in children's homes was fifteen and a half. Many of the homes in this study were multi-purpose, accommodating both short and long stay residents, which added to the problems resulting from their high levels of mental disorders (six times the level found in the general child population) and involvement with the police (Berridge et al., 2012). The majority of LAC in residential care are placed in community homes, run either by local authorities themselves or voluntary or private organisations. Community homes are usually small, open establishments which typically accommodate about half a dozen children, who attend nearby schools. The majority are also likely to be in regular contact with members of their birth family. A smaller number of LAC are also placed in residential schools and secure establishments, which are usually considerably larger and more 'institutional' in nature, taking children from a wider area and generally having fewer connections with their local communities. All forms of residential care now rely mainly on staff who work shifts (rather than living on the premises, as previously), the majority of whom are females with low levels of professional qualification but with many years of experience (ibid.).

Advantages and disadvantages of residential care

Residential care has a number of potential advantages over family-based care, including the capacity to cope with difficult behaviour and provide a range of therapeutic programmes and group activities. Many residential establishments, for example, use 'token economies', based on behavioural theory and involving systems of sanctions and rewards, as a way of promoting pro-social behaviour amongst the children who live there. Most also try to involve the children in some aspects of the everyday running of the establishment in order to promote their sense of responsibility and belonging, as well as supporting their activities and relationships outside the establishment, with particular emphasis on their educational progress and family and friendship networks.

However, residential care also faces a number of challenges, including issues of control, privacy and instability. For example, many young people in residential care only stay for a short period of time. Staff turnover is also high, so it can be difficult to establish the sort of continuity and stability that children need. There may also be problems with local residents, unhappy about having groups of 'disturbed' or 'vulnerable' teenagers living on their doorsteps. The open nature of most residential establishments also means that the children who live in them are vulnerable to sexual and other forms of exploitation by people in the local area (Stacy, 2009).

There is also a long history of physical and sexual abuse of children in residential care by the adults who are supposed to be caring for them. There have been major inquiries into cases of abuse in residential establishments, for example, in Staffordshire ('Pindown'), Leicestershire (Frank Beck), Gwent (Ty Mawr) and North Wales (Bryn Estyn). In response to ongoing concerns about the abuse of children living away from home in England, Sir

William Utting produced a report (DH, 1997) which concluded that the danger of abuse in residential homes at the time remained an ever-present threat. The report's recommendations, like those of previous reports about residential care for children in different parts of the UK (e.g. The Scottish Office, 1992) focused on the need to improve the calibre of staff and pay more attention to the health and education of all children looked after away from home. However, the costs of fully implementing recommendations like these have always been a problem in the UK, particularly when the children who live in residential care these days are often portrayed as delinquents (rather than children in need) by the media.

The effectiveness of residential care

Two recent studies, focusing on residential care in England, under-taken by David Berridge and his colleagues (2008, 2012) present a rather mixed picture of its effectiveness. Although most children were positive about the care they received, generally felt safe and showed some improvements in their behaviour, emotional and social development, and education, whilst they were in care, for others it appeared to be 'too little, too late'. Although the researchers judged the dozen homes in the second study to be comfortable, the majority also had some unnecessary institutional features, and only about half of them were providing consistently warm and caring environments.

From these and other evaluative studies which have been under-taken (e.g. Sinclair, 2006), it is clear that positive outcomes in children's residential care are likely to depend on:

- Having a range of placement options, so that children with different needs can be matched to appropriate placements.
- Providing small homes, with good management and well trained staff working to clear and agreed goals.
- Effectively controlling children's risky and antisocial behaviour (e.g. offending, bullying, absconding) and developing their pro-social skills and self-esteem.
- Promoting positive relationships between children and their families.
- Providing access to specialist services (e.g. child and adolescent mental health services).

The effectiveness of social workers responsible for children looked after in residential care is therefore likely to centre on their ability to develop a good assessment of the child's needs in the first place and to form and maintain positive relationships with the child and his or her family, as well as residential staff and other professionals, including the designated LAC teacher at the child's school and anyone else involved in providing specialist services.

Secure accommodation

Secure accommodation, which is the most restrictive placement option for LAC, can only be used for children aged 12 years or older who have a history of absconding from other forms of accommodation (when they are likely to suffer significant harm) or who are likely to harm themselves or others if they are kept in any other form of accommodation. Keeping a child in secure accommodation for all but emergency situations requires a court (or children's hearing) order, and 12-year-old children can only be detained on the direct authority of the Secretary of State.

The decision to restrict the liberty of a child, especially on welfare grounds, is a very serious one, which is usually only taken after all other options have been fully considered. It is also a very expensive option, with the Scottish government, for example, estimating that the average cost of a place in a secure unit was over £5,000 per week in 2009/10. Across the UK fewer than 330 children were accommodated in secure units on any one day during 2011. Whilst the majority of children in secure accommodation remain there for less than six months, they face considerable problems whilst they are there, not the least of which is that they are likely to be living a considerable distance from home. This inevitably increases children's unhappiness and sense of vulnerability, as well as limiting visits made by family members and restricting their involvement in planning and review meetings. It has also been found that social workers and other professionals, such as youth offending team members, are often insufficiently involved in transition planning prior to the child's discharge from secure accommodation (Ofsted, 2010).

Working with children leaving care

It will be clear from what has already been said about the disadvantages experienced by looked after children that when they come to leave care they are likely to face a number of significant challenges.

As a group their future life chances are relatively poor because their lower educational achievement means they are at heightened risk of being unemployed. Most care leavers also move to independent living at a much younger age than children living at home. Their early transition to independent living, often accompanied by a range of emotional, behavioural and mental health difficulties (Dixon, 2008), and inadequate preparation and after-care support, means they are also at greater risk of becoming homeless and engaging in risky behaviour such as offending and substance misuse.

The disadvantages experienced by care leavers have been recognised for many years, and all parts of the UK have developed improved legislation and targeted provision designed to ensure that young people do not leave care until they are ready and that they receive more effective support once they have left. Reflecting their continuing responsibilities as 'corporate parents', local authorities across the UK now have a range of duties towards care leavers. For children currently being looked after these duties include the provision of a personal adviser, who carries out an assessment of their needs and prepares a 'pathway plan' (by their sixteenth birthday), which must be regularly reviewed. Pathway plans identify how the young person's needs for accommodation, practical life skills, education, training and employment, financial support, and any other specific support needs will be met, up to the age of 21 (or 24, if the young person is in education or training), including contingency arrangements in case the plan breaks down.

Personal advisers do not have to be social workers, but they need to have good links with the range of services that care leavers require (e.g. housing, education, training and employment agencies), as well as being capable of providing ongoing advice, advocacy and support themselves. Wherever possible, a personal adviser should be someone that the young person wishes to take on this role. As most 16- and 17-year-old care leavers will not be able to claim benefits, one of the main responsibilities of the personal adviser for young people in this age group will be to coordinate the financial support provided by the local authority, which should be enough to cover the cost of the young person's accommodation and daily living expenses. Once the young person is old enough to qualify, the personal adviser should ensure that he or she claims (and receives) any benefits to which he or she is entitled.

To facilitate the work of personal advisers and improve the support available to care leavers, many local authorities have either created specialist teams themselves or contracted this work out to other agencies, as well as providing access to adult or peer volunteer mentors (Clayden and Stein, 2005). Specialist services like these have been successful in developing flexible support and a range of accommodation resources for care leavers, including staying on in their existing placements after ceasing to be 'looked after', as well as offering supported lodgings, training flats, hostels, foyers and independent tenancies. However, evidence of shortages of supply and poor quality accommodation for care leavers, in many parts of the UK, indicates that greater investment is needed in this area. The economic crisis affecting all parts of the UK has also had a devastating effect on employment opportunities for all young people, making the challenges faced by care leavers even greater. Work is particularly important for care leavers, not only because of the financial benefits that it can bring, but also because of the structure it provides in their lives and the opportunities it offers for extending their social networks and improving their self-esteem (Wade, 2003).

Key messages for practice

1. Practitioners working with LAC on a regular basis should never lose sight of just how unusual an experience it is for children in the UK to be cared for away from home. Only about 1 per cent of the total population of children in the UK ever experience being looked after away from home by a local authority, and for many of them this is likely to be a traumatic and life-changing experience.

2. Whilst much of the research about LAC identifies the major disadvantages that they are likely to experience, it is important to remember that when the effects of pre-care experiences and circumstances are taken into account, children's welfare in local authority care generally *improves* over time. The aim of social work assessments must therefore be to identify when placement away from home (and the timing of any subsequent return home) would help to promote the child's welfare and when it would be more beneficial to continue to support the child at home (or in care).

3. For children who do become looked after it is vital that social workers ensure (as far as possible) that the placement provided matches the child's needs, as well as doing everything they can to promote the child's resilience by enhancing the protective

factors and minimising the impact of any risk factors linked to the characteristics of the children themselves, as well as their families, schools and communities.

4. In the context of increasing pressures on local authority budgets, it is important for practitioners to distinguish between their sometimes conflicting responsibilities as employees and professionals, taking appropriate action to challenge decisions and policies which conflict with their (independent) status as registered social workers.

Additional resources

British Association for Adoption and Fostering (BAAF)
www.baaf.org.uk

Centre for Excellence for Looked After Children in Scotland (CELCIS)
www.celcis.org/

Fostering Network
www.fostering.net

Social Care Institute for Excellence (SCIE) Knowledge Reviews On-line
Reviews 4, 5 and 22 deal specifically with fostering, adoption and residential care, available at www.scie.org.uk/publications/knowledgereviews/

NICE
A range of expert papers EP1–23 which contributed to draft guidance (2010) for looked after children available at www.nice.org.uk/guidance/index.jsp?action=folderando=47410

CHAPTER 7

Working with disabled children and their families

CHAPTER OVERVIEW

In this chapter we begin by exploring evidence of the disadvantages and discrimination that serve as barriers to equality of opportunity and full participation in society for disabled children and their families. We then move on to examine the policies designed to address the financial disadvantages experienced by disabled children and their families, the integration of services and the role of education. Further sections take a critical look at practice developments and assessing the needs of disabled children, including safeguarding issues. We conclude with some consideration of support for carers and services designed to promote the social inclusion of disabled children.

Introduction

The first thing that practitioners working with disabled children should bear in mind is that they are children first, with all of the same rights, needs and aspirations as other children. This is important to remember because a good deal of what follows will inevitably focus on the impairments and disadvantages often associated with the lives of disabled children and their families, and the role that social workers and others can play in meeting the extra needs which arise as a result. However, the best ways of meeting these extra needs should always be considered in the context of policies and services for *all* children and families in the first instance, followed by those focused on children in need (see Chapter 4).

It was only during the 1970s and 1980s that serious notice began to be taken of the poor standards of care often provided for 'handicapped children' living away from home in hospitals and residential schools in different parts of the UK. As a result of mounting evidence of neglect and ill-treatment in these settings, specific provision for disabled children was made within legislation for all children for the first time (e.g. the Children Act 1989 and the Children (Scotland) Act 1995). Subsequent developments, including the UN Convention on the Rights of the Child, the Human Rights Act 1998, the Disability Discrimination Acts of 1995 and 2005, and the Equality Acts of 2006 and 2010 have greatly strengthened the rights of all disabled people. The changes in professional practice and public attitudes which have taken place since the 1970s mean that the vast majority of disabled children, even those with complex needs, are now cared for at home (Contact a Family, 2010).

Due to a combination of medical advances and increases in reporting, the number of children with disabilities recorded in the UK has risen in recent times. Based on the legal definition of 'disability' set out in the Disability Discrimination Act 1995 ('a physical or mental impairment which has a substantial and long-term adverse effect on a person's ability to carry out normal day-to-day activities'), it is currently estimated that nearly one million (7.3 per cent) of the UK population of children aged 0–18 years are disabled (Blackburn et al., 2010), with this figure swelling to over two million if children with 'special educational needs' (in Scotland 'additional support needs for learning') are included.

The UK government's strategy on disability for the twenty-first century, set out in the White Paper *Valuing People*, included the objective 'to ensure that disabled children gain maximum life chance benefits from educational opportunities, health care and social care while living with their families or in other appropriate settings in the community where their assessed needs are adequately met and reviewed' (DH, 2001b). However, despite a large number of policy and practice developments in different parts of the UK since then, there is continuing evidence of the disadvantages and discrimination that serve as barriers to equality of opportunity and full participation in society for disabled children and their families.

Disadvantage and social exclusion

Households which include disabled children, especially black and minority ethnic families, are more likely to experience a wide range of disadvantages compared with the rest of the population (Russell, 2003; Clarke, 2005; Blackburn et al., 2010). For example, households which include at least one disabled child are significantly more likely to live in poverty and be in debt than those without a disabled child, largely due to a combination of the extra costs of caring and more restricted employment opportunities for parents, with the result that over 20 per cent of households with a disabled child have an income of less than half the UK average (Contact a Family, 2010).

Unsuitable accommodation can also present many problems for families with disabled children, with a recent review finding that they were 50 per cent more likely than families without a disabled child to be living in accommodation which was in a poor state of repair or was overcrowded (Beresford, 2008). The majority of parents with a disabled child also report that their homes are unsuitable for the child's needs, with lack of space one of the biggest issues, alongside access and location problems (Beresford and Oldman, 2002; Cavet, 2009).

Financial and housing problems of this nature add to the extra pressures of caring experienced by the parents of disabled children, especially as disabled children typically spend more time at home than non-disabled children. This is partly because they tend to have difficulty in accessing a wide range of services, including mainstream or specialist education and training, leisure, transport, child care, short breaks and domiciliary help (Audit Commission, 2003). For example, Jenkins (2002) has highlighted the way that failure to provide leisure facilities suitable for disabled children prolongs their dependence on parents, as well as restricting their opportunities to socialise with non-disabled peers. Problems like this can be particularly acute for disabled children from minority ethnic backgrounds, who share many experiences with their white peers, but also face discrimination on the grounds of their ethnicity, with services often unable to respond to their needs in culturally appropriate ways (Hussain et al., 2002). Unfortunately, difficulties in accessing mainstream services also mean that the parents and siblings of disabled children tend to have more restricted sources of informal support via their social networks, which reduces their opportunities to enjoy natural breaks from caring responsibilities (Jenkins, 2002).

Policies to reduce financial disadvantage

Given the disadvantages faced by many disabled children and their families, policies to tackle problems such as child poverty are very important. Economic disadvantages are primarily addressed through the tax and benefit system, which for disabled children importantly includes Disability Living Allowance, as well as targeted elements within initiatives designed to improve the well-being of all children.

Disability Living Allowance (DLA) is a tax-free benefit that consists of two components intended to help with the extra costs of care and mobility, respectively. The level of payment depends on the individual's degree of impairment, with the rates in 2011 ranging from £20 to £70 per week for the care component and £20 to £50 for the mobility component. The award of DLA may also entitle children and families to additional payments under other benefits, such as income support, jobseekers allowance, council tax, housing benefit and tax credits, but practitioners should note that frequent stays away from home by a disabled child can affect the care component of DLA. Carers on low incomes who provide substantial amounts of care to their disabled children may also be entitled to Carer's Allowance, worth just over £50 a week at the time of writing.

However, as with all discretionary benefits, many of those who are entitled to claim DLA fail to do so, often because they simply don't know about it, whilst the experience for those who do claim it can be rather depressing as the forms take a medical (deficit) approach, requiring information about all of the things that the disabled person is unable to do without help. Practitioners working with low income families raising disabled children should also be aware of the Family Fund which distributed grants amounting to £33 million to approximately 56,000 families across the UK in 2011. Besides helping families to purchase essential items such as washing machines, dryers and refrigerators, grants can also be made for sensory toys, laptops, driving lessons, equipment for college and family breaks together.

Practice pointer 7.1

What information and support could be provided by social workers to maximise the take-up of benefits and other entitlements by disabled children and their families?

The development of integrated services

From an initial position of separate health, education and social care services in most parts of the UK in the 1970s, when local authority social services and social work departments were first established, there has been a gradual move towards greater coordination and integration of services for disabled children and their families. Official reports at the time drew attention to the negative effects of a fragmented approach, identifying the need for greater coordination, including the development of 'key worker' systems to provide a single point of contact for advice and services. However, despite evidence of the benefits of increased coordination, a UK-wide survey in 2003 found 'a jigsaw puzzle of services', with only about one in five teams operating care coordination schemes and far fewer providing key workers, although many stated that they planned to integrate services further in the near future (Audit Commission, 2003). Whilst most coordinated schemes which did exist at the time involved all three statutory agencies (health, education and social services), joint funding arrangements were rare, despite flexibilities introduced by the Health Act 1999 (Greco and Sloper, 2004).

Subsequent national reform programmes in different parts of the UK, including Every Child Matters (followed by the Children Act 2004) in England and Wales, and Getting it Right for Every Child in Scotland, led to the wider reorganisation and integration of services for all children, as well as reviews of services for disabled children, including *Aiming High for Disabled Children: Better Support for Families in England and Wales* (HMT/DfES, 2007), and *Caring Together in Scotland* (Scottish Government/COSLA, 2010). Whilst arguing that much had already been achieved, Aiming High acknowledged that there were still significant problems in coordinating services in some parts of the country due to differing information and referral systems and cultures, with particular difficulties involved in getting partner agencies to agree on (and stick to) shared priorities, and in routine arrangements for information sharing.

Practice pointer 7.2

How might you contribute to the improvement of joint working with other professionals and services involved in supporting disabled children and their families?

Although Aiming High set out a programme of investment, amounting to £340 million over three years (2008–11) to improve outcomes for disabled children, this did little to improve the integration of services, and a subsequent review (DCSF/DH, 2009) found that the majority of the funding had initially been allocated to extending short break services (considered later in this chapter) rather than improved integration.

The role of education

Education plays an important role in the lives of all children, but disabled children are at risk of experiencing social exclusion because of the historic investment in segregated educational provision in the UK. Until recently, one of the main aims of educational policy was to ensure that all children have the opportunity to benefit from an *inclusive* education, with the presumption that disabled children should be educated in mainstream schools unless this was incompatible with their parents' wishes or provision for other children. However, at the time of writing the Coalition Government has signalled an end to 'the bias towards inclusion' for disabled children within educational provision, arguing instead that parents should be given 'real choice' between mainstream and special schools (DfE, 2011c). The current proposals for the education of disabled children highlight one of the major issues likely to be encountered by practitioners working with any group of children. This concerns the tensions which can arise between promoting the rights and meeting the needs of children, on the one hand, whilst working in partnership with and supporting their parents, on the other. As educational policy across the UK gives priority to the views and wishes of parents (rather than children), social workers charged with responsibility for promoting the welfare of children, above all else, can face some significant practice dilemmas.

> **Practice pointer 7.3**
>
> What are your own views about the inclusion of disabled children in mainstream education? How might your personal views influence your practice?

In line with other policies, the Coalition Government is also promoting the benefits of 'reducing bureaucratic burdens', enabling professionals and services at local level to work together in more innovative and collaborative ways to improve support to children and families. However, at a time of major reductions in public spending, there are serious concerns about the impact of these policies on services and other forms of support for disabled children and their families.

Assessing the needs of disabled children

Medical and social models of disability

The medical model, which predominantly adopts an individualised approach to diagnosis and treatment, is responsible for identifying and classifying a huge range of different types of childhood disability. These include sensory and organ specific disabilities (such as those affecting eyesight, hearing or the respiratory system), disorders affecting different aspects of children's development (such as autism, Asperger's syndrome, learning disability, cerebral palsy and spina bifida), and progressive conditions (like muscular dystrophy). Whilst social workers cannot be expected to know about all of these different types of childhood disability in any detail, it is important to understand how to access information when it is needed, making use of up-to-date resources such as those provided by Contact a Family, a UK-wide organisation supporting families with disabled children, the Council for Disabled Children, which is the umbrella body for the sector in England, and For Scotland's Disabled Children, a coalition of over 50 organisations.

In contrast, the social model of disability, as its name suggests, focuses attention on the role of attitudes and other social and environmental factors in creating barriers to the full participation of disabled people in society, potentially leading to social exclusion and more limited opportunities in life (Morris, 1998; Oliver, 1999). Within this perspective, children's rights and social justice occupy central roles, with action to combat prejudice and discrimination, and other barriers to full and equal participation for disabled children primarily focused on the physical and social environment rather than the individual.

Holistic assessment practice

As noted at various points throughout the book, social workers undertaking assessments of 'children in need', the definition of which includes disabled children, have to integrate different models and approaches into holistic forms of practice capable of recognising the contributions made to children's health and well-being by interactions between their developmental needs, their parents' capacity to meet those needs, and their wider family and environmental circumstances (Jack, 1997b, 2000; DH/DfEE/HO, 2000; Horwath, 2011). However, because of the often confusing, disempowering and even pathologising experiences that disabled children and their families report having experienced in their encounters with a range of professionals, it is important for social workers involved in the assessment of disabled children to:

- Ensure that the child and his or her family are provided with full information about the purpose, process and possible outcomes of the assessment.
- Prepare well before meeting the child and family, reading any previous assessments and finding out about the child's disability and its possible impact.
- Ensure there is good inter-agency collaboration and integration of assessment processes, typically including the identification of a 'lead professional', to avoid unnecessary duplication between different professionals and agencies.
- Focus on the child's and family's strengths and encourage their active engagement in the assessment process, communicating the clear message that their views and wishes are of central importance and will be taken fully into account.
- Arrange for communication support to be available if it is needed, and ensure that it is possible for the child and his or her parents to involve an advocate or friend to support them, if they wish. (Marchant, 2010)

The ultimate aim of any assessment should be to identify the main factors which are affecting the development of *this* child, with *this* disability, in *this* family and environment. The social worker will therefore be interested in the child's views about his or her life, building an understanding of what effects the disability is having, for example, on the development of the child's emotional attachments, social relationships, behaviour, self-confidence and personal identity. Social workers will also be weighing up the various benefits and problems associated with arrangements for the child's education and health care, as well as any specific medical interventions and family support services associated with the child's disability which are either currently being provided or might be needed in the future.

Assessing the needs of parent carers and other family members

Any work with disabled children should also take into account the needs of parents and other family members, including any siblings. Legislation across the UK, including the Carers and Disabled Children Act 2000 in England and Wales, the Community Care and Health (Scotland) Act 2002, and the Carers and Direct Payments Act (Northern Ireland), gives parent carers the right to an assessment of their own needs, as well as making provision for direct payments to enable them to purchase services themselves. The aim of legislation like this is to enable local councils to support the parents of disabled children in their caring role and help them to maintain their own health and well-being. Provision to make direct payments to 16- and 17-year-old disabled children also enables them to take on more responsibility for themselves in the transition to adulthood.

Practice pointer 7.4

How might you support a disabled young person in receipt of direct payments to make the best use of the resources available to him or her?

The siblings of disabled children may also have caring responsibilities for their disabled brothers or sisters, as well as needs of their own, which should form part of a holistic 'whole family' approach to assessment. Like any other children, the siblings of disabled children should be considered as 'children in need', in their own right, if their welfare or development is likely to suffer if they are not provided with services. For example, some may be acting as 'young carers', carrying out tasks that may be inappropriate for their age or that are having a negative impact on their education and development, possibly interfering with the completion of homework or reducing opportunities to socialise with their peers and participate in activities and clubs, causing social isolation and feelings of being 'different'. Siblings of disabled children may also worry about inviting friends home from school and face teasing or even bullying by their peers, as well as perhaps experiencing feelings of embarrassment about their disabled sibling's behaviour or appearance in public. Within the household, they may also be affected by any extra stresses or particular family dynamics related to their sibling's disability, including feelings of jealousy because of the extra time and attention that their disabled sibling requires from their parents, and resentment at any limitations imposed on family activities and spending, as well as possibly having their sleep disturbed on a regular basis.

Because all of these emotions and experiences are likely to exist alongside feelings of love and concern for their disabled sibling, they are also likely to feel guilt and anxiety. Many express particular ambivalence, for example, in relation to complaining to their parents about their brother's or sister's behaviour, especially as it may simply not be acceptable to do so, perhaps having been told repeatedly that they are very lucky to have such a 'special' brother or sister. However, there can also be positive effects on a child's welfare of having a disabled sibling, including increased understanding of disability, enhanced personal skills and maturity, and stronger family relationships. Assessments of disabled children and their families should aim to gather information about all of these issues, identifying where siblings would benefit from additional information or services, possibly involving individual or group-based support (Dearden and Aldridge, 2010; Contact a Family, 2011).

Safeguarding issues

Contrary to what many people might suppose (or prefer to believe), disabled children are at least three times more likely to experience abuse or neglect than non-disabled children (Sullivan and Knutson, 2000). This heightened risk is due to a combination of factors, including: higher levels of dependence, often on a wide range of carers and away from their families; negative social attitudes towards disabled children; and communication issues (Kennedy, 2002; Miller, 2003). Disabled children in residential settings are particularly vulnerable to maltreatment. Unfortunately, child protection systems also play their part, tending to be less effective at identifying the abuse and neglect of disabled children, often because professionals lack the necessary knowledge and communication skills, or refuse to believe that it can happen, and so fail to pick up signs that would alert them to maltreatment amongst non-disabled children (Edwards and Richardson, 2003; Miller, 2003).

It is therefore important that practitioners are familiar with official guidance about safeguarding disabled children (e.g. DCSF/DH, 2009), have a good understanding of their heightened risk of experiencing neglect and abuse, and are alert to any signs, taking safeguarding action whenever appropriate.

Practice pointer 7.5

Can you identify three ways in which you could ensure that your practice with disabled children takes account of their increased vulnerability to abuse and neglect?

Communicating with disabled children

Whilst many disabled children are likely to have communication impairments, all children are capable of communicating something about their feelings and preferences at the very least. Unfortunately, children with significant communication impairments are often assumed to be incapable of communicating at all, which can result in very limited interaction with other children and adults, and perhaps 'switching off' altogether themselves. If disabled children are not understood by those around them, they are also likely to experience intense feelings of frustration. Communication problems like these can have detrimental effects on the development and well-being of disabled children, such as inhibiting their opportunities to develop literacy, as well as denying them important aspects of their human rights, such as participating in decisions which affect their lives.

When children do not use spoken language, either well or at all, practitioners may need to rely on alternative forms of communication, including any movement or behaviour that can be observed and interpreted as meaningful, or the use of a code agreed between the child and the worker in which signs and symbols are given specific meaning (Morris, 2002). Examples of what are called 'motoric' and 'gestural' forms of communication, at one end of the developmental scale, include pushing an adult's hand towards or pointing at a door in order to get it opened. Other children may be able to communicate non-verbally, either using simple vocalisations, perhaps to get an adult's attention or express excitement, or via pictures which may have been assembled specifically for the particular child to help express preferences about things like food, clothing and activities. Children further along the developmental scale may also be able to use printed words or phrases to communicate, either by pointing at words on lists specifically compiled for them, or generating their own words, for example on an electronic device. Others will be able to use gestures drawn from a manualised language, such as British Sign Language, or verbal communication, even if this is at a basic level or is difficult to understand. This is where the concept of 'total communication' can be helpful, recognizing that any one method of communication cannot provide total understanding.

In any of these cases, practitioners may either need to be supported by someone who knows the child's preferred forms of communication well, or undertake specific preparation for communicating with particular children. However, whatever forms of communication are used, practitioners need to be aware of the possibility that disabled children lack important concepts or words, which might prevent them from, for instance, accurately expressing the full range of their emotions or explaining more complex ideas. As in any work with children, practitioners should avoid using jargon or colloquial figures of speech, as well as never claiming to have understood the child when this is not the case. It is also important to bear in mind that disabled children's preferred forms of communication can change over time and in different locations, for example as a result of advances in their development, the availability of special equipment in particular settings and the presence or absence of particular people. Assessments of their communication potential may therefore be out of date, incomplete or inappropriate, running the risk of imposing an undesired communication system on the child out of habit, rather than relying on an assessment of current capabilities and preferences. Practitioners should therefore ensure that they find out how the child would prefer to communicate, adjusting the format of meetings accordingly, as well as earning the child's trust by being reliable, open and honest, as in direct work with any child.

Short breaks for carers of disabled children

As already noted, whilst most disabled children in the UK are now cared for at home, this may involve high levels of stress for their parents and other family members. Research evidence indicates that short break care can reduce the stresses on families caring for disabled children by giving them time to rest and relax (Prewett, 1999; Robertson et al., 2010). However, it is also important for practitioners to ensure that short breaks have the capacity to enhance the quality of life of disabled children, providing them, for example, with new experiences and opportunities to extend their social networks, and giving them the option of not taking part if that is their wish. This is therefore another issue, like the education of disabled children, which has the potential to create tensions between closely related, but separate, objectives for the children and adults concerned.

Practice pointer 7.6

What factors do you think ought to be taken into account when making decisions about short breaks for carers of disabled children? How can you ensure that breaks are responsive to the needs of the whole family, including siblings?

Short breaks are part of the continuum of services which can be provided by local authorities to support children in need and their families. When children are cared for continuously away from home by a local authority for over 24 hours they officially become 'looked after'. Regulations permit a planned series of short breaks – where no single placement lasts more than 17 days and the total of short breaks in a year (in that placement) does not exceed 75 days – to be treated as a *single placement*. In such circumstances, the requirements for assessment, visits, planning and review (discussed in relation to all LAC in Chapter 6) are less stringent, reflecting the fact that parents retain primary responsibility for their child. Whilst these arrangements apply to any child, in practice most short break care in the UK is provided for disabled children.

Unfortunately, despite the extra pressures experienced by families with a disabled child, only a small minority of them receive regular support from social services (CSCI, 2005). Although this is partly through choice, there is also evidence that the demand for services, such as short breaks, has always outstripped supply, particularly for Black and minority ethnic families (Flynn, 2002; Shared Care Network, 2006). Whilst increased investment in short break services across the UK over recent years has expanded capacity (Smith, 2010), as with other forms of support for disabled children and their families at the present time, there are serious doubts about their sustainability in the broader context of major cuts in public spending.

Services for disabled children

In general, disabled children do not perceive themselves to be intrinsically different to other children, but the way they are treated by others (adults and children), and the barriers that exist within disabling physical environments, can create a sense of difference and contribute to their social exclusion. The lack of opportunities to participate fully in society experienced by many disabled children can result in boredom and isolation, with more of their time typically spent at home (e.g. watching television and playing computer games) and less participating in outdoor activities (e.g. sports and leisure) than non-disabled children. Disabled children also report having limited opportunities to spend time with other children without adult supervision, and also commonly report experiencing bullying and hostility from peers (and adults), again causing feelings of isolation and lack of self-worth. When disabled children are asked what services they would like to help combat these problems, it is typically those which protect and promote their friendships, offering opportunities to spend leisure time in informal settings with their peers, that are most valued. The separation of disabled children in special schools and units within the education system, preventing them from developing the social skills necessary to integrate successfully with their non-disabled peers, is often highlighted as a particular problem (Murray, 2002; Beresford, 2002; Woolley, 2006; Martin, 2009; Knight et al., 2009; Lindsay and McPherson, 2012).

Social exclusion tends to increase as disabled children get older, especially on transfer to secondary schools, when the risk of segregation increases significantly, often severing neighbourhood friendships. As a result, there are significant differences in the lifestyles, living circumstances and expectations for the future of disabled and non-disabled young adults. Disabled young adults, for example, are more likely to be unemployed and dependent on benefits, have less control over their own finances, have more poorly developed skills for independent living, with lower self-esteem, and the perception that they have limited control over their lives. All of this underpins the disadvantages they are likely to experience throughout their adult lives (Hirst and Baldwin, 1994). The task for social workers is therefore to ensure that everything that they do on behalf of disabled children, of whatever age, is designed to reduce their potential social exclusion and maximise opportunities to achieve their full potential in society.

> ### Practice pointer 7.7
>
> What part can social workers play in ensuring that disabled children and families are involved in developing appropriate services and ensuring fair access to the services available?

Information and access to appropriate mainstream and specialist services are central to promoting the social inclusion of disabled children. Depending on their age and level of understanding, children will need to know about their disability and the management of any associated impairments, including any sources of specialist support and treatment that they may require, and the social, educational and leisure opportunities available in their local area. As they get older, children will also need information about the transition to adulthood, including the training and employment opportunities and support services available to them, their tax and benefit entitlements, and their accommodation options.

A number of initiatives in different parts of the UK, often involving disabled children in the planning and development of projects, have been explicitly designed to promote their inclusion in ordinary activities for their age group, as well as their rights as equal citizens. The PACT project in Yorkshire, for example, linked student volunteers with local disabled children and their families to help the children to access local leisure facilities and provide home-based support in the after school period, as well as bringing groups of disabled teenagers and young adults together to discuss disability issues and explore ways of expressing their views to a wider audience (Perry, 1998).

Another project, known as the GTI (Getting Teenagers Involved) Group, was set up in a seaside town in Devon where a significant number of disabled teenagers, who had attended special schools outside of the area for several years, lived. Few of them met their friends outside of school, and virtually none had any contact with their non-disabled peers in the town. Through joint work between the local secondary school, the local authority disabled children's team and youth services, and the disabled children and their parents, a new *integrated* youth club was established, with much of the extra support needed by disabled children being provided by non-disabled children also attending the group. A befriending scheme grew out of the relationships that developed within the group, enabling disabled children to extend their use of local leisure facilities, and disabled children also took active roles on the group's management committee (Jack and Jack, 2000).

More broadly, KIDS, a charity which works with disabled children, provides early intervention services for young disabled children and their families, including Portage, which involves working in partnership with parents to plan an individual education and development programme for each child, using toys and equipment loaned to the family. KIDS also operates adventure playgrounds across England, which provide opportunities for accessible and inclusive play in green spaces within urban environments in settings supportive of any special requirements that disabled children may have. Although priority is given to disabled children and their siblings, the playgrounds are also open to any other children within the age range living in the local area. Advocacy services for children in need and LAC can also play an important role in promoting the participation of disabled children in decision-making about their lives. Advocates require sufficient time to develop relationships with the children they are working with, and there also needs to be clarity about the limits of their role, including whether it is ever appropriate to go beyond pure advocacy in order to represent a child's 'best interests' (Knight and Oliver, 2007).

Practice pointer 7.8

How responsive are the services in your local area to the needs of disabled children? What information and support is available to reduce the social isolation of disabled children and promote their active participation in a full range of positive activities?

Key messages for practice

1. The overarching aim of social work with disabled children and their families, which involves the integration of knowledge and skills drawn from medical and social perspectives, should be to reduce the disadvantages commonly experienced by disabled children and their families by promoting their social inclusion.

2. Assessments of the needs of disabled children should always consider not only their needs, but also those of their parents and other family members (especially siblings), who are likely to be undertaking significant caring duties, and therefore to have specific additional needs of their own.

3. For a variety of reasons, disabled children are at increased risk of experiencing abuse and neglect at the hands of their carers. Social workers therefore need to be constantly vigilant about this possibility and be willing to take safeguarding action, including challenging any complacency or denial on the part of others, when appropriate.
4. Perhaps more than in any other area of social work with children, practitioners working with disabled children need to develop a wide range of communication skills, as well as being alert to situations that require the involvement of other workers with specialist skills.

Additional resources

Contact a Family
   A national organisation offering support, information and advice to help disabled children and their families to live the lives they want for themselves
   www.cafamily.org.uk

For Scotland's Disabled Children
   www.fsdc.org.uk

Barnardo's Policy and Research Unit
   A range of resources to help practitioners working with disabled children
   www.barnardos.org.uk/what_we_do/policy_research_unit/research_and_publications/disability_policy_research.htm

Family Fund
   The UK's largest provider of grants to low income families raising disabled and seriously ill children
   www.familyfund.org.uk

The Council for Disabled Children
   An umbrella body for the disabled children's sector in England (with links to the other UK countries), which aims to promote disabled children's rights and inclusion, and influence national policy
   www.councilfordisabledchildren.org.uk

KIDS
   A national charity working with disabled children and their families across England
   www.kids.org.uk

CHAPTER 8

Working with young offenders

Introduction

The balance between what are usually contrasted as 'welfare' and 'justice' approaches to offending by young people depends upon the extent to which they are considered to be responsible for their actions. This means that the age of criminal responsibility and the policies developed to address offending by children vary from country to country. In this chapter the term 'young offenders' is used to refer to children aged ten to seventeen years who commit a crime, defined as any act which is proscribed by criminal law within the country in which it takes place. However, as will be apparent when the systems which have evolved to deal with young offenders across the UK are examined, interventions to reduce the likelihood of criminal behaviour by young people are not restricted to children who have reached the age of ten. Furthermore, it will also be necessary to consider antisocial behaviour, which does not necessarily constitute a crime but can result in official sanctions for children with many of the same characteristics and circumstances as young offenders.

Children's antisocial and offending behaviour

There are difficulties involved in any attempt to quantify the true levels of antisocial and offending behaviour by children, with significant differences between estimates based on population surveys and official crime statistics. For these reasons, reporting of trends in crime in different parts of the UK usually involves the simultaneous release of data about the number of arrests and convictions of offenders for different categories of crime alongside information from the British Crime Survey, which is based on population-level self-reports from the victims of crimes, many of which may never have been reported to the police. In relation to this last point, it should be borne in mind by practitioners working in this area that children are more often the victims than the perpetrators of antisocial behaviour and crime, and that any young offender may also be a 'child in need' (see Chapter 4).

Practice pointer 8.1

How can social workers ensure that young people identified as 'offenders' are also recognised and provided with services as 'children in need'?

Some of the most reliable information about children's offending and antisocial behaviour in the UK can be found in two self-report surveys, one involving a representative sample of over 14,000 11- to 16-year-olds in secondary schools across England, Scotland and Wales, and the other involving over 11,000 children in the same age range in six disadvantaged inner London boroughs (Beinart et al., 2002; Communities that Care, 2005). Although nearly half (48.5 per cent) of the children in the national samples reported having committed a criminal offence at some time in their lives, the numbers who reported having done so in the previous 12 months were much smaller. For example, approximately one in five children reported that they had stolen something from a shop in the last year, with similar proportions reporting that they had stolen something from elsewhere, handled stolen goods or vandalised property in the same period. Approximately one in ten children also reported having carried a weapon to school or in the neighbourhood in the last 12 months, and a similar proportion reported having attacked someone intending to cause them serious harm. Much smaller proportions of children reported either burglary (3 per cent) or theft of a vehicle (2 per cent) in the previous 12 months.

Levels of self-reported offending in these two surveys varied significantly according to factors such as age, gender and ethnic background. The peak age for reporting involvement in the two most common offences amongst children, vandalism and shoplifting, for example, was 14 to 15 years. Approximately one in three children of this age reported having been involved in an act of vandalism, and one in four reported having stolen from a shop in the last 12 months, compared with approximately one in five for both of these offences across the whole age range. However, even at this age most types of offending were reported to be infrequent, with only one in ten 14- to 15-year-old boys, for example, reporting having stolen from a shop on three or more occasions in the past year.

Boys significantly outnumbered girls in relation to most types of self-reported offending and antisocial behaviour, although the differences between them diminished with age, and girls in the inner London survey were more likely to report smoking tobacco and drinking alcohol than boys. Some level of alcohol consumption was relatively common amongst children across the whole age range in the national samples, with the highest levels of consumption reported by 15- to 16-year-old boys and girls, four out of five of whom reported having drunk alcohol in the previous four weeks, with more than half of them reporting at least one episode of 'binge drinking' (five or more alcoholic drinks in one session), and over one in four reporting three or more episodes over the same period. Levels of tobacco and illegal drug use were much lower, with only about 3 per cent of children aged 11 to 16 in the London survey, for example, reporting regular cigarette smoking, and a similar proportion reporting that they had smoked cannabis in the previous four weeks. However, the use of these substances, like alcohol consumption, varied between boys and girls, with nearly one in ten (9 per cent) of 15- to 16-year-old boys in the national samples, for example, reporting having smoked cannabis on three or more occasions in the last year, compared with only one in twenty girls in the same age range. Even fewer children reported ever having taken ecstasy or amphetamines, and reported use of cocaine and heroin was rare. Although more (and younger) children reported having used solvents, frequent use was again rare. Finally, in relation to variations according to ethnic background, the offending rates reported by black Caribbean and white British children were significantly higher than those for black African and, especially, south Asian children across the age range.

Data like these tells us that, if children are involved in any form of offending or antisocial behaviour at all, as approximately half of the 11- to 16-year-olds in these two surveys reported, this is likely to be a relatively minor and isolated incident which, on its own, is unlikely to be an indicator of more serious problems. If any of these children come to official attention as a result of their offending behaviour, the most sensible course of action will normally involve dealing with them in as informal a way as possible, ensuring that they are not inappropriately drawn into the systems designed to deal with more persistent or serious offenders. Labelling theory (Becker, 1963) serves to remind us that identifying children as 'offenders' runs the risk of making this a significant part of their personal identity, thereby *increasing* the risk of future offending behaviour rather than reducing it. Knowledge like this provides the justification for the diversionary principles which underpin the early stages of the youth justice systems developed in all parts of the UK, which are discussed later in this chapter.

Across the UK, levels of recorded crime involving children aged ten to seventeen years have been declining in recent years. For example, whilst nearly 200,000 offences involving children were recorded in England and Wales in 2009/10, this represented a fall of 19 per cent on the previous year (and 33 per cent since 2006/07), with the number of children receiving a first official sanction for criminal offences falling by nearly a quarter, from just under 80,000 in 2008/09 to just over 60,000 in 2009/10. The most common offences committed by children in England and Wales in 2009/10 were theft (21 per cent), violence against the person (20 per cent) and criminal damage (12 per cent). Almost two-thirds of these offences were committed by young males aged 15 to 17 years, with nearly eight out of every ten offences overall having been committed by males. Typically, children from black ethnic backgrounds are over-represented in the population of young offenders, accounting for only 3 per cent of the overall population of 10 to 17-year-olds, but 6 per cent of the young offenders identified in England and Wales in 2009/10 (YJB/MJ, 2011).

Practice pointer 8.2

Why do you think children from black ethnic backgrounds (but not other minority ethnic groups) are over-represented amongst young offenders?

Risk and protective factors

Throughout the book we have stressed the value of using the concept of risk and protective factors, within an ecological framework, to understand the roots of much human behaviour. Nowhere is this more relevant than in the field of children's anti-social and offending behaviour. For example, in their self-report study of secondary school children across England, Scotland and Wales, Beinart and colleagues (2002) found that, for every risk factor identified, increased exposure was significantly associated with a greater likelihood of reporting antisocial and offending behaviour, and that, conversely, the more exposure children had to protective factors the less likely they were to report such behaviour.

Evidence from several prospective, longitudinal studies of large cohorts of children (Anderson et al., 2001; Smith, 2004; Armstrong et al., 2005; McVie and Norris, 2006) clearly shows that there is no single 'cause' of antisocial or criminal behaviour, but there is a range of interacting risk and protective factors at individual, family, school and community levels:

Individual risk factors
- Hyperactivity/impulsivity: consistently and robustly associated with anti-social behaviour in childhood and adolescence.
- Low intelligence/cognitive impairment: found to be risk factors even after controlling for variables such as low household income and large family size.
- Personal attitudes: alienation, lack of social commitment and condoning offending or drug use are all associated with higher risk.
- Early signs of problem behaviour: but only in combination with other risk factors.
- Friends with problem behaviour: antisocial children tend to form friendships with one another, with peer influences on behaviour strongest in adolescence (see Chapter 3).

Family risk factors
- Low birth weight/birth complications: associated with conduct problems if children are subsequently raised in disadvantaged family circumstances.
- Young mother: increased risk of low achievement in school, antisocial behaviour and early use of tobacco, alcohol and illegal drugs.
- Poor parental supervision/discipline: lax supervision by parents is linked to 'early onset' offending (which itself is linked to more persistent offending), and harsh, inconsistent or neglectful parenting is associated with antisocial and offending behaviour in teenagers.
- Family conflict: identified by most studies as a major risk factor, whether it occurs in 'broken' or 'intact' homes.
- Family involvement/condoning criminal behaviour: having a parent or older sibling who is (or was) involved in criminal behaviour is an important risk factor, especially in relation to the use of illegal drugs.
- Disadvantaged family circumstances: factors such as low household income, unemployment, poor housing and large family size, *in combination*, represent a risk factor (probably because of their influence on parental supervision and discipline, and the stress they place on family relationships). Parents with more limited personal resources, who also live in deprived neighbourhoods, find it hardest to be effective parents.

School risk factors
- Low achievement (beginning in primary school): consistent risk factor for offending behaviour and illegal drug use (probably through its effects on self-esteem).
- Aggressive behaviour/bullying: consistent factors in the lives of boys who go on to display antisocial behaviour.
- Lack of commitment to school/truancy: alienation and disengagement from school are risk factors.
- School disorganisation: different aspects of school cultures (even after controlling for their intakes) are associated with low achievement, truancy and poor behaviour.

Community risk factors
- Disadvantaged neighbourhood: economically deprived areas tend to have higher levels of crime (even after controlling for selection effects).

- Community disorganisation/neglect: areas characterised by a poor physical environment and lacking informal social controls over the behaviour of their residents demonstrate higher levels of offending behaviour and illegal drug use by children (and adults).
- Availability of drugs: increases the risk of their use in local areas.
- Transience: high population turnover, which undermines neighbourhood attachment and trust in neighbours, is also associated with heightened risk of antisocial and offending behaviour by children.

Whilst some protective factors are simply the opposites of the risk factors identified above, there are also a number that have been found to moderate the effects of children's exposure to risk, either by preventing risk factors from occurring in the first place or by interacting with them in ways that block or interrupt their adverse effects. At the *individual level*, for example, female gender is a protective factor, particularly in relation to offences involving theft and violence. A resilient temperament and sense of self-efficacy also serve to protect children from developing antisocial or offending behaviour, especially when they are allied to social and reasoning skills. At the *family level*, secure attachments and confiding relationships with parents (or other adult relatives) are protective, as are parents who closely monitor the behaviour of their children, limiting their exposure to high-risk local environments and providing them with opportunities to participate in positive, organised activities. At the *school level*, positive relationships with teachers and peers are protective, as are good standards set by teachers and opportunities for children's involvement in the life of the school. The protective potential of pro-social bonds with adults and children also extends to the *community level*, with involvement and recognition for positive behaviour playing a part in reducing the risk of children becoming involved in antisocial activities and offending. Once again emphasising the interconnectedness of many risk and protective factors, some relationships and opportunities within communities offer potential 'turning points' in a child's life *only if* the child has the personal skills to take advantage of them.

The balance between the risk and protective factors operating in the lives of children varies according to factors such as their age, gender and ethnic background. For example, in the study of secondary school pupils living in deprived areas of inner London already discussed (Communities that Care, 2005), the risk factors reported by the children increased and the protective factors decreased as they got older. Overall, girls reported more exposure to poor parental supervision and discipline, and family conflict, whereas boys were much more likely, for example, to have access to a weapon. There were also some striking differences by ethnic group, with significantly fewer south Asian children, for example, reporting exposure to risk factors such as poor parental supervision and discipline, and families or peers with a history of problem behaviour. White British children, however, were significantly more likely than those of other ethnic groups to engage in truancy, have a low commitment to school, be exposed to weapons and live in a disorganised community, whilst black Caribbean children were less likely than others to report experiencing strong family attachments or to have been rewarded at school for pro-social behaviour. Overall, white British children in this survey were more likely to report exposure to high levels of risk factors than other children, with south Asian and, to a lesser extent, black African respondents at the other end of the scale. However, these heightened risks for white British children were offset, to some extent, by the higher levels of protective factors which they also reported.

Complex information of this nature, illustrating some of the chains of interacting factors which help to shape children's behaviour, could easily become overwhelming if it were not systematically organised within frameworks based on ecological theory. This is the foundation of the tools (e.g. ASSET) which are now commonly used for assessing the risk of future offending by children who become involved in youth justice systems, which are considered next.

Practice pointer 8.3

How do you think you can use knowledge about the risk and protective factors involved in shaping children's antisocial and offending behaviour in your own practice?

Youth justice policies and systems across the UK

In England, Wales and Northern Ireland, 'youth justice' is an umbrella term used to describe the actions of the police, courts and welfare agencies in relation to children aged ten to seventeen years who commit criminal offences. In Scotland, the age of criminal responsibility has recently risen from eight to twelve years, although nearly all children (up to the age of 16) involved in anti-social and offending behaviour are dealt with via the Children's Hearing system rather than the courts.

Children arrested by the police on suspicion of committing criminal offences have a range of rights set out primarily in the Police and Criminal Evidence (PACE) Act 1984 and the accompanying codes of practice issued by the Home Office. For example, the custody officer at the police station must contact the child's parents or, if they are unavailable or refuse to attend, another 'appropriate adult', who will often be a trained volunteer, but could be a social worker, for example if the child is being looked after by a local authority. The role of the appropriate adult involves supporting, guiding and protecting the child. However, research has shown that social workers acting in this role often do not intervene effectively to promote children's rights (Pierpoint, 2006), so this is an area of practice which could be improved. Children also have a right to have a solicitor present at the police station, and they should not be detained in police cells unless there is nowhere else they can be properly supervised, and must not be placed in a cell with a detained adult. The consent of a parent or guardian is required before 10- to 16-year-olds can be fingerprinted or DNA tested.

Youth justice in England and Wales

The roots of much of the present youth justice system in England and Wales can be traced back to an Audit Commission report, *Misspent Youth*, published in 1996. This pointed out that something like £1 billion was being spent each year processing a relatively small number of children, mainly convicted of minor offences, through the system. The report argued that prevention of offending behaviour should be given higher priority, focusing on earlier intervention and the provision of more support for parents and vulnerable children.

Misspent Youth was followed by a White Paper, *No More Excuses* (HO, 1997) and the Crime and Disorder Act (CDA) 1998, which created the Youth Justice Board, an executive non-departmental public body, as well as multi-disciplinary Youth Offending Teams (YOTs). Local authorities in England and Wales are required to have a YOT which, besides a local authority social worker, must include a probation officer, police officer and persons nominated by the local health and education authorities. The role of YOTs is governed by national standards covering the prevention of offending and the needs of the victims of crime, as well as the supervision of offenders and involvement in court processes. Social workers seconded to YOTs draw on many of the multi-professional working and communication and relationship building skills in work with children and families discussed in previous chapters. However, they also need to be comfortable both in exercising the control elements of the role and defending the rights of young people, as well as having good knowledge of the risk and protective factors associated with antisocial and offending behaviour by children, awareness of the impact of offending on victims and communities, and detailed understanding of the youth justice system in the country in which they are practising (Littlechild and Smith, 2008).

Practice pointer 8.4

What tensions or contradictions do you think might exist between the care and control elements of a social worker's role within the youth justice system? How do you think these issues can best be resolved?

In England and Wales, the Criminal Justice and Immigration (CJ&I) Act 2008 sets out the sanctions which can be imposed on young people involved in offending or antisocial behaviour. For less serious offences, first-time offenders who admit to it will normally receive a Reprimand, given by a police officer in the presence of an appropriate adult. Repeat offenders will either receive a Final Warning or be charged. A record of these sanctions is kept at least until the offender is 18, and may be cited in any future criminal proceedings. Young offenders who receive a warning are automatically referred to the local YOT for assessment and possible participation in a programme of rehabilitation.

Youth courts, which involve panels of three lay magistrates, deal with all but the most serious offences committed by children which result in prosecution. For young offenders who go to the youth court, Pre-Sentence Reports (PSRs) are prepared by the YOT, setting out the circumstances leading up to the offence, background information about the child, and sentencing options. PSRs are based on a structured assessment tool (ASSET) used by all YOTs in England and Wales, which consists of a Core Profile, identifying key risk and protective factors in relation to offending behaviour, with numerical ratings provided for each of them alongside evidence to support the rating. The final score produced indicates the overall likelihood of reoffending, although not the type or seriousness of any future offences. Where it is deemed that there is a 'risk of serious harm', a separate form is completed. As with any assessment tool, the validity and reliability of the conclusions reached depend on factors such as the skills and knowledge of practitioners, the quality of the evidence used and the organisational context (Baker, 2008).

YOTs are also required to provide a bail information service to assist the Crown Prosecution Service to decide if they wish to seek a remand on bail or a remand to local authority (or secure) accommodation. Many YOTs provide bail support schemes to try to avoid the necessity of accommodating young offenders away from their families in appropriate cases.

Youth court disposals begin with an Absolute Discharge, where no further punishment is considered necessary, or a Conditional Discharge, where another conviction within a period of three years leads to sentencing for the original offence as well as the new one. With a few exceptions, those appearing in the youth court for the first time must also be referred to a Youth Offending Panel, consisting of two community volunteers and a named YOT member, under the terms of a Referral Order. The aim of these panels is to promote restorative justice and help to reintegrate offenders into the community, for example by getting them to accept personal responsibility for their crimes and make appropriate reparation to their victims. Young offenders appearing before them are required to sign a contract to participate in an agreed programme of activities aimed at preventing further offending, for a period of time specified by the court. The contract is reviewed and amended as necessary at subsequent panel meetings.

Young offenders appearing before the youth court may also receive a Fine, normally payable by their parents or guardians, with the sum involved governed by set maximums, the financial means and age of the defendant, and the seriousness of the offence. In appropriate cases a Reparation Order can also be made, which involves up to 24 hours of work by young offenders, such as repairing damage to property or cleaning graffiti, designed to make them aware of the distress their actions have caused. Disposals of this nature, commonly referred to as 'restorative justice', may also involve either direct dialogue between the offender and victim (if willing) or participation in a victim awareness scheme. An evaluation of over 40 projects funded by the Youth Justice Board found most offered a mixture of restorative elements, including community reparation (35 per cent) and victim awareness (21 per cent), although less than one in seven cases (13.5 per cent) involved direct meetings between victim and offender. Over three-quarters of victims and offenders whose views were sought considered that the intervention had helped the offender to understand better the impact of the offence on the victim (Wilcox, 2004).

Practice pointer 8.5

What are your own thoughts about the restorative justice approach to youth offending? Can you identify two advantages and two disadvantages of this approach?

The CJ&I Act 2008 also includes a range of orders intended to prevent offending before it occurs. For example, the Child Safety Order (CSO) allows for the supervision (by YOT members) of children up to the age of nine who commit an act which would constitute an offence if the child was ten years or over; and the Anti-Social Behaviour Order (ASBO) allows for a civil rather than a criminal measure to be taken against individuals or groups of children (aged ten years and over) when courts decide that there is a likelihood of an offence being committed. However, the boundaries between antisocial behaviour and offending are often rather blurred, with examples of what can constitute antisocial behaviour including things like racial harassment, vandalism and threatening behaviour, all of which may also be treated as criminal behaviour. Whilst sanctions for antisocial behaviour are civil rather than criminal, it is important for practitioners to realise that non-compliance can result in criminal sanctions. Children involved in antisocial behaviour can also be asked to sign a voluntary Acceptable Behaviour Contract. Although it is an informal procedure, practitioners again need to be alert to the fact that breaking it can be used as evidence in applying for an ASBO. Parenting Orders (POs), lasting for up to 12 months, can also be used in conjunction with CSOs and ASBOs (as well as the full range of community sentences). POs require parents to attend classes or counselling sessions for up to 12 weeks, as well as complying with any other specified requirements, such as ensuring the child's school attendance or return home by a specified time. Further information about parenting programmes is included in the next section of this chapter.

Practice pointer 8.6

What do you think about preventive approaches to antisocial and offending behaviour that involve interventions with children below the age of criminal responsibility?

For more serious crimes in England and Wales, punishable by imprisonment, the courts have a range of community sentences (as alternatives to custody) at their disposal. The Youth Rehabilitation Order, for example, can include requirements for young offenders to:

- Undertake a short, intensive, individually tailored programme, supervised by the YOT.
- Take part in activities at an 'attendance centre', usually run by the police on Saturday afternoons.
- Be subject to a curfew or exclusion order, requiring that they are either in, or avoid entering, a specified place for a specified period of time.
- Comply with supervision by a designated YOT member, often with requirements about where and with whom they must live, participation in (or refraining from) specified activities, making reparation, being subject to a curfew or wearing an 'electronic tag' to monitor their whereabouts.

Children aged 16 and 17 can also receive 'adult' community sentences, including Community Rehabilitation, Community Punishment, and Drug Treatment and Testing Orders.

The main custodial sentence available to youth courts in England and Wales is the Detention and Training Order (DTO). This can only be imposed when the offence is either so serious that only a custodial sentence is appropriate or where it is of a violent or sexual nature requiring custody to protect the public from serious harm (or the offender refuses to accept a community sentence that requires their consent). Children aged 12 to 15 years must be classed as 'persistent offenders' in order to receive a custodial sentence. DTOs involve a specified period of detention, followed by an equal period of supervision in the community, amounting to a total of between four and twenty-four months. The period of custody can be spent in a Secure Training Centre, a Young

Offender Institution, a Youth Treatment Centre or other prison service accommodation.

Custody poses particular risks for young offenders, who are typically disadvantaged and vulnerable as a result of a combination of factors such as poverty, family conflict, educational under-achievement, emotional and behavioural disorders, drug and alcohol misuse, and self-harm (Goldson, 2002). Social workers and other professionals responsible for children in custody therefore need to assess carefully the risks that they face (Littlechild and Smith, 2008). Supervision in the second half of the sentence is normally undertaken by a YOT member, who needs to be fully aware of the wide range of needs which young people are likely to have at this point in their lives, as well as ensuring that they comply with the requirements (set out in national standards) governing, for example, contact arrangements, in the knowledge that any significant or repeated breach will normally result in a return to custody. For grave crimes, where the youth court considers that a greater penalty than 24 months detention and training is likely to be needed, children are sent for trial in the Crown Court.

Youth justice in Scotland

The Children's Hearing system in Scotland, established in the wake of the Kilbrandon Report in 1964, recognises the similarities between young offenders and children in need and treats the welfare of the child rather than the reduction of offending as its paramount consideration. Children's Hearings deal with children under 16 years of age who have committed all but the most serious offences (e.g. murder or serious assault), with 16- and 17-year-olds normally being dealt with by the adult criminal justice system. All children who may require compulsory supervision are referred to a Reporter, who can decide that no further action is required, refer the child to the local authority, or bring the child before a Children's Hearing, which consists of a panel of three trained lay members. The Children's Hearings (Scotland) Act 2011 strengthens and modernises the system, making provision for the development of an advocacy service for children and requiring that children's views are conveyed to panel members (normally in social work reports), as well as giving Hearings greater powers to hold local authorities to account in implementing their decisions.

After considering the information provided by those attending the hearing, including the child and his or her parents and reports prepared by the child's social worker, school and any appropriate specialists, the panel decide on any measures of supervision which are in the child's best interests. Supervision requirements, if made, can include conditions for the child to live at home under the supervision of a social worker or away from home with relatives, foster carers, in a children's home or in secure accommodation, as well as arrangements for contact. The Antisocial Behaviour etc. (Scotland) Act 2004 also gives Children's Hearings powers to restrict a child's movements through intensive support and monitoring (including the use of electronic tags) in or away from specified places. However, there is not intended to be any element of punishment in hearing decisions, and no fines, for example, can be imposed. Legal representation is only provided when there is the risk of the child being placed in secure accommodation or when it is deemed necessary to facilitate the child's effective participation in the hearing.

Youth justice in Northern Ireland

Northern Ireland's youth justice system also differs in some significant respects from those in the rest of the UK. Prosecution of young offenders is very much the exception rather than the rule, with the majority of cases dealt with through diversionary processes, and 'nuisance behaviour' by children dealt with through the Youth Diversion Scheme (YDS). The Justice (Northern Ireland) Act 2002 also introduced Youth Conferences (YCs), which normally operate as an alternative to prosecution, although they can also be ordered by the youth court.

For less serious offences, the YDS usually involves the use of an Informed Warning, which stays on record for 12 months (unless further offending takes place). For more serious offences, a Restorative Caution can be issued, which normally involves a meeting between the offender and the victim, and remains on record for two and a half years (again, unless further offending takes place). Where the offence is very serious, or follows two or more previous 'disposals' (or is denied), the matter can be referred for prosecution, with the Public Prosecution Service deciding what action to take, including referral to the youth or crown court, or to a YC. YCs are organised by the Youth Justice Services and involve meetings between the offender, the victim and others affected by the crime. The plans agreed at these meetings can include an apology, reparation or compensation payment to the victim, supervision by an adult, work for the community, participation in activities (e.g.

to address offending behaviour or provide education and training), restrictions on conduct or whereabouts, and treatment (e.g. for mental health problems or drug and alcohol dependency). The sentences available to the courts in Northern Ireland are similar to those already discussed in relation to England and Wales.

Young offenders from BME groups

Whichever country practitioners are working in, it is important to recognise the disadvantages typically experienced by young offenders from black and minority ethnic groups within youth justice systems, especially those of Afro-Caribbean and mixed racial heritage (YJB, 2004; Lovell, 2006; Sender et al., 2006). Social workers involved in this area of work therefore need to practise in reflexive and culturally competent ways, which include recognising their own attitudes and assumptions (together with those of their employing organisations and the other agencies involved in the youth justice system), as well as being committed to addressing any issues relating to unfair discrimination. Amongst other things, this commitment involves being ready to challenge any signs of individual or institutional racism that come to light, as well as making it known to the children they are working with that they are open to being challenged about their own practice and willing to support them in complaints about any unfair treatment by others (Littlechild and Smith, 2008).

Interventions and programmes to prevent or reduce antisocial and offending behaviour by children

Besides the formal sanctions and mandated interventions discussed above, there are a large number of voluntary schemes which are designed to prevent or reduce antisocial and offending behaviour by children within the community. Most of these interventions use knowledge about the risk and protective factors known to be associated with such behaviour by children to target high-risk individuals, groups or communities.

Cognitive behavioural projects

Cognitive behavioural approaches are based on the understanding that most young offenders do not foresee the impact of their behaviour on their victims, the community or themselves. Role play, experimental exercises and interactive computer games are used to help young offenders understand the factors that trigger their offending behaviour, realise the consequences of their actions and achieve greater self-control. Evaluation of 23 cognitive behavioural projects, which involved more than a thousand young people, found that they had some impact on reducing reconviction rates and significantly improved behaviour, but had difficulties engaging or maintaining the involvement of significant numbers of the young people referred to them (YJB, 2004). The engagement problems are perhaps partly because these projects place the responsibility for offending on the individual, thereby failing to recognise some of the other risk (and protective) factors known to be associated with offending behaviour over which individuals have little or no control.

Mentoring schemes

Mentoring schemes also focus on individual offenders, but, unlike cognitive behavioural approaches, they also include some consideration of risk factors beyond the offender's personal characteristics. Mentors, who are normally trained volunteers, act as role models and provide support and advice to the young people to help them address any problems they are experiencing with things like their education, training and employment, relationships, accommodation, and drug and alcohol use. The Youth Justice Board invested £10 million in the development of mentoring schemes across England and Wales between 2001 and 2005, with 50 schemes targeted at children with literacy and numeracy problems and a further 30 aimed at young offenders from minority ethnic and hard-to-reach groups. Unfortunately, because the schemes were only able to provide an average of 20 hours of mentoring to each of the children they successfully engaged, the results were rather limited. For example, a third of the young people re-entered education and training, and there was also an increase in their involvement in community activities, but over half of those referred either refused to participate at all or did not engage successfully with their allocated mentor (YJB, 2005).

Parenting programmes

Parenting programmes can either be ordered by the courts or offered on a voluntary basis. They are often run by YOTs in partnership with other local agencies and typically involve a combination of personal advice and support alongside group work, with the aim of addressing the parental risk factors (and increasing the protective factors) associated with offending behaviour by children, in particular trying to reduce harsh or erratic discipline, poor supervision and family conflict. Most of the parents involved in the 34 programmes evaluated on behalf of the Youth Justice Board by Ghate and Ramella (2002) reported significant positive changes, including improved communication, supervision and monitoring of their children's activities, and the way that they dealt with the (lower number of) family conflicts which arose, as well as giving their children more praise and approval, with less criticism and loss of temper, and being able to influence their behaviour more effectively. There were also some measurable reductions in their children's offending.

Positive activities for young people (PAYP)

PAYP programmes can be targeted at either high-risk individuals or high-risk areas. Community consultations with children and adults living in disadvantaged areas repeatedly identify the availability of more leisure facilities for young people as one of the keys to improving their lives and reducing youth crime. Positive activities can build the self-esteem and self-confidence of young people, thereby helping to improve their attitudes towards school and peers, as well as reducing their opportunities to engage in antisocial and offending behaviour, and promoting opportunities to make a positive contribution to their local communities. They can also help to build bridges between different groups of children and enable individuals to access more specialist help if they need it. Evaluation of PAYP schemes running in England and Wales between 2003 and 2006, which between them had engaged nearly 300,000 young people, found that they had contributed to reductions in antisocial behaviour and offending by children in the targeted areas, as well as improving levels of re-entry to education and training (CRG, 2006).

A ten-year government strategy to extend the provision of PAYP programmes in England and Wales (HO, 2007) was based on an understanding that changes in the labour market, wider society, family structures and the use of leisure time over the previous 30 years had made the transition from adolescence to early adulthood increasingly challenging. It was therefore considered important that all young people develop the social and emotional skills to take advantage of the opportunities that were available, as well as the resilience to cope with the risks. Research informing the PAYP strategy indicated that the best outcomes were associated with structured leisure time activities which had a clear underlying purpose and element of organisation by adults, with young people who had only attended unstructured activities found to be at the most risk of poor outcomes (Feinstein et al., 2005). Other features of successful PAYP programmes include:

- Being creative and inclusive.
- Not treating young people as problems.
- Involving young people (and parents) in their design and delivery.
- Taking a holistic approach to meeting young people's needs.
- Ensuring appropriate supervision.
- Adequate resourcing and good management.

Community programmes

Community programmes, which typically involve several interrelated components, have also been developed to reduce antisocial and offending behaviour by children, often in high risk areas. Geographical variations in youth crime have been the subject of long-standing sociological and criminological interest. Whilst much of the variation which is found can be explained by population differences, variations in crime rates are often still evident after these factors have been taken into account. Several research studies comparing areas matched for their population characteristics have demonstrated that crime rates are also related to the levels of social organisation and informal social controls over behaviour which exist in different neighbourhoods. For example, two large-scale studies by Sampson and colleagues have shown that areas with higher than predicted crime rates for their socio-economic profiles were characterised by sparse friendship networks, unsupervised groups of teenagers and low levels of organisational participation (Sampson and Groves, 1989). Variations in what the researchers termed 'collective efficacy' (a form of enacted social capital), consisting of a combination of the level of mutual trust which existed between residents and their willingness to intervene to maintain public order in the local area, were identified as the key factor in the different levels of crime found in otherwise similar areas (Sampson et al., 1997).

As a result of research of this nature, community programmes have been developed which aim to increase opportunities for local residents to interact with one another in ways which increase trust and develop informal controls over antisocial and offending behaviour (Donnelly and Kimble, 1997). One of these, the On Track (OT) programme funded by the Home Office, aimed to provide a range of early intervention services (including home–school partnerships, parent support and training, family therapy, home visiting and pre-school education) to children aged four to twelve years and their families living in high crime areas. The first phase of a longitudinal study comparing the 24 OT areas with a similar number of matched non-OT areas found that, although most of the children and families who used OT services thought they were helpful, their use was lower than anticipated and they were no more effective in reducing antisocial and offending behaviour by young people than the alternative services available in non-OT areas (Finch et al., 2006).

Part of the explanation for these rather disappointing results can no doubt be attributed to targeting problems, with high crime areas identified by the presence of risk factors not guaranteeing the engagement of high risk *individuals* (and their parents) in the services provided. There are also problems associated with trying to implement a national programme like OT in different local contexts, as well as identifying effective interventions from the available evidence (Camina, 2004; Hine, 2005). These problems have also apparently undermined the effectiveness of Communities that Care (CtC), the other major multi-component community programme designed to reduce antisocial and offending behaviour by children which has been implemented across the UK in recent years. Based on local audits of the risk and protective factors affecting children and families, CtC aims to address children's offending behaviour, as well as associated problems such as school failure, drug use and teenage pregnancy, by reducing the risk factors and increasing the protective factors operating in particular communities (Catalano and Hawkins, 1996). By involving key members of the local community in this process, CtC programmes aim to increase the level of informal social organisation, promoting a sense of ownership and engagement in action to improve children's circumstances and behaviour (France and Crow, 2001). Whilst early evaluations of CtC programmes across the UK have found that they are reasonably good at engaging and maintaining community involvement, evidence of measurable improvements in the circumstances and behaviour of young people has been more difficult to identify (Crow et al., 2004: Banister and Dillane, 2005).

Key messages for practice

1. Although engagement in some form of antisocial or criminal behaviour is fairly common during the teenage years, for most children this is likely to involve relatively minor and isolated incidents. This is why diversion, rather than prosecution, is the most appropriate way of dealing with the majority of young offenders.
2. Use of ecological theory provides the best way of identifying and understanding the interactions between the risk and protective factors associated with children who go on to establish more serious or persistent patterns of offending behaviour. The characteristics and circumstances typical of young offenders should alert practitioners to the fact that they are also likely to be 'children in need' (see Chapter 4).
3. Practitioners working with more serious or persistent young offenders need to feel comfortable exercising the control elements of their role, as well as balancing the rights and needs of young offenders with those of their victims and the wider community.
4. Certain groups of young offenders are in particularly disadvantaged or vulnerable positions, including children of black and minority ethnic backgrounds, who are over-represented within youth justice systems, and young offenders in custody, especially if they are living at a distance from their natural support systems, including their relatives and friends.

Additional resources

NACRO
  Provides resources about crime reduction
  www.nacro.org.uk

Children's Hearings website
  Provides up-to-date information about the reform programme in Scotland
  www.chscotland.gov.uk

Youth Justice Board in England and Wales: Toolkits
> Designed to help YOTs understand causes and contributory factors in offending behaviour
> www.justice.gov.uk/youth-justice/toolkits

The CJ&I Act 2008
> Further information about sentencing options for young offenders
> www.justice.gov.uk/youth-justice/courts-and-orders/disposals

Youth Justice in Northern Ireland
> In formation about sentencing options for young offenders in Northern Ireland
> www.youthjusticeagencyni.gov.uk

CHAPTER 9

Working with children with mental health problems

CHAPTER OVERVIEW

In this chapter we begin by examining what is known about the prevalence and persistence of mental disorders amongst children in the UK. We take a look at the risk and protective factors involved, the longer-term consequences of childhood mental disorders and trends in children's mental health over time. This is followed by a section examining the role of schools in the promotion of children's mental health and the provision of early help when problems first appear, including partnership work with mental health specialists. We then consider approaches to working with children and parents where the problems are more serious, including the provision of child and adolescent mental health services (CAMHS) and work with particularly vulnerable and disadvantaged groups, including children looked after by local authorities.

Introduction

As with other aspects of development, different perspectives exist when it comes to considering children's mental health. Social approaches emphasise that ideas about mental health and illness are socially constructed and culturally defined, and focus on the importance of promoting children's mental health within an under-standing of the wider social causes of mental distress, whereas medical approaches tend to focus on the individual diagnosis and treatment of 'mental disorders' which are causing significant personal distress or impairment. Population surveys estimate that as many as one in five children in the UK experience significant psychological problems at any one time, with about half of them suffering from a classifiable mental disorder. The task for social workers and other child welfare professionals is to achieve a 'constructive synthesis' between these two perspectives (RIP, 2003), doing everything that they can to promote children's mental health, as well as recognising and helping children who experience significant problems. In much of what follows in this chapter, as throughout the rest of the book, it is argued that this is best achieved by using an ecological framework, within which children's mental health, like all other aspects of their development, is understood to be the result of interactions between risk and protective factors operating at child, family, school, community and society levels.

Childhood mental disorders

Medical definitions

The widely used International Classification of Diseases (ICD-10) identifies a number of childhood mental disorders which cause individuals significant distress or impairment of functioning. The main disorders (and their sub-categories) are:

Emotional disorders
- Separation anxiety: child feels sick, anxious or has nightmares about the possibility of separation from their attachment figure(s).
- Specific phobia: child becomes very upset about and tries to avoid particular objects or situations (e.g. animals, storms, the dark).
- Generalised anxiety: child worries excessively about a wide range of past, present or future events and situations (e.g. own appearance, death/dying), often resulting in physical symptoms such as fatigue, poor concentration and insomnia.
- Depression: child has persistent feelings of sadness, irritability, lack of interest and worthlessness, and thoughts about self-harm and death, often associated with physical symptoms such as tiredness, insomnia, agitation and changes in appetite.

Conduct disorders
- Oppositional defiant disorder: characterised by frequent outbursts of temper, arguments with/disobedience of adults, vindictive behaviour, and persistent feelings of anger and resentment.
- Socialised/unsocialised conduct disorders: both are characterised by persistent lying, fighting, bullying, running away from home, truanting from school, cruelty to animals or

people, and criminal acts (socialised: acting with others; unsocialised: acting alone).

Hyperkinetic disorder
- The characteristics typical of hyperkinetic disorder are hyperactivity (child constantly fidgets, runs around, climbs on furniture and makes a lot of noise), impulsive behaviour (child can't wait his or her turn, constantly talks, butts into conversations or games, and blurts out answers) and inattentiveness (child can't concentrate, makes careless mistakes and does not listen).

Autistic spectrum disorder
- Characterised by impaired social interaction, lack of social or emotional reciprocity, delayed speech development, repetitive language and mannerisms, impoverished play, inflexible routines and rituals, and unusual preoccupation with particular objects or parts of objects.

Practice pointer 9.1

As a social worker, how comfortable do you feel with the medical approach to mental health, which classifies children's psychological problems as diagnosable disorders?

Prevalence

It is estimated that around 20 per cent of children in the UK experience psychological problems at any one time, with half of them having a clinically diagnosable mental disorder (Kay, 1999; Meltzer et al., 2000). In the most recent population survey of children (aged 5–16 years) conducted on behalf of the Office for National Statistics (ONS), 4 per cent were found to have a classifiable emotional disorder, 6 per cent a conduct disorder, 2 per cent hyperactivity disorder and 1 per cent another form of disorder, with one in five of these children experiencing more than one disorder. Boys were more likely to have a mental disorder (especially a conduct or hyperactivity disorder) than girls, and older children were at greater risk than younger children. Other risk factors associated with all forms of mental disorder included being a member of a lone-parent or reconstituted family, having a parent with no educational qualifications, belonging to a family in which neither parent was in work, living in rented accommodation, and belonging to a low income household or living in a disadvantaged area (Green et al., 2005).

Children with any form of mental disorder were much more likely to have had time off school, often resulting in significant delays in their intellectual development. They also had much lower scores on parent-reported measures of their general health and development, including their strengths and social aptitude (e.g. not having close relationships with family members or other children). The parents of children with mental disorders were more likely to be in poor emotional health themselves and to be part of a family that was assessed as functioning 'unhealthily'. In the previous 12 months the majority of parents of children with a mental disorder had sought professional advice or help for their child, but this was most frequently from a teacher rather than a mental health specialist (ibid.).

Whilst the children identified as suffering from Autistic Spectrum Disorder (ASD) were also predominantly boys (82 per cent), in contrast to other forms of mental disorder their parents were *more* likely to be highly qualified and *less* likely to be on low incomes, although nearly one in three children with ASD still lived in a family in which no parent was working. In other respects, the disadvantages experienced by these children (and their parents) were similar to those identified in relation to children with other forms of mental disorder, although children with ASD were much more likely to be rated by their parents as having 'no friends at all' (ibid.).

Before moving on to consider what follow-up surveys reveal about the persistence of childhood mental disorders, it is also worth noting another useful source of information about children's psychological health. This is the annual Tellus survey conducted on behalf of the Department for Education, the most recent of which at the time of writing, Tellus4, was based on over a quarter of a million on-line responses from children (10, 12 and 14 years of age) in 3,700 primary and secondary schools across all local authorities in England. Whilst the survey includes questions about a wide range of issues affecting children, the section on emotional health revealed that over 80 per cent considered they had supportive relationships and someone to talk to, such as a parent or a friend, when they were worried. What this means, of course, is that nearly two in every ten children who participated in the survey reported that they *didn't* have access to this form of support when worried.

Tellus4 also reveals that children who identified themselves as disabled were less likely to report being happy or to have supportive relationships with their parents and peers, and that bullying was a common experience for many children. Just over half of children, for example, reported having experienced bullying at some time in the previous 12 months, and almost one in five in the previous four weeks. Incidents of bullying for those who experienced it were also fairly frequent, with four in ten of these children reporting they experienced bullying in school at least weekly. Only 60 per cent of children across the whole sample thought that their schools were dealing well with this issue (Chamberlain et al., 2010).

Practice pointer 9.2

What steps would you take if you thought a child with whom you were working was being bullied by other children?

Persistence

In addition to carrying out large-scale, UK-wide surveys of children's mental health, the ONS has also undertaken follow-up surveys which demonstrate that significant numbers of children identified as having a mental disorder at one point in time no longer have the same disorder three years later. The level of persistence is lowest for emotional disorders, with only a quarter of the children assessed as having such a disorder in 1999 or 2004 found to be suffering from it three years later. Although the persistence of conduct disorders was higher in both follow-up studies (43 per cent), this still means that nearly six out of ten children diagnosed with a conduct disorder in 1999 or 2004 were not suffering from it three years later. However, as the overall level of mental disorder found amongst 5- to 16-year-olds in 1999 and 2004 was the same (10 per cent), for every child whose mental disorder did not persist over the three-year period of the follow-up studies, there was another child who experienced the onset of a disorder (Meltzer et al., 2003a; ONS, 2008).

In the most recent study, the persistence of all childhood mental disorders was found to be independently associated with the mother's poor mental health, whilst the persistence of emotional disorders was associated with living in rented accommodation, and that of conduct disorders with the mother's poor educational qualifications, older children, boys, those with special educational needs, and children living in lower income households. Importantly, several factors which *protected* against the persistence of mental disorders were also identified. In relation to the persistence of all disorders, parents' positive ratings of their child's strengths and social aptitude were found to be protective, as were parents' ratings of their child's capacity to make and sustain friendships and the child's positive views about the neighbourhood in which they lived (ONS, 2008).

Other protective factors identified in the wider research literature on children's mental health include characteristics and circumstances operating at all ecological levels of influence (e.g. Kay, 1999; Gutman et al., 2010). For example, at the individual level, children with good communication skills, the capacity for reflection, a sense of humour, religious faith or at least one secure and confiding relationship with a parent are all less likely to develop mental health problems. Similarly, a range of family and household level factors have also been found to be protective, including a family environment that provides appropriate and consistent discipline, support for children's education, good housing and a higher standard of living. Several protective factors operating outside of the home have also been identified, including having a good social support network (parents and children), involvement in a range of positive sport and leisure activities and attending a school offering a safe and disciplined environment alongside good academic and non-academic opportunities.

Information like this about the risk and protective factors associated with the onset and persistence of childhood mental disorders highlights a range of targets for intervention designed to promote children's mental health. However, before going on to consider the role that schools and specialist services can play in promoting children's mental health, as well as responding appropriately when significant problems are identified, it is also important to understand the longer-term consequences of childhood mental health problems and the trends which have occurred over recent decades.

Practice pointer 9.3

How might you use knowledge about the risk and protective factors involved in the onset and persistence of childhood mental ill-health in your own practice?

Long-term consequences

Longitudinal research using the national birth cohorts of people born in the UK in 1946, 1958 and 1970 has identified the main long-term consequences of childhood mental disorders (Richards and Abbot, 2009). Given the greater persistence of childhood conduct disorders than emotional disorders over follow-up periods of three years, it is not surprising to find that the adverse long-term consequences of childhood conduct problems are generally more significant than those associated with emotional problems.

As you would expect, the risk of adverse long-term consequences associated with childhood conduct problems generally increases with the severity (or earlier onset) of the original problem. For example, children with mild conduct problems were found to be twice as likely to have no educational qualifications by early adulthood, whilst those with severe conduct problems were four times as likely. Both mild and severe conduct problems in childhood were also found to be associated with a significantly increased risk of long-term unemployment, while those in work earned 30 per cent less than others who had not experienced conduct problems in childhood. By early adulthood, conduct problems during childhood were also strongly associated with never marrying (for women), divorce, teenage parenthood and criminal conviction.

Although emotional problems in childhood were generally found to be associated with similar problems in adulthood, other long-term effects were generally less pronounced than those associated with conduct problems, and in some cases *better* outcomes were identified.

Trends over time

Evidence from two longitudinal studies suggests that there has been an upward trend in the prevalence of childhood mental health problems over the past 50 years. The first study used similar assessment methods and instruments to measure levels of emotional, conduct and hyperactivity problems in three general population samples of UK children aged 15 and 16 in 1974, 1986 and 1999 (Collishaw et al., 2004). The researchers found there had been a substantial increase in conduct problems amongst males and females of all social classes and family types over this 25-year period. The data also revealed that there had been a more recent rise in the prevalence of emotional problems, but mixed evidence in relation to hyperactive behaviour. The second study, based on data drawn from three samples of 15-year-olds living in the west of Scotland, used the same self-completion questionnaire with large numbers of adolescents in 1987, 1999 and 2006 (Sweeting and West, 2003: Sweeting et al., 2009). The researchers found that all forms of psychological distress among boys rose from nearly 13 per cent in 1987 to over 21 per cent in 2006, whilst the rate for girls rose even more sharply, from nearly 19 per cent in 1987 to over 44 per cent in 2006. The 1999 data revealed that gender differences in self-esteem, body image, gender role orientation, body mass index, smoking and physical activity were largely responsible for the much higher levels of depressive mood reported by females, and also partially explained the higher levels of psychosomatic symptoms, such as headaches, dizziness, stomach aches and sickness reported by them. These explanations for the gender differences in levels of psychological distress were supported by the 2006 survey in which over a third of females reported feeling 'constantly under strain', with over a quarter of them feeling that they could not overcome their difficulties, and the number thinking of themselves as worthless having trebled between 1987 and 2006 (Sweeting et al., 2007).

Practice pointer 9.4

What factors in modern society might be responsible for the finding that teenage girls are experiencing increasing levels of emotional problems? What can be done to address the issues that you have identified?

Although evidence from the two ONS surveys suggests that there was no significant rise in mental *disorders* amongst children aged 5–16 years between 1999 and 2004, these two longitudinal studies of mental health *problems* amongst teenagers clearly indicate a significant rising trend, particularly amongst girls. Taken together, the evidence suggests that an average sized school class is likely to include three children with a classifiable mental disorder, and at least a further three children with a significant mental health problem, amongst whom teenage girls are at particular risk. Evidence like this makes it imperative that teachers and other professionals, including social workers and child mental health specialists, do everything possible to promote children's mental health, as well as taking appropriate action when problems first appear.

Mental health promotion and early intervention

Children who experience mental health problems (and their parents) may be reluctant to admit it or seek help due to a combination of factors including denial, fear, guilt, shame, stigma, lack of knowledge and concern about professional interventions. Those who seek help are most likely to talk to a friend or relative, and if they seek help from a professional, it is likely to be a teacher rather than a mental health specialist they approach (Farmer et al., 2003). However, teachers typically report that they already feel stretched in their educational role and lack the knowledge and skills to recognise and manage psychological distress in children (Rothi and Leavey, 2006; Dagley et al., 2007).

Traditionally, schools have tended to focus on managing disruptive behaviour by children through discipline and control measures, rather than by exploring the mental health problems which may lie behind it. Children whose behaviour cannot be managed successfully in this way are often placed in special schools for children with 'emotional and behavioural difficulties' or pupil referral units. However, more recently policy across the UK, in line with guidance from the World Health Organization (WHO, 2001) about 'child-friendly schools', has emphasised the importance of developing learning environments that are supportive and nurturing. Schools are increasingly expected to encourage tolerance, equality, diversity and creativity, promote active involvement, cooperation, self-esteem and self confidence, and make positive connections with families and local communities. However, it is acknowledged that all of this requires significant developments in the cultures, structures and facilities of many schools, as well as changes to the role of teachers themselves (Shucksmith et al., 2005; Spratt et al., 2006).

The evidence available indicates that the promotion of children's mental health requires a 'whole school' approach, with additional support provided for children with particular needs (Weare and Gray, 2003). An example of such an approach is the Social and Emotional Aspects of Learning (SEAL) programme adopted by the majority of primary and secondary schools in England. Unfortunately the early results from the national evaluations of the implementation of SEAL have been rather mixed, with only a few statistically significant but small improvements identified in junior school pupils' skills and emotional literacy, and no significant improvements detected in the social and emotional skills, mental health difficulties or behaviour of secondary school pupils (Humphrey et al., 2008, 2010). The secondary school SEAL evaluation team suggested that their findings, which are at odds with the significant improvements in pupil outcomes identified within the broader (largely US-based) literature on school-based social and emotional learning programmes, may be attributable to shortcomings in the way in which the SEAL programme has been implemented in the UK.

More broadly, evidence from different parts of the UK (e.g. Huddart, 2006; Connelly et al., 2008) suggests that many schools and teachers are increasingly involved in providing a wide range of responses to the mental health needs of their pupils. Activities include workshops for parents of pre-school children, one-to-one sessions with children designed to promote their trust and self-esteem, 'buddy schemes' which facilitate peer support, 'time-out' sanctuaries, advocacy on behalf of pupils with mental health difficulties, and closer partnership working with child mental health specialists. However, the study by Connelly and colleagues (2008), which was based on questionnaires completed by 365 teachers across Scotland, revealed that providing a good quality education to all children, at the same time as dealing effectively with children with mental health problems, was challenging. Specialist services (e.g. child and adolescent mental health services – CAMHS) were generally perceived to be too slow and inflexible, with gaps in provision due to inadequate resourcing. Feelings of 'powerlessness' amongst teachers were common, as was confusion over the roles of different professionals, and many teachers said that they needed better training and access to advice.

In response to some of these issues, new government-funded initiatives were introduced in different parts of the UK, including mental health link workers based in schools in parts of Scotland and the Targeted Mental Health in Schools (TaMHS) programme across England. The role of mental health link workers within schools in one area of Scotland (West Lothian), for example, included providing training, consultations to school staff and parents, and direct work with individual pupils and groups of children. The greatest impact was reported for children in the early stages of emotional (but not behavioural) problems, with the assessment of children and access to other CAMHS perceived to have speeded up. In relation to conduct problems, social models of intervention, typically involving social work services and support systems, appeared to be more effective than the medical model involving diagnosis and treatment favoured by the CAMHS link workers. Teachers reported feeling more competent to deal with children's mental health problems within school support systems, rather than referring them for outside help, although some children preferred to go to the link workers because they were *not* members of school staff. However, the most consistent concern expressed by those consulted about this scheme, in line with the findings of an earlier large-scale survey in schools across Scotland (Pettitt, 2003) was about inadequate and short-term funding (Huddart, 2006).

The government-supported TaMHS programme in England, which also involved short-term funding (2008–11), was used to enhance some of the social and emotional learning programmes already in place, as well as increasing training, supervision and consultancy for staff, individual and group therapy for children, peer support for pupils, and information for parents and children. However, the initial findings from the evaluation of this programme have also been rather mixed. For example, some evidence suggests that inter-agency working, links with CAMHS and the provision of information to pupils all improved and were independently associated with reductions in behaviour problems amongst secondary school pupils. However, other evidence suggested that TaMHS interventions had not resulted in significant reductions in either behavioural or emotional problems amongst secondary school pupils. Furthermore, whilst there was evidence that TaMHS led to a significant reduction in problems for primary pupils with behaviour problems, there was no evidence of similar improvements for children with emotional problems. Overall, the TaMHS programme was well received by pupils, parents and staff, and the national evaluation team concluded that some of the mixed evidence may have been due to the fact that schools had not been using evidence-based interventions. Some respondents also commented on the problems caused by differences in philosophy and language between education and mental health staff, and expressed concern that TaMHS services were substituting for, rather than supplementing, existing services and support (DCSF, 2010c). Results from the evaluation of the educational impact of the TaMHS programme had not been published at the time of writing.

In summary, the evidence suggests that, whilst schools potentially occupy a key position in the promotion of children's mental health, they have difficulties in fully realising that potential. Teachers appear to need more support, training and guidance (Atkinson and Hornby, 2002), while schools would benefit from strengthened policy guidance, as well as better and more sustainable funding, to enable them to deliver successfully effective evidence-based intervention programmes.

Specialist mental health services for children

Child and adolescent mental health services (CAMHS)

CAMHS cover a range of interventions provided primarily by the NHS, but also involving local authority social services, education and other departments, and voluntary and independent sector organisations. CAMHS are normally described within a four-tiered model, with Tier 1 services being provided by GPs and other primary health care staff, teachers, social workers and voluntary agencies for children with the least severe problems. Tier 2 and 3 services, for children with more significant problems and mental disorders respectively, are usually provided by child mental health specialists, including child psychiatrists and psychotherapists, clinical and educational psychologists and family therapists, either working on their own or in multi-disciplinary teams (which may also include teachers and social workers). Tier 4 comprises highly specialised services, such as in-patient or residential facilities. The services provided to children within schools, discussed in the previous section, can be seen to span the first two tiers within this framework.

Prior to the major reductions in public spending implemented across the UK since the financial crisis in 2008, CAMHS had received significant levels of investment. In England and Wales, for example, new resources were provided to health trusts and local authorities to facilitate the development of a comprehensive range of services in all areas, including an appropriately trained workforce, multi-agency assessments of need, 24-hour services for all children who need them, and effective multi-agency commissioning of services (Health Services/Local Authority Circular, 2003). However, when CAMHS were reviewed five years after the introduction of this strategy there were still some significant problems, including insufficient understanding amongst professionals (and parents) about a range of issues relevant to children's mental health and effective services, with some entrenched views amongst different groups of professionals. Services also needed to be more accessible, responsive and holistic, with greater attention paid to meeting the needs of some particularly vulnerable children (DH, 2008).

The review argued that the whole children's workforce needed to be appropriately trained and informed about children's psychological well-being, with everyone recognising the importance of children's mental health and the part that they and others could play in promoting it. In response, the government established a National Advisory Council (and a National Support Team) for Children's Mental Health and Psychological Wellbeing to hold them to account in implementing the review's recommendations, with Personal, Social, Health and Economic education to be compulsory in schools from 2011 and dedicated CAMHS to be available for vulnerable groups such as looked after children. In addition, funding was made available for Improving Access to Psychological Therapies (IAPT), a cognitive behavioural programme already in place for adults, to be extended to children (DCSF/DH, 2010).

Cognitive behavioural therapy programmes

The IAPT programme in England was launched in 2009 to provide cognitive behavioural therapy (CBT), via GP surgeries, for an estimated 900,000 adults with common mental health problems such as anxiety and depression. The services offered range from low intensity interventions, such as computerised CBT and guided self-help for people with less severe problems, through to high intensity therapist-led CBT and access to advice about employment, housing, drug and benefit issues for people with more serious problems. Evidence of the effectiveness of this approach was demonstrated in pilot programmes like the one in Doncaster, where depression rates amongst the 2,300 people who used the service over a seven-month period dropped from 78 to 24 per cent. The majority of 'patients' needed only low level guided self-help, with just 4 per cent needing high intensity CBT. Other non-medical CBT approaches have also been developed around the UK, including the Living Life to the Full programme in Glasgow, based on CBT self-help workbooks and delivered via an eight-week course at local adult education colleges, and the Book Prescription scheme in Wales, which uses the public library system to loan out selected psychological self-help books to adults seeking help with mental health problems from their GPs (Pollock, 2009).

Andrew McCulloch, chief executive of the Mental Health Foundation, believes that every child should be taught basic CBT skills at school to improve their mental health and build their resilience. More specifically, CBT has been used widely in programmes for young offenders, either to improve their general coping and problem-solving skills or to address specific mental health problems such as depression and post-traumatic stress (Townsend, 2007).

Vulnerable and disadvantaged groups

Post-traumatic stress, anxiety and depression are also commonly experienced by refugee and asylum-seeking children, amongst whom rates of mental health disorders are estimated to be as high as 40 to 50 per cent (Leavey et al., 2004). CBT approaches may therefore be helpful for these children, but the literature also emphasises the importance of family and social networks to them and the need for coordinated multi-agency working across statutory and voluntary agencies and community groups (Elliott, 2007). These findings serve to remind us that social approaches to promoting children's mental health are often at least as important as medical approaches.

Many children with whom social workers are involved are likely to have experience of the social and familial risk factors associated with increased rates of childhood mental health problems, whilst also lacking significant protective factors. For example, homeless children (and their parents) tend to experience higher levels of mental health problems, including both emotional and behavioural disorders, because of the constellation of risk factors to which they are exposed. In particular, they may require help to overcome traumatic experiences, such as domestic abuse, but their mobility and social exclusion means that they often do not receive the help that they need, either from mainstream or specialist services (Vostanis, 2007).

As noted earlier in this chapter, there is also a significant overlap between mental disorders and physical illness in children, and learning disabled children are also at increased risk of developing mental health problems (McCarthy and Boyd, 2002). Unfortunately, the added stresses often experienced by disabled children and their parents can increase the risk factors and decrease the protective factors associated with mental health problems, including family and social support (Karim, 2007). Furthermore, children's physical and learning disabilities can result in their mental health needs being overlooked or in the provision of inappropriate services. For example, learning disabled children may need interventions to be adapted to match their cognitive, emotional and linguistic abilities (Baum and Lyngaard, 2006), with effective services typically depending on relationships built on trust, provided by professionals with appropriate communication skills, and delivered in familiar surroundings (Pote et al., 2006). Effective services for all children with disabilities also require a level of interagency collaboration and integrated provision which is not easy to achieve, even when service responses are coordinated through key workers or lead professionals.

Black and minority ethnic children may also be more vulnerable to mental health problems, either because of the effects of racism and discrimination or the stigma associated with mental illness within some cultures, which is often accompanied by pressure not to go outside the family for help. Unfortunately, research has revealed that service providers often lack understanding of the culture-specific nature of family life, as well as being unable to provide staff from appropriate cultural backgrounds (Kurtz and Street, 2006). This is therefore an area where the importance of culturally competent practice (see p. 86) amongst *all* staff working in children's services is highlighted (Lewis and Ippen, 2004; Jack and Gill, 2012).

Practice pointer 9.5

How might you develop your own cultural competence to ensure that you are able to work effectively with children from different backgrounds?

Looked after children

Many of these issues are also relevant when it comes to considering the provision of mental health services to children looked after by local authorities. Evidence from national surveys across the UK (Meltzer et al., 2003b, 2004a, 2004b) reveals that approximately 45 per cent of looked after children aged five to seventeen are likely to have a classifiable mental disorder at any one time, more than four times the level amongst the general population of children in this age range. On top of this, over 40 per cent of looked after children without a mental disorder in the English survey were considered by their carers to have significant emotional, behavioural or hyperkinetic problems, twice the level of these problems found in the general population. However, the use of CAMHS by looked after children across the UK has generally been considerably lower than expected for their levels of need (Minnis and Del Priore, 2001; Meltzer et al., 2003a).

Looked after children with mental disorders also tend to have other health, education and social needs, making holistic assessments and coordinated multi-agency responses particularly important (McAuley and Davis, 2009). For children on the edge of care (or custody), interventions include Multi-Systemic Therapy, which typically involves a combination of family therapy, CBT and family support services (Utting et al., 2007), whilst for looked after children with challenging behaviour, Multi-Dimensional Treatment Foster Care (MDTFC) is often used. This is a highly structured programme, based on social learning theory, involving the provision of a consistent environment with clear boundaries, close monitoring of children's behaviour and whereabouts, and diversion from anti-social peers, along with the development of positive social skills. Evaluation of pilot MDTFC schemes in England found that they had improved outcomes for 11- to 16-year-olds with serious conduct problems, including reductions in their behaviour problems and improvements in their overall social adjustment (Biehal et al., 2012). Other local authorities have used the Fostering Changes programme, a CBT approach designed to help foster carers manage children's behaviour more effectively (Pallett et al., 2002; Warman et al., 2006).

Parenting programmes

Besides the individually focused work discussed already, a number of parenting programmes have also been developed to help families in which children have significant behaviour problems, including conduct disorders (e.g. see NICE, 2006; Hutchings et al., 2008). However, some children and parents with complex needs, which often include living in very disadvantaged circumstances, typically do not participate in or respond positively to such interventions and therefore require more specialised programmes (Nock and Ferriter, 2005).

One such programme, Empowering Parents Empowering Communities trains parents to deliver support in their own communities for families whose children are displaying behavioural difficulties (Day et al., 2012). Peer trainers are selected on the basis of their capacity for self-reflection, understanding and empathy with the difficulties of others, as well as aptitude for the trainer role. New facilitators are normally paired with a more experienced worker, and all receive fortnightly supervision, invitations to workshops, payment and independent accreditation. They deliver a manualised programme specifically designed for use in socially and economically disadvantaged areas with parents of 2- to 11-year-olds, which aims to improve parent–child relationships, reduce children's disruptive behaviour and other problems, and increase participants' confidence in their parenting abilities (Penney et al., 2010). Based on a range of theories and methods (attachment, social learning, structural, relational and cognitive behavioural), it consists of eight weekly two-hour sessions for groups of between six and fourteen parents, covering: being a parent; feelings, communication and culture; play and listening; avoiding labels and using praise; understanding children's behaviour; setting boundaries; and coping with stress. Parents who have attended the programme report high levels of satisfaction, including significant improvements in their children's behaviour and reductions in their own stress levels (Day et al., 2012).

For children aged five to eleven years with more severe and persistent conduct problems the Helping Families Programme has been developed (Day et al., 2011). This is a strengths-based, multi-component programme designed to address many of the key risk and protective factors which have an impact on children's behaviour and parents' ability to achieve change. It is delivered by staff specifically trained to build and maintain purposeful relationships with disadvantaged parents and focuses on issues such as respect, integrity, empathy and communication skills. This provides the starting point for exploring parents' problems, strengths and circumstances, with the aim of developing a shared understanding about how their present difficulties have arisen and are maintained, as well as the potential for change. Subsequent tasks involve: goal setting; identification and guided implementation of agreed intervention strategies; review of goal attainments, partnership working and practitioner effectiveness; and negotiating the programme ending. The programme targets changes in parents' behaviour, cognitions and emotion regulation, aiming to: increase their capacity to develop and maintain warm and purposeful relationships with their children; successfully manage crises and daily hassles; cope with stressful feelings by adopting personal and family activities that improve well-being; minimise harm arising from parental use of drugs and alcohol; and build a social support network that reinforces resilience and buffers against risk. Contact occurs over a minimum of 20 weeks, normally in the family's own home. Although it is too early to identify any long-term outcomes, parents involved in the pilot programmes generally reported high levels of satisfaction, often contrasting it with other services they had received which had been experienced as hostile and persecutory, with priority given to practitioner opinions and little of practical benefit offered to facilitate change (Dawe and Harnett, 2007).

Key messages for practice

1. The prevalence of mental health problems amongst children in the UK is much higher than most people probably realise, with around 20 per cent of children estimated to be experiencing psychological problems at any one time, and 10 per cent having a mental disorder causing significant personal distress or impairment.

2. Practitioners need to be familiar with the evidence about the risk and protective factors associated with children's mental health, using an ecological framework to understand the way that individual, family, community and society level factors interact to influence outcomes for children (and their families).

3. Schools are in a key position when it comes to promoting children's mental health and responding when problems first arise, but to be effective in this area teachers need more support and training, and schools need strengthened policy guidance and more sustainable funding.

4. Various groups of children, particularly those looked after by local authorities (but also including children who are homeless, disabled, refugees, seeking asylum or of black and minority ethnic origin), are over-represented in statistics about childhood mental health problems, but under-represented amongst users of child and adolescent mental health services. Social workers and other child welfare practitioners therefore need to ensure that they work effectively together in the promotion of children's mental health, as well as recognising when children have significant problems and ensuring that they have access to appropriate services.

5. The evidence indicates that conduct problems are not only more persistent than other childhood mental health problems, but also have the most serious consequences for children's future well-being and life chances as adults. Early intervention is therefore crucial, ideally involving a combination of individual work,

typically based on CBT principles, and family work, perhaps utilising parenting programmes specifically designed to help families in which children are displaying significant behaviour problems.

Additional resources

YoungMinds
  www.youngminds.org.uk/

Beatbullying
  www.beatbullying.org/

Department for Education (DfE)
  Annual Tellus surveys gather national information about children's well-being, including their emotional health
  www.dfe.gov.uk

Conclusion: the organisational context for social work practice

Introduction

The great majority of social workers embark on their careers with high expectations, motivated to become knowledgeable and skilled professionals, capable of making a positive difference to the lives of the people with whom they are working (Jack and Donnellan, 2010). So how can they be supported to achieve these goals, developing into fully established professionals who can enjoy successful long-term careers? Having considered the environment within which children are growing up in the UK today and the main components of child development in Part I, and social work as a professional activity with different groups of children in Part II, we conclude the book by considering the organisational contexts of social work practice.

The Social Work Task Force (2009) identified five key working conditions, applicable to all employment settings, that they considered necessary for effective social work practice: enough time to spend working directly with children, adults and families; the right working environment; appropriate ICT systems; meaningful professional support; and access to learning and evidence. Each of these is considered below.

Time for direct work

After many years in which the care management model has dominated the delivery of personal social services across the UK, it is not surprising to find that surveys of front-line social workers consistently identify that their work is increasingly bureaucratic, with a limited proportion of their time spent in direct work with service users. At the same time, research with social workers in the early stages of their careers has found that direct work with service users is the factor which contributes most to their job satisfaction, and the degree to which they consider they have made a difference in people's lives is an important factor in sustaining their morale (Jack and Donnellan, 2010). Unfortunately, whilst recent policy documents (e.g. Social Work Task Force, 2009; Munro, 2011b) have emphasised the central role of relationships in social work, the capacity of social work organisations to ensure that their staff have sufficient time available for direct work, at a time of severe cuts in public spending across the UK, is debatable.

Working environment

As well as becoming more bureaucratic, social work organisations have been subject to almost endemic change over the last decade, and it is perhaps not surprising that they have tended to respond by adopting 'managerialist' approaches, standardising processes and creating audit trails in an attempt to reduce risk and protect themselves from criticism and litigation. Sadly, such approaches frequently conflict with the motivations and value base of social workers, resulting in a significant gap between their 'ideals' and the 'reality' of day-to-day practice. The socialisation process which occurs whilst individuals are making the transition from student to qualified social worker and on to established professional is therefore likely to require considerable support if it is to be satisfactorily negotiated.

One of the ways in which this process can be helped is through the annual 'health check' that employers of social workers are required to undertake, in England at least (TCSW, 2012). This involves assessing the practice conditions within the organisation and planning improvements, drawing on feedback gathered from their staff. Although only a small minority of student and newly-qualified social workers in a survey carried out by the authors in 2011, soon after this requirement was introduced, had taken part in an assessment of this sort, practitioners need to be ready to engage actively in any process that gives them the chance to influence the quality of their working environment.

ICT systems

As pressure to collect more information to meet the needs of regulation and inspection has increased, the requirement for data-gathering via electronic recording systems has also increased, along with a high level of dissatisfaction amongst social workers with the amount of time they have to spend in front of a computer screen. A common problem with many ICT systems used by social workers is the restrictions which they place on the amount and type of information that can typically be entered, so that using them often feels like something of a 'tick box' exercise, rather than a useful professional task. Incompatibility problems between the ICT systems used by different organisations are also common, so that transferring or sharing information is not as straightforward as it ought to be. Practitioners new to an ICT system should ensure that they access training as soon as possible and draw on the 'know how' of more experienced colleagues to establish the most effective ways of using the system, maximising the extent to which it can serve their needs and ways of working, rather than the other way around.

Reflecting what has been available for some time to teachers, the Standards Framework in England (SWRB, 2011) also sets out the expectation that employers will provide skilled administrative staff to support social workers in order to maximise the time they have for direct work. Where these arrangements are properly implemented, practitioners should be able to delegate a range of data input and record-keeping tasks to others. Where this is not the case, it may be an issue which practitioners need to raise at team meetings or with their line manager.

Professional support

Formal supervision

Supervision is central to effective social work practice, providing an important opportunity for the development and support of critical thinking, the capacity to use experiences to improve practice, to receive feedback on performance, to build emotional resilience, and to think reflectively about the relationships involved in professional practice. Although the quality of supervision will always be difficult to assure, there is a growing consensus about the minimum expectations of the quantity and content of supervision. For newly-qualified social workers, employers are expected to ensure weekly supervision for the first six weeks and fortnightly sessions for the first six months, with a minimum of monthly supervision for all staff beyond this point. Each supervision session should comprise at least an hour and a half of uninterrupted time, and cover four key issues: workload management; the quality of decision-making and interventions; line management and accountability; and further personal learning, career and development opportunities (SWRB, 2011).

It is important to remember that the overall purpose of supervision is to improve the quality of services and outcomes for children, adults and families. Supervision can contribute both directly, by exploring different ways of helping in individual situations, and indirectly, as better services are known to be delivered by social workers who feel valued. Effective supervision should be individually tailored to practitioners' experience and stage of development, confidence and abilities, as well as their range of work and the level of responsibility held. To facilitate this process, practitioners should be proactive in:

- Formulating a supervision agreement that specifies appropriate roles and responsibilities.
- Giving supervision the priority it deserves by booking a schedule of appointments that is adhered to in all but the most exceptional circumstances.
- Preparing for each session, including playing a full part in agreeing the agenda and ensuring that personal needs are discussed as well as organisational requirements, recognising that both are of equal importance.
- Discussing further learning and development needs (see section on access to learning and evidence below).
- Remembering to discuss what has gone well, alongside any problems that have arisen – reflecting positively on achievements is an important way of building confidence and maintaining motivation to take on new tasks and challenges.

In relation to this final point, it is important not to regard supervision as an arena for dealing exclusively with problems. With high expectations at the start of a new career, it is easy to be over-sensitive to what may be minor failings and become overwhelmed by emotion. Supervision should help in formulating realistic expectations and reframing feelings of failure as a natural part of professional development. Challenging situations often provide the experiences from which the most significant developments in practice emerge, but only when sufficient time for recovery and reflection has been offered as part of supportive supervision arrangements. However, even highly supportive supervision cannot overcome an excessively demanding workload. Where demands outstrip the ability to cope, it is imperative to use supervision to address the issue of workload and agree strategies that will remove or at least ameliorate the main sources of stress. This might include, for example, reallocating work, reviewing priorities, adjusting deadlines or sharing responsibilities by co-working.

Informal support

Whilst formal supervision is a primary source of professional support, a range of other sources may also be needed to meet different situations. These are likely to include colleagues who can provide invaluable advice and opportunities for observing, shadowing or co-working, as well as someone with whom simply to let off steam occasionally. Agencies may provide a named mentor (ideally outside line management structures) as part of an induction or 'buddying' system, and opportunities for peer-group support, which may be particularly important for those who are home-based, in dispersed teams or lone social workers in multi-professional teams. Staff in a similar situation, for example newly-qualified social workers, may also be facilitated to come together on a regular basis outside supervision and line management arrangements, and it is important to take advantage of these opportunities if they exist. Special interest networks and trade unions may also be useful sources of information and advice, and family and friends can be vital 'resources' when personal support, reassurance and understanding are needed.

There is little doubt that social work can be an extremely demanding job at times and some degree of stress is therefore to be expected. There are several ways in which social workers can help to regulate their own levels of stress, including managing their workload and use of time, establishing a healthy work/life balance and developing their personal coping strategies:

- *Workload and time management*: social workers often refer to the variety of their work as a positive factor in their level of job satisfaction, but this requires successfully managing the plethora of demands that arise within a typical working day, thereby helping to develop a sense of control. This means being clear about priorities, setting deadlines for important pieces of work and delegating or sharing work with others as an integral part of professional practice.

- *Work/life balance*: evidence shows that those working extended hours are not necessarily more productive. It is important to limit the occasions on which the working day is extended or work taken home, and to resist the temptation to 'prove' commitment by accepting every task offered; in other words, learning to say 'no'.
- *Personal coping strategies*: workplace stress is typically the result of an inappropriate level of pressure resulting from the interaction of organisational demands and the individual's ability to cope with those demands. Even where demands are high, levels of stress may be low if a person's coping ability is high. Effective coping strategies of two types may be helpful in dealing with stress and maintaining job satisfaction: 'emotion-focused coping', when the cause of the stress is beyond personal control and coping is aimed at reducing or managing distress; and 'problem-focused coping', which involves taking action when something can be done to alter the cause of the stress.

Expanding on this last point, emotion-focused strategies include: *acceptance*, where a stressor cannot be changed but is accommodated in a more acceptable way by adjusting expectations and attitudes; *positive reappraisal*, talking about feelings and putting stressful circumstances into a wider context so that they appear in a more favourable light; and *stress inoculation*, consciously ensuring time to plan and prepare for a difficult situation, perhaps rehearsing options in supervision. By way of contrast, problem-focused strategies involve seeking out support and active engagement in thinking about and implementing whatever practical steps can be taken to reduce the stress being experienced. By stepping back from the situation causing the stress it is often easier to employ restraint, avoid acting prematurely and set more realistic goals that help to restore feelings of self-efficacy and control in working towards them. Unfortunately, the dominant coping strategy found amongst social workers is the internalisation of difficulties, with anxiety allowed to build up in the vain hope that it will eventually disappear or be released elsewhere. Failing to acknowledge or attempting to deal with stress in this way often means that the situation has no chance to improve, and is in fact more likely to deteriorate (Collins, 2007).

Access to learning and evidence

The final aspect of organisational requirements considered here is access to learning and evidence. All social workers should remain open to learning throughout their careers, actively seeking out new knowledge as part of the process of their continuing professional development (CPD). As social workers are likely to change jobs several times throughout the course of their careers, it is also essential that they develop expertise and specialist skills appropriate to the new settings in which they are working.

In 2012, a new Professional Capabilities Framework (PCF) was adopted by the College of Social Work as the single way in which social workers in England would demonstrate and plan their CPD at both pre- and post-qualifying levels, defining a range of capabilities in nine domains of development (www.tcsw.org.uk/). Progression between levels is characterised by the ability to manage increasing complexity, risk, ambiguity and autonomy. At the time of writing different arrangements for registration, regulation and CPD, based on the National Occupational Standards (NOS) for social work, apply in Wales (www.ccwales.org.uk), Scotland (www.sssc.uk.com) and Northern Ireland (www.niscc.info).

Whether linking to the PCF or NOS, there are four related elements that should guide practitioners in their CPD:

- *Personal development planning (PDP)*: this is a useful way of making the connection between learning at different stages of professional development. Templates for developing PDPs are available from most universities and employers, with pre-qualifying programmes, for example, required to provide graduating students with a statement of their achievements and areas for further development. Where practitioners share their PDP in supervision, it can make an important contribution to identifying their training needs and informing decisions about the allocation of different types of work to build confidence and broaden experience in a coherent way.
- *Post-registration training and learning (PRTL)*: this is a condition for continued registration as a professional social worker. Each of the four UK councils regulating social work has developed slightly different approaches to the specific requirements, with details available from the relevant websites (England – Health & Care Professions Council: www.hpc-uk.org; Northern Ireland Social Care Council:

www.niscc.info; Care Council for Wales: www.ccwales.org.uk; Scottish Social Services Council: www.sssc.uk.com). Whatever the specific arrangements in different countries, practitioners should be provided with time, resources and support to complete the relevant requirements for PRTL with employers expected to have mechanisms in place for recording and tracking the CPD activities undertaken by their staff, either as a paper or electronic portfolio.

- *Post-qualifying (PQ) education and training*: PRTL fits within the broader PQ frameworks for education and training, which aim to create learning and development opportunities that are: *flexible*, allowing for individual circumstances; *a shared responsibility*, focusing equally on the needs of the individual, team and employer, as well as policy and wider workforce requirements; and *available via a range of routes of equal value*, based on three 'modes' of learning: informal learning in the course of daily practice; unassessed courses and training, including short courses and in-house programmes, usually delivered away from the workplace for a specified number of days; and certificated learning through higher education institutions. Again, in developing the specific PQ requirements, the four UK countries have taken different approaches; more details can be found on the respective councils' websites.

- *Reflexive journal*: especially in the early stages of professional development, keeping a reflexive journal, with a central focus on personal ideas, feelings and actions, can be a very useful way of recording what influences an individual's practice. This might include trends or patterns in thinking or action that might not otherwise be apparent, but that would benefit from further exploration, either in supervision or discussion with colleagues.

Summary

It is important for practitioners to be aware of the influence that the organisational requirements of the setting in which they are working are likely to have on their professional practice and development, as well as their personal well-being. They need to establish effective support systems for themselves, as well as being prepared to challenge any inappropriate aspects of their working arrangements.

All social workers should also recognise that a key element of their continuing professional development and their capacity to provide the best possible quality of social work practice is effective supervision. To be effective, supervision should be tailored to each person's stage of development, confidence and abilities, the types of learning opportunities undertaken, and the range of work and level of responsibility held. To facilitate this process, practitioners should play an active role in setting the agenda, ensuring that they get what they need from supervision, and preventing practice audit and performance management from dominating. The quality of services provided to vulnerable children and families depends on effective processes for encouraging and supporting the capacity of practitioners to reflect on their practice and pay appropriate attention to their personal well-being and professional development.

Fully developed professional practice involves the flexible and creative use of knowledge and skills, applied in the context of practitioners' professional identity and the organisational requirements of their work settings. This enables practitioners to form autonomous professional judgements which they are able to explain clearly and justify, taking account of the complexities and uncertainties of a given situation and recognising the importance of context, in which actions are mediated by circumstances that change over time and place.

References

Action for Children (2012) *Child Neglect in 2011*. Watford: Action for Children.

Ainsworth, M., Blehar, M., Waters, E., and Wall, S. (1978) *Patterns of Attachment*. Hillsdale, NJ: Erlbaum.

Allen, G. (2011) *Early Intervention: The Next Steps*. London: HM Government.

Anderson, B., Beinart, S., Farrington, D. Langman, J., Sturgis, P. and Utting, D. (2001) *Risk and Protective Factors Associated with Youth Crime and Effective Interventions to Prevent It*. London: Youth Justice Board.

Armsden, G., and Greenberg, M. (1987) The inventory of parent and peer attachment: Individual differences and their relationship to psychological well-being in adolescence. *Journal of Youth and Adolescence,* 16 (5): 427–454.

Armstrong, D., Hine, J., Hacking, S., Armaos, R., Jones, R., Klessinger, N. and France, A. (2005) *Children, Risk and Crime: The On Track Youth Lifestyles Surveys*. London: Home Office.

Atkinson, M. and Hornby, G. (2002) *Mental Health Handbook for Schools*. London: Routledge Falmer.

Attree, P. (2004) Growing up in disadvantage: A systematic review of the qualitative evidence. *Child: Care, Health and Development,* 30 (6): 679–689.

Attwood, G., and Croll, P. (2006) Truancy in secondary school pupils: prevalence, trajectories and pupil perspectives. *Research Papers in Education,* 21 (4): 467–484.

Audit Commission (1996) *Misspent Youth*. London: Audit Commission.

Audit Commission (2003) *Services for Disabled Children: A Review of Services for Disabled Children and their Families*. London: Audit Commission.

Baker, K. (2008) Risk, uncertainty and public protection: Assessments of young people who offend. *British Journal of Social Work,* 38:1463–1480.

Bakermans-Kranenburg, M.J., IJzendoor, M.H., van and Juffer, F. (2003) Less is more: Meta-analyses of sensitivity and attachment interventions in early childhood. *Psychological Bulletin,* 129 (2):195–215.

Balbernie, R., (2009) Guide to infant mental health services, *Community Care Inform*, retrieved from www.ccinform.co.uk/articles (accessed 25 July 2010).

Banister, J. and Dillane, J. (2005) *Communities That Care: An Evaluation of the Scottish Pilot Programme*. Research Findings No. 17. Edinburgh: Scottish Executive

Banks, S. (2010) Integrity in professional life: Issues of conduct, commitment and capacity. *British Journal of Social Work,* 40 (7): 2168–2184.

Barlow, J., Simkiss, D. and Stewart-Brown, S. (2006) Interventions to prevent or ameliorate child physical abuse and neglect: Findings from a systematic review of reviews. *Journal of Children's Services*, 1 (3): 6–28.

Barnes, J., Ball, M., Meadows, P. Howden, B., Jackson, A., Henderson, J. and Niven, L. (2011) *The Family-Nurse Partnership Programme in England: Wave 1 Implementation in Toddlerhood and a Comparison Between Waves 1 and 2a of Implementation in Pregnancy and Infancy*. London: Department of Health.

Bartlett, J., and Miller, C. (2011) *Truth, Lies and the Internet – A Report into Young People's Digital Fluency*. London: Demos.

BASW (2009) *Code of Ethics*. United Kingdom: British Association of Social Workers.

Baum, S. and Lyngaard, H. (2006) *Intellectual Disabilities: A Systemic Approach*. London: Karnac Books.

Baumrind, D. (1972) Socialisation and instrumental competence in young children. In W. W. Hartup (ed.) *The Young Child: Reviews of Research Volume 2*. Washington, DC: National Association for the Education of Young Children, 202–224.

Baumrind, D. (2005) Patterns of parental authority and adolescent autonomy. *New Directions for Child and Adolescent Development,* 108: 61–69.

Baynes, P. (2008) Untold stories: A discussion of life story work. *Adoption and Fostering*, 32 (2): 43–49.

Beatbullying (2006) Bullying and truancy report, 2006 www.beatbullying. org/pdfs/bullying-truancy-report-2006.pdf (accessed 12 December 2012)

Becker, H. (1963) *Outsiders: Studies in the Sociology of Deviance*. New York: Free Press.

Bee, H., and Boyd, D. (2010) *The Developing Child* (12th edn). Boston, MA: Pearson.

Beinart, S., Anderson, B., Lee, S. and Utting, D. (2002) *Youth at Risk? A National Survey of Risk Factors, Protective Factors and Problem Behaviour among Young People in England, Scotland and Wales*. London: Communities that Care.

Bell, M. (2003) Case conferences in child protection. In K. Wilson and A. James (eds) *The Child Protection Handbook*. London: Ballière Tindall, 288–304

Belsky, J. (1993) Etiology of child maltreatment: A developmental-ecological analysis. *Psychological Bulletin*, 114 (3): 413–434.

Belsky, J. and Jaffee, S.R. (2006) The multiple determinants of parenting. In D. Cicchetti and D.J. Cohen (eds), *Developmental Psychopathology: (Vol. 3) Risk, Disorder and Adaptation*, Hoboken, NJ: John Wiley & Sons, 38–85.

Belsky, J., Burchinal, M., McCartney, K., Lowe Vandell, D., Clarke-Stewart, A. and Tresch Owen, M. (2007) Are there long-term effects of early child care? *Child Development*, 78 (2): 681–701.

Beresford, B. (2002) Preventing the social exclusion of disabled children. In D. McNeish, T. Newman, and H. Roberts (eds) *What Works for Children?* Buckingham: Open University Press, 147–164.

Beresford, B. (2008) *Housing and Disabled Children.* York, Joseph Rowntree Foundation.

Beresford, B. and Oldman, C. (2002) *Housing Matters: National Evidence Relating to Disabled Children and their Housing.* Bristol: Policy Press.

Berridge, D. (2000) *Placement Stability* (Quality Protects Research Briefing). Dartington: Research in Practice.

Berridge, D., Dance, C., Beecham, J. and Field, S. (2008) *Educating Difficult Adolescents. Effective Education for Children in Public Care or with Emotional and Behavioural Difficulties.* London: Jessica Kingsley Publishers.

Berridge, D., Biehal, N. and Henry, L. (2012) *Living in Children's Residential Homes.* (Research Report DFE-RR201). London: Department for Education.

Biehal, N. (2006) *Reuniting Looked-after Children with their Families: A Research Review.* London: National Children's Bureau.

Biehal, N. and Parry, E. (2010) *Maltreatment and Allegations of Maltreatment in Foster Care: A Review of Evidence.* York: Social Policy Research Unit, University of York/The Fostering Network.

Biehal, N., Dixon, J., Parry, E., Sinclair, I., Green, J., Roberts, C., Kay, C., Rothwell, J., Kapadia, D. and Roby, A. (2012) *The Care Placements Evaluation (CaPE) Evaluation of Multidimensional Treatment Foster Care for Adolescents (MTFC-A).* London: Department for Education.

Black, K., (2012) The relationship between companion animals and loneliness among rural adolescents, *Journal of Pediatric Nursing*, 27(2), 103–112

Blackburn, C.M., Spencer, N.J. and Read, J.M. (2010) Prevalence of childhood disability and the characteristics and circumstances of disabled children in the UK: Secondary analysis of the Family Resources Survey. *BMC Pediatrics*, 10: 21.

Blanden, J., and Gibbons, S. (2006) *The persistence of poverty across generations: A view from two British cohorts.* Bristol: JRF/Policy Press.

Blos, P. (1967) The second individuation process of adolescence. In R. S. Eissler (ed.), *Psychoanalytic Study of the Child* (Vol. 15). New York: International Universities Press, 369–374.

Bostock, L. (2004) *Promoting Resilience in Fostered Children and Young People* (Resource Guide No 4). London: SCIE.

Boushel, M., Fawcett, M., and Selwyn, J. (eds) (2000) *Focus on Early Childhood*. London: Blackwell Science Ltd.

Bowlby, J. (1969) *Attachment and Loss: Volume 1 Attachment*. New York: Basic Books.

Bradshaw, J. and Richardson, D. (2009) An index of child well-being in Europe. *Child Indicators Research*, 2: 319–351.

Bradshaw, P. and Martin, C., with Cunningham-Burley, S. (2008) *Growing Up in Scotland: Explaining the Experiences and Outcomes of Advantaged and Disadvantaged Families*. Edinburgh: Scottish Government.

Brandon, M. and Thoburn, J. (2008) Safeguarding children in the UK: A longitudinal study of services to children suffering or likely to suffer significant harm. *Child and Family Social Work*, 13: 365–377.

Brandon, M., Dodsworth, J., and Rumball, D. (2005) Serious case reviews: learning to use expertise. *Child Abuse Review*, 14 (3): 160–176.

Bronfenbrenner, U. (1979) *The Experimental Ecology of Human Development*. Cambridge, MA: Harvard University Press.

Brooks, R. B. (1994) Children at risk: Fostering resilience and hope. *American Journal of Orthpsychiatry*, 64 (4): 545–553.

Brown, B. (1990). Peer groups. In S. Feldman and G. Elliott (eds) *At the Threshold: The Developing Adolescent*. Cambridge: Harvard University Press, 255–276.

Brown, B., Mory, M., and Kenney, D. (1994) Casting crowds in a relational perspective: Caricature, channel and context. In R. Monemayor, G. Adams and T. Gullotta (eds) *Advances in Adolescent Development (Vol. 5: Personal Relationships during Adolescence)*. Newbury Park, MA: Sage, 123–137.

Browne (1993) Home visitation and child abuse: The British experience. *American Professional Society on the Abuse of Children*, 6 (4): 11–31

BSA. (2010) *British Social Attitudes Survey, 27th Report*. From www.natcen.ac.uk/study/british-social-attitudes-27th-report

Buchanan, C. M., Eccles, J. S., and Becker, J. B. (1992) Are adolescents the victims of raging hormones? Evidence for activational effects of hormones on moods and behavior at adolescence. *Psychological Bulletin*, 111 (1): 62–107.

Buckley, H., Whelan, S., Carer, N. and Murphy, C. (2008) *Service Users' Perceptions of the Irish Child Protection System*. Dublin: Office of the Minister for Children and Youth Affairs.

Bull, J., McCormick, G., Swann, C. and Mulvihill, C. (2004) *Ante- and Post-natal Home-Visiting Programmes: A Review of Reviews: Evidence Briefing*. London: Health Development Agency.

Burt, M., and Worsley, A. (2008) Social work, professionalism and the regulatory framework. In S. Fraser and S. Matthews (eds), *The Critical Practitioner in Social Work and Health Care*. London: Sage/OU: 27–42.

Butler, I. and Williamson, H. (1994) *Children Speak: Children, Trauma and Social Work.* Harlow: Longman.

Butler-Sloss, Lord Justice (1988) *Report on the Inquiry into Child Abuse in Cleveland 1987.* London: HMSO.

Bywaters, T., Hutchings, J., Daley, D., Whitaker, C., Yeo, S.T., Jones, K., Eames, C. and Tudor Edwards, R. (2009) Long-term effectiveness of a parenting intervention for children at risk of developing conduct disorder. *British Journal of Psychiatry*, 195: 1–7.

C4EO (2010a) *Grasping the Nettle: Early Intervention for Children, Families and Communities (Executive Summary).* London: Centre for Excellence and Outcomes in Children and Young People's Services.

C4EO (2010b) *The Views and Experiences of Children and Young People Who Have Been Through the Child Protection/Safeguarding System.* London: Centre for Excellence in Outcomes in Children and Young People's Services.

Calder, M.C. and Hackett, S. (2003) The Assessment Framework: A critique and reformulation. In M.C. Calder and S. Hackett (eds) *Assessment in Child Care: Using and Developing Frameworks for Practice.* Lyme Regis: Russell House Publishing, 3–60.

Camina, M. (2004) *Understanding and Engaging Deprived Communities.* London: Home Office.

Campbell, B. (1988) *Unofficial Secrets. Child Sexual Abuse: The Cleveland Case.* London: Virago.

Catalano, R. and Hawkins, J.D. (1996) The social development model: A theory of antisocial behaviour. In J.D. Hawkins (ed.) *Delinquency and Crime.* Cambridge: Cambridge University Press, 57–86.

Cavet, J. (2009) *Housing for Disabled Children and their Families.* York: Joseph Rowntree Foundation.

Chamberlain, T., George, N., Golden, S., Walker, F., and Benton, T. (2010) *Tellus4 National Report.* London: Department for Children, Schools and Families.

Cicchetti, D. and Valentino, K. (2006) An ecological-transactional perspective on child maltreatment: Failure of the average expectable environment and its influence on child development. In D. Cicchetti and D.J. Cohen (eds) *Developmental Psychopathology: Risk, Disorder and Adaptation*, Hoboken, NJ: John Wiley & Sons, 129–201.

Clarke, H. (2005) *Preventing Social Exclusion of Disabled Children and their Families.* National Evaluation of the Children's Fund (www.ne-cf.org).

Cleaver, H. and Walker, S., with Meadows, P. (2004) *Assessing Children's Needs and Circumstances: The Impact of the Assessment Framework.* London: Jessica Kingsley Publishers.

Cleaver, H., Unell, I. and Aldgate, J. (2011) *Children's Needs – Parenting Capacity: Parental Mental Illness, Learning Disability, Substance Misuse, and Domestic Violence* (2nd edn). London: The Stationery Office.

Clayden, J. and Stein, M. (2005) *Mentoring Young People Leaving Care: 'Someone For Me'*. York: Joseph Rowntree Foundation.

CLS (2005) *Parenting*. London: Institute of Education/Centre for Longitudinal Studies.

Collins, S. (2007) Social workers, resilience, positive emotions and optimism. *Practice*, 19 (4), 255–269.

Collishaw, S., Maughan, B., Goodman, R. and Pickles, A. (2004) Time trends in adolescent mental health. *Journal of Child Psychology and Psychiatry*, 45(8): 1350–1362.

Communities that Care (2005) *Findings from the Safer London Youth Survey 2004*. London: Communities That Care.

Connelly, G., Lockhart, E., Wilson, P., Furnivall, J., Bryce, G., Barbour, R. and Phin, L. (2008) Teachers' responses to the emotional needs of children and young people – results from the Scottish Needs Assessment Programme. *Emotional and Behavioural Difficulties*, 13 (1): 7–19.

Contact a Family (2010) *Information about Families with Disabled Children*. London: Contact a Family.

Contact a Family (2011) *Siblings: Information for Families*. London: Contact a Family.

Corby, B. (2000) *Child Abuse: Towards a Knowledge Base* (2nd edn). Buckingham: Open University Press.

Cote, S. and Healy, T. (2001) *The Well-Being of Nations. The Role of Human and Social Capital*. Paris: Organisation for Economic Co-operation and Development.

CRG (2006) *Positive Activities for Young People: National Evaluation*. Cardiff: CRG Research Limited.

Cross, E.J., Richardson, B., Douglas, T., and Vonkaenel-Platt, J. (2009) *Virtual Violence: Protecting Children from Cyberbullying*. London: Beatbullying.

Crow, I., France, A., Hacking, S., and Hart, M (2004) *Does Communities That Care Work? An Evaluation of a Community-based Risk Prevention Programme in Three Neighbourhoods*. York: Joseph Rowntree Foundation.

CSCI (2005) *Social Services Performance Assessment Framework Indicators*. London: Commission for Social Care Inspection.

Dagley, V., Howe, A., Salter, C., Brandon, M., Warren, C. and Black, J. (2007) Implications of the new Common Assessment Framework and lead professional working for pastoral care staff in schools. *Pastoral Care*, March: 4–10.

Dale, P. (2004) 'Like a fish in a bowl'. Parents' perceptions of child protection services. *Child Abuse Review*, 13: 137–157.

Daly, B., and Morton, L.L., (2006) An investigation of human-animal interactions and empathy as related to pet preference, owenership, attachment and attitudes in children, *Anthrozoös*, 19(2), 113–127

Daniel, B., and Wassell, S. (2002) *The School Years: Assessing and Promoting Resilience in Vulnerable Children 2*. London: Jessica Kingsley.

Daniel, B., Wassell, S., and Gilligan, R. (1999) *Child Development for Child Care and Protection Workers*. London: Jessica Kingsley.

Davey Smith, G. (ed.) (2003) *Health Inequalities: Lifecourse Approaches*. Bristol: The Policy Press.

Dawe, S. and Harnett, P.H. (2007) Improving family functioning in methadone maintained families: Results from a randomised controlled trial. *Journal of Substance Abuse Treatment*, 32: 381–390.

Dawson, G., Panagiotides, H., Klinger, L. G., and Spieker, S. (1997) Infants of depressed and non-depressed mothers exhibit differences in frontal brain electrical activity during the expression of negative emotions. *Developmental Psychology*, 33: 650–656.

Day, C., Kowalenko, S., Ellis, M., Dawe, S., Harnett, P. and Scott, S. (2011) The Helping Families Programme: A new parenting intervention for children with severe and persistent conduct problems. *Child and Adolescent Mental Health*, 16 (3): 167–171.

Day, C., Michelson, D., Thomson, S., Penney, C. and Draper, L. (2012) Innovations in Practice: Empowering Parents, Empowering Communities: A pilot evaluation of a peer-led parenting programme. *Child and Adolescent Mental Health*, 17 (1): 52–57.

DCLG (2009) *Local Index of Child Well-Being: Summary Report*. London: Department for Communities and Local Government.

DCLG (2010) *The English Indices of Deprivation 2010*. London: Department for Communities and Local Government.

DCSF (2008) *The Impact of Parental Involvement on Children's Education*. Nottingham: Department for Children Schools and Families.

DCSF (2010a) *Working Together to Safeguard Chidlren: A guide to interagency working to safeguard and promote the welfare of children*. Nottingham: Department for Children, Schools and Families.

DCSF (2010b) *Teenage Pregnancy Strategy: Beyond 2010*. Nottingham: Department for Children Schools and Families.

DCSF (2010c) *Me and My School: Preliminary Findings from the First Year of the National Evaluation of Targeted Mental Health in Schools (2008–2009)*. London: Department for Children, Schools and Families.

DCSF/DH (2009) *Aiming High for Disabled Children: Best Practice to Common Practice*. Nottingham: Department for Children, Schools and Families.

DCSF/DH (2010) *Keeping Children and Young People in Mind: The Government's Full Response to the Independent Review of CAMHS*. Nottingham: Department for Children, Schools and Families.

Dearden, C. and Aldridge, J. (2010) Young carers: Needs, rights and assessments. In Horwath, J. (ed.) *The Child's World: The*

Comprehensive Guide to Assessing Children in Need. London: Jessica Kingsley Publishers, 214–228.

Desforges, C., with Abouchaar, A., (2003) *The Impact of Parental Involvement, Parental Support and Family Education on Pupil Achievement and Adjustment: A Review of the Literature* (Research Brief No: 433). London: Department for Education and Skills.

DfE (2010) *Children in Need in England: Year Ending 31 March 2010*. London: Department for Education.

DfE (2011a) *Children Looked After in England (Including Adoption and Care Leavers) Year Ending 31 March 2011*. London: Department for Education.

DfE (2011b) *Outcomes for Children Looked After by Local Authorities in England, as at 31 March 2010*. London: Department for Education.

DfE (2011c) *Support and Aspiration: A New Approach to Special Educational Needs and Disability*. Green Paper, Cm 8027. London: The Stationery Office.

DfE/DH (2000) *Education Protects*. London: Department for Education and Department of Health.

DfE/DH (2011) *Supporting Families in the Foundation Years*. London: Department for Education/Department of Health.

DfES (2003) *Every Child Matters*. London: Department for Education and Skills, HMSO.

DH (1989) *An Introduction to the Children Act 1989*. London: Department of Health, HMSO.

DH (1997) *People Like Us: The Report of the Review of Safeguards for Children Living Away From Home*. London: Department of Health, The Stationery Office.

DH (2001a) *Private Fostering: A Cause for Concern*. London: Department of Health.

DH (2001b) *Valuing People: A New Strategy for Learning Disability for the 21st Century*. White Paper, Cm5086. London: Department of Health, The Stationery Office.

DH (2008) *Children and Young People in Mind: The Final Report of the National CAMHS Review*. London: Department of Health.

DH/DfEE/HO (2000) *Framework for the Assessment of Children in Need and their Families*. London: Department of Health, Department for Education and Employment, and Home Office, The Stationery Office.

DHSS (1974) *Maria Colwell Inquiry Report*. London: Department of Health and Social Security, HMSO.

DHSSPS (2008) *Standards for Child Protection Services*. Belfast: Department of Health, Social Services and Public Safety.

DHSSPS (2011) *Publication of 'Children Order Statistical Trends for Northern Ireland 2004/05 to 2009/10'*. Belfast: Department of Health, Social Services and Public Safety.

Dixon, J. (2008) Young people leaving care: Health, well-being and outcomes. *Child and Family Social Work*, 13: 207–217.

Donnellan, H. and Jack, G. (2010) *Hitting the Ground Running: The Survival Guide for Newly Qualified Child and Family Social Workers*. London: Jessica Kingsley Publishers.

Donnelly, P.G. and Kimble, C.E. (1997) Community organizing, environmental change, and neighbourhood crime. *Crime and Delinquency*, 43: 493–511.

Dowling. M. (1999) *Social Work and Poverty: Attitudes and Actions*. Aldershot: Ashgate.

Dunn, J. and Deater-Deckard, K. (2001) *Children's Views of their Changing Families*. York: Joseph Rowntree Foundation/York Publishing Services.

DWP (2005) *Households Below Average Income 2004*. London: Department for Work and Pensions.

DWP (2010) *Households Below Average Income: An Analysis of the Income Distribution 1994/95–2008/09*. London: Department for Work and Pensions

Dyson, A., Hertzman, C., Roberts, H., Tunstill, J., and Vaghri, Z. (2010) Childhood development, education and health inequalities – Report of Task Group Submission to the Marmot Review. www.marmotreview.org/AssetLibrary/pdfs/full%20tg%20reports/early%20years%20and%20education%20t.g.%20full%20report.pdf (accessed 18 February 2012).

Edwards, H. and Richardson, K. (2003) The child protection system and disabled children. In J. Morris (ed.) *'It Doesn't Happen to Disabled Children' Child Protection and Disabled Children – Report of the National Working Group on Child Protection and Disability*. London: NSPCC, 31–44.

Edwards, P., Roberts, I., Green, J., and Lutchmun, S. (2006) Deaths from injury in children and employment status in family: analysis of trends in class specific death rates. *British Medical Journal*, 333 (7559): 119.

Edwards, R., Hadfield, L., and Mauthner, M. (2005) *Children's Understanding of their Sibling Relationships*. York: Joseph Rowntree Foundation.

Eisenberg, N., Morris, A., McDaniel, B., and Spinrad, D. (2009) Moral cognitions and pro-social responding in adolescence. In R. Lerner and L. Steinberg (eds), *Handbook of Adolescent Psychology* (3rd edn, Vol. 1). New York: Wiley, 229–265.

Elkind, D. (1967) Egocentrism in adolescence. *Child Development*, 38: 1023–1034.

Elliott, V. (2007) Interventions and services for refugee and asylum-seeking children and families. In P. Vostanis (ed.) *Mental Health Interventions and Services for Vulnerable Children and Young People*. London: Jessica Kingsley Publishers, 132–148.

Ellis, B. J. (2004). Timing of pubertal maturation in girls: An integrated life history approach. *Psychological Bulletin,* 130 (6): 920–958.

Erikson, E. H. (1968) *Identity: Youth and Crisis.* New York: Norton.

Erikson, E. H. (1995) *Childhood and Society.* London: Vintage.

Evangelou, M., Sylva, K., Kyriacou, M., Wild, M., and Glenny, G. (2009) *Early Years Learning and Development Literature Review Research Report 176.* London: Department of Education.

Fahlberg, V. (1991). *A Child's Journey through Placement.* London: British Association of Adoption and Fostering.

Falkov, A. (2002) Addressing family needs when a parent is mentally ill. In H. Ward and W. Rose (eds) *Approaches to Needs Assessment in Children's Services.* London: Jessica Kingsley Publishers, 235–260.

Farmer, E. and Moyers, S. (2005) *Children Placed with Family and Friends: Placement Patterns and Outcomes.* Bristol: School for Policy Studies, University of Bristol.

Farmer, E., Burns, B., Philips, S., Angold, A. and Costello, J. (2003) Pathways into and through mental health services for children and adolescents. *Psychiatric Services,* 54 (1): 60–66.

Farmer, E., Sturgess, W. and O'Neill, T. (2008) *Reunification of Looked After Children with their Parents: Patterns, Interventions and Outcomes.* London: Department for Children, Schools and Families.

Farmer, E., Sturgess, W., O'Neill, T and Wijedasa, D. (2011) *Achieving Successful Returns from Care: What Makes Reunification Work?* London: British Association of Adoption and Fostering (BAAF).

Feinstein, L. and J. Bynner (2004) The importance of cognitive development in middle childhood for adult socio-economic status, mental health and problem behaviour, *Child Development* 75 (5), 1329–1339.

Feinstein, L., Bynner, J. and Duckworth, K. (2005) *Leisure Contexts in Adolescence and their Effects on Adult Outcomes.* London: Institute of Education.

Fergus, S., and Zimmerman, M. A. (2005) Adolescent resilience: A framework for understanding healthy development in the face of risk. *Annual Review of Public Health,* 26: 399–419.

Finch, S., Maung, N.A., Jones, A., Tipping, S., and Blom, A., with Ghate, D. (2006) *National Evaluation of On Track Phase Two: Report of the First Wave of the Longitudinal Cohort Study.* London: Department for Education and Skills.

Flavell, J. H. (1985) *Cognitive Development.* Englewood Cliffs, NJ: Prentice-Hall.

Fletcher-Campbell, F., Archer, T. and Tomlinson, K. (2003) *The Role of the School in Supporting the Education of Children in Public Care* (Research Brief No: RB498). London: Department for Education and Skills.

Flouri, E. (2006) Parental interest in children's education, children's self-esteem and locus of control and later educational attainment: twenty six year follow up of the 1970 British birth cohort. *British Journal of Educational Psychology,* 76 (1): 41–55.

Flouri, E., Tzavidis, N., and Kallis, C. (2010) Area and family effects on the psychopathology of the Millennium Cohort Study children and their older siblings. *Journal of Child Psychology and Psychiatry*, 51 (2): 152-161.

Flynn, R. (2002) *Short Breaks: Providing Better Access and More Choice for Black Disabled Children and their Parents.* Bristol: Policy Press.

Fonagy, P., Steele, M., Steele, H., Higgit, A., and Target, M. (1994). The theory and practice of resilience. *Journal of Child Psychology and Psychiatry,* 35(2), 231-257.

Fook, J. (2002) *Social Work: Critical Theory and Practice.* London: Sage.

Forrester, D., Kershaw, S., Moss, H. and Hughes, L. (2008) Communication skills in child protection: How do social workers talk to parents? *Child and Family Social Work*, 13: 41–51.

Forrester, D., Goodman, K., Cocker, C., Binnie, C. and Jensch, G. (2009) What is the impact of public care on children's welfare? A review of research findings from England and Wales and their policy implications. *Journal of Social Policy*, 38 (3): 439–456.

Fostering Network, The (2008) *Fostering Families: Supporting Sons and Daughters of Foster Carers.* London: The Fostering Network.

Fostering Network, The (2011) *Crisis Looms for Foster Care in 2012.* www.fostering.net/news/2011/crisis-looms-foster-care-in-2012 (accessed 29 December 2011).

Fortin, J. (2009) *Children's Rights and the Developing Law* (3rd edn). Cambridge: Cambridge University Press.

4Children (2007) *Free Range Childhoods: Creating Good Neighbourhoods for Children to Grow Up In.* London: www.4Children.org.uk

Fox Harding, L. (1996) *Family, State and Social Policy.* Basingstoke: Macmillan.

FPA (2010) Teenage Pregnancy Factsheet. www.fpa.org.uk/professionals/factsheets/teenagepregnancy (accessed 25 November 2011).

France, A. and Crow, I. (2001) *CTC: The Story So Far. An Interim Evaluation of Communities That Care.* York: York Publishing Services.

Fredriksen, K., Rhodes, J., Reddy, R., and Way, N. (2004). Sleepless in Chicago: Tracking the effects of adolescent sleep loss during the middle school years. *Child Development,* 75 (1): 84–95.

Fuligni, A. J., and Hardway, C. (2006) Daily variation in adolescents' sleep, activities, and psychological well-being. *Journal of Research on Adolescence,* 16 (3): 353–378.

Gable, S., Belsky, J., and Crnic, K. (1992) Marriage, parenting, and child development: Progress and prospects. *Journal of Family Psychology*, 5 (3–4): 276–294.

Garces, E.D., Thomas, D. and Currie, J. (2002) Longer-term effects of Head Start. *American Economic Review,* 92 (4): 999–1012.

Gesell, A. (1952) *Infant Development: The Embryology of Early Behaviour*. New York: Harper & Brothers.

Ghaffar, W., Manby, M. and Race, T. (2011) Exploring the experiences of parents and carers whose children have been subject to child protection plans. *British Journal of Social Work* (doi:10.1093/bjsw/bcr132).

Ghate, D. and Hazel, N (2002) *Parenting in Poor Environments: Stress, Support and Coping*. London: Jessica Kingsley Publishers.

Ghate, D. and Ramella, M. (2002) *Positive Parenting: The National Evaluation of the Youth Justice Board's Parenting Programme*. London: Youth Justice Board.

Gilbert, R., Kemp, A., Thoburn, J., Sidebotham, P., Radford, L. Glaser, D. and MacMillan, H.L. (2009) Recognising and responding to child maltreatment. *The Lancet*, 373: 167–180.

Gill, O. (1988) Integrated work in a neighbourhood family centre. *Practice*, 2 (3): 243–255.

Gill, O. and Jack, G. (2007) *The Child and Family in Context: Developing Ecological Practice in Disadvantaged Communities*. Lyme Regis: Russell House Publishing.

Gilligan, R. (2000) Adversity, resilience and young people: The protective value of positive school and spare time experiences. *Children and Society*, 14: 37–47.

Glass, N. (1999) Sure Start: The development of an early intervention programme for young children in the United Kingdom. *Children and Society*, 13: 257–264.

Glass, N. (2005) Surely some mistake? *The Guardian*, www.society.guardian.co.uk/print/0,3858,5095487-108861,00.html (accessed 10 January 2005).

Goldson, B. (2002) *Vulnerable Inside: Children in Secure and Penal Settings*. London: The Children's Society.

Goodman, A., and Gregg, P. (2010) *Poorer Children's Educational Attainment: How Important are Attitudes and Behaviour?* York: Joseph Rowntree Foundation.

Graham, H. (ed.) (2000) *Understanding Health Inequalities*. Buckingham: Open University Press.

Greco, V. and Sloper, P. (2004) Care co-ordination and key worker schemes for disabled children: Results of a UK-wide survey. *Child: Care, Health and Development*, 30: 13–20.

Green, H., McGinnity, A., Meltzer, H., Ford, T. and Goodman, R. (2005) *Mental Health of Children and Young People in Great Britain, 2004*. London: National Statistics.

Green, M. (2007) *Voices of People Experiencing Poverty in Scotland*. York: Joseph Rowntree Foundation

Greenberg, M.T., Siegel, J M., and Leitch, C.J. (1983) The nature and importance of attachment relationships to parents and peers during adolescence. *Journal of Youth and Adolescence,* 12 (5): 373–386.

GSCC (2011) *Professional Boundaries – Guidance for Social Workers*. London: General Social Care Council.

Gutman, L.M., Brown, J., Akerman, R. and Obolenskaya, P. (2010) *Change in Wellbeing from Childhood to Adolescence: Risk and Resilience*. London: Department for Children, Schools and Families.

Hall, G.S. (1904) *Adolescence: Its Psychology and Its Relations to Anthropology, Sex, Crime, Religion and Education*. New York: Appleton.

Hannon, C., Bazalgette, L. and Wood, C. (2010) *In Loco Parentis*. London: Demos.

Hansen, K. (2010) *Millennium Cohort Study Briefing 6: Teacher Assesment at Age 5*. London: Centre for Longitudinal Studies, Institute of Education.

Harper, R. (2001) *Social Capital: A Review of the Literature*. London: Office for National Statistics.

Harrist, A.W., and Waugh, R.M. (2002) Dyadic synchrony: Its structure and function in children's development. *Developmental Review*, 22 (4): 555–592.

Harter, S. (1998) The development of self-representations. In W. Damon (ed.), *Handbook of Child Psychology* (5th edn, Vol. 3). New York: Wiley, 553–617.

Harter, S., Marold, D. B., Whitesell, N. R., and Cobbs, G. (1996) A model of the effects of perceived parent and peer support on adolescent false self behavior. *Child Development*, 67 (2): 360–374.

Hartup, W.W. (1996) The company they keep: Friendships and their developmental significance. *Child Development*, 67: 1–13.

Hawthorne, J., Jessop, J. Pryor, J. and Richards, M. (2003) *Supporting Children Through Family Change: A Review of Interventions and Services for Children of Divorcing and Separating Parents*. York: Joseph Rowntree Foundation/York Publishing Services.

Health Services/Local Authority Circular (2003) *A Comprehensive CAMHS*. HSC 2003/003: LAC (2003)2.

Herrenkohl, E. C., Herrenkohl, R. C., Toedter, L., and Yanushefski, A. M. (1984) Parent–child interactions in abusive and nonabusive families. *Journal of the American Academy of Child Psychiatry*, 23 (6): 641–648.

Hildyard, K. L., and Wolfe, D. A. (2002) Child neglect: developmental issues and outcomes. *Child Abuse and Neglect*, 26 (6–7): 679–695.

Hills, J. (2004) *Inequality and the State*. Oxford: Oxford University Press

Hine, J. (2005) Early multiple intervention: A view from On Track. *Children and Society*, 19: 117–130.

Hirst, M. and Baldwin, S. (1994) *Unequal Opportunities: Growing Up Disabled*. London: HMSO.

HM Government (2005) *Statutory Guidance on Making Arrangements to Safeguard and Promote the Welfare of Children under Section 11 of the Children Act 2004*. London: Department for Education and Skills.

HMT/DfES (2007) *Aiming High for Disabled Children: Better Support for Families*. London: HM Treasury and Department for Education and Skills.

HO (1997) *No More Excuses: A New Approach to Tackling Youth Crime in England and Wales*, CM 3809. London: Home Office, HMSO.

HO (2007) *Aiming High for Young People: A Ten Year Strategy for Positive Activities*. London: Home Office.

Home-Start (2010) *A Report of the Statistical Information Collected from 334 Schemes 2009/2010*. Leicester: Home-Start.

Hooper, C-A., Gorin, S., Cabral, C. and Dyson, C. (2007) *Living with Hardship 24/7: The Diverse Experiences of Families in Poverty in England*. London: The Frank Buttle Trust.

Horwath, J. (2002) Maintaining a focus on the child? First impressions of the Framework for the Assessment of Children in Need and their Families in cases of child neglect. *Child Abuse Review*, 11 (4): 195–213.

Horwath, J. (ed.) (2011) *The Child's World: The Comprehensive Guide to Assessing Children in Need*. London: Jessica Kingsley Publishers.

Howe, D. (1995) *Attachment Theory for Social Work Practice*. Basingstoke: Macmillan.

Huddart, P. (2006) Insiders on the outside: Primary mental health work in schools. *Journal of Public Mental Health*, 5 (2): 28–35.

Humphrey, N., Kalambouka, A., Bolton, J., Lendrum, A., Wigelsworth, M., Lennie, C. and Farrell, P. (2008) *Primary Social and Emotional Aspects of Learning (SEAL): Evaluation of Small Group Work*. London: Department for Children, Schools and Families.

Humphrey, N., Lendrum, A. and Wigelsworth, M. (2010) *Social and Emotional Aspects of Learning (SEAL) Programme in Secondary Schools: National Evaluation*. London: Department for Education.

Hussain, Y., Atkin, K. and Ahmad, W. (2002) *South Asian Disabled Young People and their Families*. Bristol: Policy Press.

Hutchings, J., Bywater, T., Daley, D., Gardner, F., Whitaker, C., Jones, K., Eames, C., and Edwards, R.T. (2007) Parenting intervention in Sure Start services for children at risk of developing conduct disorder: Pragmatic randomised controlled trial. *British Medical Journal* (doi10.1136/bmj.39126.620799.55).

Hutchings, J., Bywater, T., Eames, C. and Martin, P. (2008) Implementing child mental health interventions in service settings: Lessons from three pragmatic randomised controlled trials in Wales. *Journal of Children's Services*, 3 (2): 17–27.

Iwaniec, D., Larkin, E., and McSherry, D. (2007) Emotionally Harmful Parenting. *Child Care in Practice,* 13 (3): 203–220.

Jack, G. (1997a) Discourses of child protection and child welfare. *British Journal of Social Work*, 27: 659–678.

Jack, G. (1997b) An ecological approach to social work with children and families. *Child and Family Social Work*, 2 (2): 109–120.

Jack, G. (2000) Ecological influences on parenting and child development. *British Journal of Social Work*, 30: 703–720.

Jack, G. (2006) The area and community components of children's well-being. *Children and Society*, 20: 334–347.

Jack, G. (2010) Place matters: The significance of place attachments for children's well-being. *British Journal of Social Work*, 40: 755–771.

Jack, G. (2011) Using local area data to improve the lives of disadvantaged children and families. *Child and Family Social Work*, 16: 61–70.

Jack, G. and Donnellan, H. (2010) Recognising the person within the developing professional – tracking the early careers of newly-qualified child care social workers in three local authorities in England. *Social Work Education*, 29:3: 305–318.

Jack, G. and Gill, O. (2003) *The Missing Side of the Triangle: Assessing the Importance of Family and Environmental Factors in the Lives of Children*. Barkingside: Barnardo's.

Jack, G. and Gill, O. (2010a) The impact of family and community support on parents or caregivers and children. In J. Horwath (ed.) *The Child's World: The Comprehensive Guide to Assessing Children in Need* (2nd edn). London: Jessica Kingsley Publishers, 382–396.

Jack, G. and Gill, O. (2010b) The impact of economic factors on parents or caregivers and children. In J. Horwath (ed.) *The Child's World: The Comprehensive Guide to Assessing Children in Need* (2nd edn). London: Jessica Kingsley Publishers, 368–381.

Jack, G. and Gill, O. (2010c) The role of communities in safeguarding children and young people. *Child Abuse Review*, 19: 82–96.

Jack, G. and Gill, O. (2012) Developing cultural competence for social work with families living in poverty. *European Journal of Social Work* (doi10.1080/13691457.2011.649347).

Jack, G. and Jack, D. (2000) Ecological social work: The application of a systems model of development in context. In P. Stepney and D. Ford (eds) *Social Work Models, Methods and Theories: A Framework for Practice*. Lyme Regis: Russell House Publishing, 93–104.

Jack, G. and Stepney, P. (1995) The Children Act 1989 – protection or persecution? Family support and child protection in the 1990s. *Critical Social Policy*, 43: 26–39.

Jackson, S. and Nixon, P. (1999) Family group conferences: A challenge to the old order? In L. Dominelli (ed.), *Community Approaches to Child Welfare: International Perspectives*. Aldershot: Ashgate, 117–146.

Jackson, S. and Thomas, N. (1999) *On the Move Again. What Works in Creating Stability for Looked After Children*. Barkingside: Barnardo's.

Jenkins, N. (2002) *Promoting Safe Play and 'Hanging Out'*. Barkingside: Barnardo's.

Jenks, C. (ed.) (1982) *The Sociology of Childhood*. London: Batsford.

Johns, G. (2010) Presenteeism in the workplace: A review and research agenda. *Journal of Organisational Behaviour,* 31: 519–542.

Johnson, S.B. and Jones, V.C. (2011) Adolescent development and risk of injury: Using developmental science to improve interventions. *Injury Prevention,* 17 (1): 50–54.

Joseph, S., Becker, F., and Becker, S. (2009) *Manual of Measures of Caring Activities and Outcomes for Children and Young People.* Woodford Green: Princess Royal Trust for Carers.

Joyce, R., Muriel, A., Phillips, D. and Sibieta, L. (2010) *Poverty and Inequality in UK: 2010.* London: Institute for Fiscal Studies.

Karim, K. (2007) Children with physical illness. In P. Vostanis (ed.) *Mental Health Interventions and Services for Vulnerable Children and Young People.* London: Jessica Kingsley Publishers, 193–202.

Kay, H. (1999) *Bright Futures: Promoting Children and Young People's Mental Health.* London: Mental Health Foundation.

Kennedy, M. (2002) Disability and child abuse. In K. Wilson and A. James (eds) *The Child Protection Handbook.* London: Ballière & Tindall, 201–224.

Knight, A. and Oliver, C. (2007) Advocacy for disabled children and young people: Benefits and dilemmas. *Child and Family Social Work,* 12 (4): 417–425.

Knight, A., Petrie, P., Zuurmond, M. and Potts, P. (2009) 'Mingling together': Promoting the social inclusion of disabled children and young people during the school holidays. *Child and Family Social Work,* 14 (1): 15–24.

Kohlberg, L. (1969) Stages and sequence: The cognitive developmental approach to socialization. In D. A. Goslin (ed.), *Handbook of Socialisation Theory and Research.* Chicago: Rand McNally, 347–480.

Korbin, J.E. (2002) Culture and child maltreatment: Cultural competence and beyond. *Child Abuse and Neglect,* 26: 637–644.

Kroll, B. and Taylor, A. (2003) *Parental Substance Misuse and Child Welfare.* London: Jessica Kingsley Publishers.

Kuhn, D. (2008) Formal operations from a twenty-first century perspective. *Human Development,* 51 (1): 48–55.

Kurtz, Z. and Street, C. (2006) Mental health services for young people from black and minority ethnic backgrounds: The current challenge. *Journal of Children's Services,* 1(3): 40–49.

Ladd, G.W. (2006) Peer rejection, aggressive or withdrawn behavior, and psychological maladjustment from ages 5 to 12: An examination of four predictive models. *Child Development,* 77 (4): 822–846.

Lader, D. (2009) *Contraception and Sexual Health.* London: Office of National Statistics.

Laible, D.J., and Thompson, R.A. (1998) Attachment and emotional understanding in preschool children. *Developmental Psychology,* 34 (5): 1038–1045.

Laird, S.E. (2008) *Anti-Oppressive Social Work: A Guide for Developing Cultural Competence*. London: Sage.

Laming, The Lord (2003) *The Victoria Climbié Inquiry*, Cm5730. London: The Stationery Office.

Laming, The Lord (2009) *The Laming Review*. London: HMSO.

Leavey, G., Hollins, H., King, M., Papadopoulos, C. and Barnes, J. (2004) Psychological disorder amongst refugee and migrant children in London. *Social Psychiatry and Psychiatric Epidemiology*, 39: 191–195.

Lewis, M.L. and Ippen, C.G. (2004) Rainbows of tears, souls full of hope: Cultural issues related to young children and trauma. In J.D. Osofsky (ed.) *Young Children and Trauma: Treatment and Intervention*. New York: Guilford Press, 145–152.

Lindsay, S. and McPherson, A.C. (2012) Strategies for improving disability awareness and social inclusion of children and young people with cerebral palsy. *Child: Care, Health and Development*, 38(6): 809–816.

Little, M., Axford, N. and Morpeth, L. (2003) Children's services in the UK 1997–2003: Problems, developments and challenges for the future. *Children and Society*, 17: 205–214.

Littlechild, B. and Smith, R. (2008) Social work with young offenders. In K. Wilson, G. Ruch, M. Lymbery and A. Cooper (eds), *Social Work: An Introduction to Contemporary Practice*. Harlow: Pearson Education Limited, 512–536.

Lloyd, S. (1993) Facing the facts: Self-help as a response to child sexual abuse. In L. Waterhouse (ed.), *Child Abuse and Child Abusers*, London: Jessica Kingsley Publishers, 191–207

Lovell, E. (2006) Just justice: A study into young black people's experience of the youth justice system. *Childright*, 227: 20–23.

Maccoby, E., and Martin, J. (1983) Socialization in the context of the family: Parent–child interaction. In E. M. Hetherington (ed.), *Handbook of Child Psychology: Socialization, Personality and Social Development Vol. 4*. New York: Wiley, 1–101.

Macdonald, G. and Turner, W. (2007) *Treatment Foster Care for Improving Outcomes in Children and Young People*. http://online library.wiley.com/doi/10.1002/14651858.CD005649.pub2/full (accessed 29 December 2011).

Maclean, M. (2004) *Together and Apart: Children and Parents Experiencing Separation and Divorce*. York: Joseph Rowntree Foundation.

Maclean, K. and Connelly, G. (2005) Still room for improvement? The educational experiences of looked after children in Scotland. In D. Crimmens and I. Milligan (eds) *Facing Forward: Residential Child Care in the 21st Century*. Lyme Regis: Russell House Publishing, 135–144.

MacMillan, H.L., Wathen, C.N., Barlow, J., Fergusson, D.M., Leventhal, J.M. and Taussig, H.N. (2009) Interventions to prevent child maltreatment and associated impairment. *The Lancet*, 373: 250–266.

Marchant, R. (2010) *Making Assessment Work for Children with Complex Needs.* In J. Horwath (ed.) *The Child's World: The Comprehensive Guide to Assessing Children in Need.* London: Jessica Kingsley Publishers, 199–213.

Marcia, J.E. (1980) Identity in adolescence. In J. Adelson (ed.), *Handbook of Adolescent Psychology.* New York: Wiley, 159–187.

Markiewicz, D., Lawford, H., Doyle, A.B., and Haggart, N. (2006). Developmental differences in adolescents' and young adults' use of mothers, fathers, best friends, and romantic partners to fulfill attachment needs. *Journal of Youth and Adolescence,* 35 (1): 121–134.

Marsh, P. and Crow, G. (1998) *Family Group Conferences in Child Welfare.* Oxford: Blackwell.

Martin, K. (2009) *Making Ourselves Heard: Exploring Disabled Children's Participation.* London: National Children's Bureau.

McAnarney, E.R. (2008) Adolescent brain development: Forging new links? *Journal of Adolescent Health,* 42 (4): 321–323.

McAuley, C. and Davis, T. (2009) Emotional well-being and mental health of looked after children in England. *Child and Family Social Work,* 14: 147–155.

McAuley, C., Knapp, M., Beecham, J., McCurry, N. and Steed, M. (2004) *Young Families under Stress: Outcomes and Costs of Home-Start Support.* York: Joseph Rowntree Foundation.

McCarthy, J. and Boyd, J. (2002) Mental health services and young people with intellectual disability: Is it time to do better? *Journal of Intellectual Disability Research,* 46: 250–256.

McHale, S.M., Crouter, A.C., and Tucker, C.J. (2001) Free-time activities in middle childhood: Links with adjustment in early adolescence. *Child Development,* 72 (6): 1764–1778.

McSweeney, F. (2012) Student, practitioner, or both? Separation and integration of identities in professional social care education. *Social Work Education,* 31 (3): 364–382.

McVie, S. and Norris, P. (2006) *Neighbourhood Effects on Youth Delinquency and Drug Use.* Edinburgh: Centre for Law and Society, University of Edinburgh.

Melhuish, E., Belsky, J., MacPherson, K., and Cullis, A. (2010) *The Quality of Group Childcare Settings Used by 3–4 year old Children in Sure Start Local Programme Areas and the Relationship with Child Outcomes.* London: Department for Children, Schools and Families.

Meltzer, H. and Gatward, R, with Goodman, R. and Ford, T. (2000) *The Mental Health of Children and Adolescents in Great Britain.* London: The Stationery Office.

Meltzer, H., Gatward, R., Corbin, T., Goodman, R. and Ford, T. (2003a) *Persistence, Onset, Risk Factors and Outcomes of Childhood Mental Disorders.* London: The Stationary Office.

Meltzer, H., Corbin, T., Gatward, R., Goodman, R. and Ford, T. (2003b) *The Mental Health of Young People Looked After by Local Authorities in England*. London: The Stationery Office.

Meltzer. H., Lader, D., Corbin, T., Goodman, R. and Ford T. (2004a) *The Mental Health of Young People Looked After by Local Authorities in Scotland*. London: The Stationery Office.

Meltzer. H., Lader, D., Corbin, T., Goodman, R. and Ford T. (2004b) *The Mental Health of Young People Looked After by Local Authorities in Wales*. London: The Stationery Office.

MHF (2010) *MyCare: The Challenges Facing Young Carers of Parents with a Severe Mental Illness*. London: Mental Health Foundation.

Miller, D. (2003) Disabled children and abuse. In J. Morris (ed.) *'It Doesn't Happen to Disabled Children' Child Protection and Disabled Children – Report of the National Working Group on Child Protection and Disability*. London: NSPCC, 19–30.

Minnis, H. and Del Priore, C. (2001) Mental health services for looked after children. *Adoption and Fostering*, 25 (4): 27–38.

Moffitt, T.M. (1993). Adolescence-limited and life-course-persistent anti-social behaviour: A developmental taxonomy. *Psychological Review*, 100 (4): 674–701.

Monck, E., Reynolds, J. and Wigfall, V. (2003) *The Role of Concurrent Planning: Making Permanent Placements for Young Children*. London: BAAF.

Mooney, A., Oliver, C. and Smith. M. (2009) *Impact of Family Breakdown on Children's Wellbeing: Evidence Review*. London: Department for Children, Schools and Families.

Moran, P. and Ghate, D. (2005) The effectiveness of parenting support. *Children and Society*, 19 (4): 329–336.

Morris, J. (1998) *Accessing Human Rights: Disabled Children and the Children Act*. Barkingside: Barnardo's.

Morris, J. (2002) *A Lot to Say: A Guide for Social Workers, Personal Advisors and Others Working with Disabled Children and Young People with Communication Impairments*. London: Scope.

Mumford, K. and Power, A. (2003) *East Enders: Family and Community in East London*, Bristol: The Policy Press.

Munro, E. (2010) *The Munro Report of Child Protection Part One: A Systems Analysis*. London: Department for Education.

Munro, E. (2011a) *The Munro Review of Child Protection Interim Report: The Child's Journey*. London: Department for Education.

Munro, E. (2011b) *The Munro Review of Child Protection: Final Report. A Child-Centred System*. Cm8062. London: Department for Education.

Murray, P. (2002) *Hello! Are You Listening? Disabled Teenagers' Experience of Access to Inclusive Leisure*. York: York Publishing Services.

NAO (2005) *Improving School Attendance In England*. London: National Audit Office, England, The Stationery Office.

Natsal (2000) *National Survey of Sexual Attitudes and Lifestyles*. London: National Centre for Social Research.

NAW/HO (2001) *The Framework for Assessing Children in Need and their Families*. London: National Assembly for Wales and Home Office, The Stationery Office.

Newman, T., Yates, T., and Masten, A. (2004) *What Works in Building Resilience?* Barkingside: Barnardo's.

NICE (2006) *Parent Training/Education Programmes in the Management of Children with Conduct Problems*. London: National Institute for Health and Clinical Excellence.

NICE/SCIE (2010) *Looked-after Children and Young People: Quick Reference Guide*. London: National Institute for Health and Clinical Excellence and Social Care Institute for Excellence.

NISRA (2010) *Northern Ireland Multiple Deprivation 2010*. Belfast: Northern Ireland Statistics and Research Agency (www.nisra.gov.uk/deprivation.htm).

Nixon. P. (2007) *Relatively Speaking: Developments in Research and Practice in Kinship Care*. Dartington: Research in Practice.

Nixon, P., Burford, G. and Quinn, A. with Edelbaum, J. (2005) *A Survey of International Practices, Policy and Research on Family Group Conferencing and Related Practices*. London: Family Rights Group.

Nock, M.K. and Ferriter, C. (2005) Parent management of attendance and adherence in child and adolescent therapy: A conceptual and empirical review. *Clinical Child and Family Psychology Review*, 8: 149–166.

NSPCC (2000) *Child Maltreatment in the UK: A Study of the Prevalence of Child Abuse and Neglect*. London: National Society for the Prevention of Cruelty to Children.

NSPCC (2006) *Old Heads on Young Shoulders*. London: National Society for the Prevention of Cruelty to Children/ChildLine.

Oakley, A., Rajan, L. and Grant, A. (1990) Social support and pregnancy outcome. *British Journal of Obstetrics and Gynaecology*, 97: 155–162.

Oakley, A., Rigby, D., Rajan, L. and Hickey, D. (1996) Social support in pregnancy: Does it have long term effects? *Journal of Reproductive and Infant Psychology*, 14 (7):22.

O'Connor, T. and Scott, S. (2007) *Parenting and Outcomes for Children*. York: Joseph Rowntree Foundation.

OECD (2008) *Growing Unequal? Income Distribution and Poverty in OECD Countries*. Paris: Organisation for Economic Co-operation and Development.

Ofsted (2010) *Admission and Discharge from Secure Accommodation*. Manchester: Ofsted.

Ofsted (2011) *Edging Away From Care – How Services Successfully Prevent Young People Entering Care*. Manchester: Ofsted.

Olds, D.L., Eckenrode, J., Henderson, C.R., Kitzman, C.R., Powers, J., Cole, R., Sidora, K., Morris, L.M. and Luckey, D. (1997) Long-term effects of home visitation on maternal life course and child abuse and neglect: Fifteen-year follow up of a randomized trial. *Journal of the American Medical Association*, 278: 637–643.

Oliver, M. (1999) *Understanding Disability: From Theory to Practice*. London: Macmillan.

ONS (2004) *Focus on Social Inequalities*. London: Office for National Statistics.

ONS (2008) *Three Years On: Survey of the Development and Emotional Well-being of Children and Young People*. London: Office for National Statistics.

ONS (2010) *Social Trends 41*. London: Office for National Statistics.

Owen, C. and Statham, J. (2009) *Disproportionality in Child Welfare: The Prevalence of Black and Ethnic Minority Children within the 'Looked After' and 'Children in Need' Populations and on Child Protection Registers in England* (Research Brief DCSF-RB124). London: Department for Children, Schools and Families.

Pallett, C., Scott, S., Blackeby, K., Yule, W. and Weissman, R. (2002) Fostering changes: A cognitive-behavioural approach to help foster carers manage children. *Adoption and Fostering*, 30: 1–10.

Parton, N. (1979) The natural history of child abuse: A study in social problem definition. *British Journal of Social Work*, 9: 431–451.

Parton, N. (1985) *The Politics of Child Abuse*. London: Macmillan.

Paus, T., Keshavan, M., and Giedd, J.N. (2008) Why do many psychiatric disorders emerge during adolescence? *Nature Reviews Neuroscience, 9* (12): 947–957.

Penney, C., Wilson, C., Draper, L., Day, C., and Kearney, C. (2010) *Being a Parent: Manual for Course Facilitators*. London: The Parenting Centre and The Centre for Parent and Child Support.

Perrott, S. (2009) *Protecting Our Children: An Expert Seminar on Improving Safeguarding Practice and Social Work Education*. Durham: Durham University, School of Applied Social Sciences.

Perry, A., Douglas, G. Murch, M., Bader, K. and Borkowski, M. (2000) *How Families Cope Financially on Marriage Breakdown*. York: Joseph Rowntree Foundation.

Perry, F. (1998) *Children Belong Together: Working Towards the Inclusion of Children and Young People with Disabilities in their Communities*. London: The Children's Society.

Petrosino, A., Turpin-Petrosino, C., and Buehler, J. (2002) *'Scared Straight' and Other Juvenile Awareness Programs for Preventing Juvenile Delinquency (Review)*. London: The Cochrane Collection/Wiley.

Pettitt, B. (2003) *Effective Joint Working between Child and Adolescent Mental Health Services (CAMHS) and Schools*. London: Mental Health Foundation and Department for Education and Skills.

Piaget, J. (1932) *The Moral Judgement of the Child*. New York: Macmillan.

Piaget, J. (2001) *The Language and Thought of the Child* (3rd edn). London: Routledge.

Piaget, J., and Inhelder, B. (1969) *The Psychology of the Child*. New York: Basic Books.

Pickett, K.E. and Wilkinson, R.G. (2008) Child wellbeing and income inequality in rich countries: Ecological cross sectional study. *British Medical Journal* (doi:10.1136/bmj.39377.580162.55).

Pierpoint, H. (2006) Reconstructing the role of the appropriate adult in England and Wales. *Criminology and Criminal Justice*, 6 (2): 219–237.

Pithouse, A. and Lindsell, S. (1996) Child protection services: Comparison of a referred family centre and a field social work service in South Wales. *Research on Social Work Practice*, 6 (4): 473–491.

Pollock, L.A. (2009) Fit for purpose? *The Guardian*, 18 February.

Pote, H., Bureau, J. and Goodban, D. (2006) *Mental Health Services for Children with Learning Disabilities – Developing Local Services: A Resource Pack*. London: CAMHS Publications.

Prewett, P. (1999) *Short-term Break, Long-term Benefit: Family-based Short Breaks for Disabled Children and Adults*. Sheffield: Joint Unit for Social Services Research, University of Sheffield.

Puckering, C., Mills, M., Cox, A., Maddox, H., Evans, J. and Rogers, J. (1999) *Improving the Quality of Family Support: An Intensive Parenting Programme: Mellow Parenting*. London: Department of Health.

Radford, L., Corral, S., Bradley, C., Fisher, H., Bassett, C., Howatt, N. and Collishaw, S. (2011) *Child Cruelty in the UK 2011*. London: NSPCC.

Rah, Y. and Parke, R. (2008) Pathways between parent–child interactions and peer acceptance. The role of children's social information processing. *Social Development, 17*, 341–357.

Raikes, H., Luze, G., Brooks-Gunn, J., Pan, B.A., Tamis-LeMona, C.S., Constantine, J., Tarullo, L.B., and Rodriguez, E.T. (2006) Mother–child book-reading in low-income familes: Correlates and outcomes during the first three years of life. *Child Development, 77* (4), 924–953.

Ramey, C.T, and Ramey, S.L. (2004) Early learning and school readiness: can early intervention make a difference? *Merrill-Palmer Quarterly* 50 (4): 471–91.

Richards, M. and Abbott, R. (n.d.) *Childhood Mental Health and Life Chances in Post-war Britain*. London: Medical Research Council Unit for Lifelong Health and Ageing.

Ridge, T. (2009) *Living with Poverty: A Review of the Literature on Children's and Families' Experiences of Poverty*. London: Department for Work and Pensions.

RIP (2003) *Promoting the Mental Health of Children in Need*. Dartington: Research in Practice.

RIP (2009) *Under 18 Conception Rate*. Dartington: Research in Practice.

Roberts, I. (1996) Family support and the health of children. *Children and Society*, 10 (3): 217–224.

Roberts, F., Mathers, S., Joshi, H., Sylva, K., and Jones, E. (2010) *Millennium Cohort Study Briefing 8: Childcare in the Pre-school Years*. London: Centre for Longitudinal Studies, Institute of Education.

Robertson, J., Hatton, C., Emerson, E., Wells, E., Collins, M., Langer, S. and Welh, V. (2010) *The Impacts of Short Break Provision on Disabled Children and their Families: An International Literature Review.* Lancaster: Centre for Disability Research, Lancaster University.

Robinson, M. (2008) *Child Development from Birth to Eight – A Journey Through the Early Years.* Maidenhead: OU Press/McGraw Hill.

Rodgers, B and Pryor, J. (1998) *Divorce and Separation: The Outcomes for Children.* York: Joseph Rowntree Foundation.

Rose, W. (2010) The assessment framework. In J. Horwath (ed.) *The Child's World (2nd edition): The Comprehensive Guide to Assessing Children in Need.* London: Jessica Kingsley Publishers, 34–55.

Rothbart, M., Sheese, B., and Posner, M. (2007) Executive attention and effortful control: linking temperament, brain networks and genes. *Child Development Perspectives*, 1 (1), 2–7.

Rothi, D.M. and Leavey, G. (2006) Mental health help-seeking and young people: A review. *Pastoral Care*, September: 4–13.

Roulstone, S., Law, J., Rush, R., Clegg, J., and Peters, T. (2011) *The Role of Language in Children's Early Educational Outcomes – Research Report 134.* London: Department of Education.

Rowe, M. (2008) Child-directed speech: relation to socioeconomic status, knowledge of child development and child vocabulary skill. *Journal of Child Language*, 35 (1), 185–205.

Rowe, J. and Lambert, L. (1973) *Children Who Wait.* London: British Agencies for Adoption and Fostering.

Russell, P. (2003) Access and achievement or social exclusion. Are the government's policies working for disabled children and their families? *Children and Society*, 17 (3): 215–225.

Rutter, M (1989) Intergenerational continuities and discontinuities in serious parenting difficulties. In D. Cicchetti and V. Carlson (eds) *Child Maltreatment: Theory and Research on the Causes and Consequences of Child Abuse and Neglect.* Cambridge: Cambridge University Press, 317–348.

Rutter, M., (1991) A fresh look at maternal deprivation. In P. Bateson (ed.) *The Development and Integration of Behaviour.* Cambridge: Cambridge University Press, 331–376.

Rutter, M. and Rutter, M. (1992). *Developing Minds – Challenge and Continuity Across the Life Span.* London: Penguin.

Ryan, T and Walker, R. (2007) *Life Story Work: A Practical Guide to Helping Children Understand their Past.* London: British Association of Adoption and Fostering.

Sammons, P., Sylva, K., Melhuish, E., Siraj-Blatchford, I., Taggart, B., Marsh, A. and Elliott, K. (2004) *Technical Paper 11: Report of the Continuing Effects of Pre-School Education at Age 7 (EPPE Project).* London: DfES/Institute of Education, University of London.

Sampson, R.J. and Groves, W.B. (1989) Community structure and crime: Testing social-disorganization theory. *American Journal of Sociology,* 94 (4): 774–802.

Sampson, R.J., Raudenbush, S.W. and Earls, J. (1997) Neighbourhoods and violent crime: A multi-level study of collective efficacy. *Science,* 277: 1–7.

Schneider, B., J. Wiener, and Murphy, K. (1994). Children's friendships: The giant step beyond peer acceptance, *The Journal of Social and Personal Relationships* 11(3), 323–340.

Schön, D. (1995) *The Reflective Practitioner – How Professionals Think in Action.* Aldershot: Arena.

SCIE (2003) *Knowledge Review 5: Fostering Success. An Exploration of the Research Literature in Foster Care.* London: Social Care Institute for Excellence.

Scott, S., O'Connor, T. and Futh, A. (2006) *What Makes Parenting Programmes Work in Disadvantaged Areas? The PALS Trial.* York: Joseph Rowntree Foundation.

Scottish Executive (2002) *'It's Everyone's Job to Make Sure I'm Alright'. Report of the Child Protection Audit and Review.* Edinburgh: Scottish Executive.

Scottish Executive (2007) *Examining the Use and Impact of Family Group Conferencing.* Edinburgh: Scottish Executive.

Scottish Executive (2008) *Getting it Right for Every Child.* Edinburgh: Scottish Executive.

Scottish Executive (2010) *National Guidance for Child Protection in Scotland.* Edinburgh: The Scottish Government.

Scottish Government (2008) *A Guide to Getting it Right for Every Child.* Edinburgh: Scottish Government.

Scottish Government (2009) *Scottish Index of Multiple Deprivation: 2009 General Report.* Edinburgh: The Scottish Government.

Scottish Government (2011) *Children Looked After Statistics 2009–10.* Edinburgh: The Scottish Government.

Scottish Government/COSLA (2010) *Caring Together.* Edinburgh: Scottish Government and Convention of Scottish Local Authorities.

Scottish Office, The (1992) *Another Kind of Home: A Review of Residential Child Care.* London: HMSO.

Scottish Refugee Council (2006) *Poverty in Scotland.* Glasgow: Scottish Refugee Council.

Seaman, P., Turner, K., Hill, M., Stafford, A. and Walker, M. (2006) *Parenting and Children's Resilience in Disadvantaged Communities.* London: National Children's Bureau.

Sellick, C., Thoburn, J. and Philpot, T. (2004) *What Works in Adoption and Foster Care?* Barkingside: Barnardo's.

Sender, H., Littlechild, B. and Smith, N. (2006) Black and minority ethnic groups and youth offending. *Youth and Policy,* 93: 61–76.

Settersten, R.A. (2011) Becoming adult: Meanings and markers for young Americans. In M. Waters, P. Carr, M. Kefalas and J. Holdaway (ed.), *Coming of Age in America: The Transition to Adulthood in 21st Century*. Berkeley: University of California Press, 169–190

Shared Care Network (2006) *Still Waiting? Families of Disabled Children in the UK Waiting for Short Break Services*. Bristol: Shared Care Network.

Shonkoff, J.P. and Phillips, D.A. (eds) (2000) *From Neurons to Neighbourhoods: The Science of Early Childhood Development*. Washington DC: National Research Council and Institute of Medicine, National Academy Press.

Shucksmith, J., Philip, K., Spratt, J. and Watson, C. (2005) *Investigating the Links Between Mental Health and Behaviour in Schools*. Edinburgh: Scottish Executive.

Sidebotham, P.D., Golding, J., and the ALSPAC Study Team (2001) Child maltreatment in the 'children of the nineties': A longitudinal study of parental risk factors. *Child Abuse and Neglect*, 25: 1177–1200.

Sidebotham, P.D., Heron, J. and the ALSPAC Study Team (2006) Child maltreatment in the 'children of the nineties': A cohort study of risk factors. *Child Abuse and Neglect*, 30: 497–522.

Sidebotham, P.D., Heron, J., Golding, J. and the ALSPAC Study Team (2002) Child maltreatment in the 'children of the nineties': Deprivation, social class and social networks in a UK sample. *Child Abuse and Neglect*, 26: 1243–1259.

Sinclair, I. (2005) *Fostering Now: Messages from Research*. London: Jessica Kingsley Publishers.

Sinclair, I. (2006) Residential care in the UK. In C. McAuley, P.J. Pecora and W. Rose (eds) *Enhancing the Well-being of Children and Families through Effective Interventions: International Evidence for Practice*. London: Jessica Kingsley Publishers, 203–216.

Siraj-Blatchford, I., (2009) Learning in the home and at school: how working class children 'succeed against the odds', *British Educational Research Journal*, 36:3, 463–482.

Siraj-Blatchford, I., and Siraj-Blatchford, J. (2010) *Improving Children's Attainment through Better Quality Family-based Support for Early Learning – Early Years Knowledge Review 2*. London: C4EO.

Skinner, B.F. (1948). *Walden Two* New York: Macmillan.

Smith, D. (2004) *Parenting and Delinquency at Ages 12 to 15*. Edinburgh: Centre for Law and Society, University of Edinburgh.

Smith, P.M. (2010) Disabled children and the Children Act 1989. *Journal of Children's Services*, 5 (3): 61–68.

Smith, R., Purdon, S., Schneider, V., La Velle, I., Wollny, I., Owen, R., Bryson, C., Mathers, S. and Sylva, K. (2009). *Early Education Pilot for Two Year Old Children: Research Report 134*. London: Department for Children, Schools and Families.

Snell, E.K., Adam, E.K., and Duncan, G J. (2007) Sleep and the body mass index and overweight status of children and adolescents. *Child Development*, 78 (1), 309–323.

Social Work Task Force (2009) *Building a Safe, Confident Future: The Final Report of the Social Work Task Force*. London: Department for Children, Schools and Families.

Southwell, P. (1994) The integrated family centre. *Practice*, 7 (1): 45–54.

Spear, L.P. (2000) The adolescent brain and age-related behavioral manifestations. *Neuroscience and Biobehavioral Reviews*, 24 (4): 417–463.

Spear, L.P. (2010) *The Behavioural Neuroscience of Adolescence*. New York: Norton.

Speight, S., Smith, R., Lloyd, E., and Coshall, C. (2010). *Families Experiencing Multiple Disadvantage: Thier Use and Views of Childcare Provision: Research Report 191*. London: Department for Children, Schools and Families.

Spratt, T. and Callan, J. (2004) Parents' views on social work interventions in child welfare cases. *British Journal of Social Work*, 34:199–224.

Spratt, J., Shucksmith, J., Philip, K. and Watson, C. (2006) 'Part of who we are as a school should include responsibility for well-being': Links between the school environment, mental health and behaviour. *Pastoral Care*, September: 14–21.

SSIA (2008) *Improving Social Care in Wales*. Cardiff: SSIA.

Stacy, L. (2009) *Who's Child Now?* Barkingside: Barnardo's.

Stang, J., and Story, M. (2005) Adolescent growth and development. In J. Stang and M. Story (eds) *Guidelines for Adolescent Nutrition Services*. Minneapolis: University of Minnesota, 1–8.

Statham, J. (2000) *Outcomes and Effectiveness of Family Support Services: A Research Review*. London: Institute of Education, University of London.

Statistics for Wales (2008) *Welsh Index of Multiple Deprivation (WIMD) 2008*. Cardiff: Welsh Assembly Government.

Statistics for Wales (2011) *Wales Children in Need Census 2010*. Cardiff: Statistics Directorate, Welsh Assembly Government.

Steinberg, L. (2011) *Adolescence* (9th edn). New York: McGraw-Hill.

Steinberg, L, and Morris, A.S., (2001) Adolescent development, *Annual Reviews of Psychology*, 52, 83–110

Stroud, J. (1997) Mental disorder and the homicide of children. *Social Work and Social Services Review*, 6 (3): 149–162.

Sugarman, L. (2001) *Life-Span Development – Frameworks, Accounts and Strategies*. Hove: Taylor & Francis.

Sullivan, P.M. and Knutson, J.F. (2000) Maltreatment and disabilities: A population based epidemiological study. *Child Abuse and Neglect*, 24 (10): 1275–1288.

Sutton, C., Utting, D., and Farrington, D. (2004) *Support from the Start: Working with Young Children and their Families to Reduce the Risks of Crime and Anti-social Behaviour Research Report 524.* Nottingham: Department for Education and Skills.

Sutton, L., Smith, N., Dearden, C., and Middleton, S. (2007) *A Child's Eye View of Social Difference.* York: Joseph Rowntree Foundation.

Sweeting, H. and West, P. (2003) Sex differences in health at ages 11, 13 and 15. *Social Science and Medicine,* 56 (1): 31–39.

Sweeting, H.N., West, P.B. and Der, G.J. (2007) Explanations for female excess psychosomatic symptoms in adolescence: Evidence from a school-based cohort in the West of Scotland. *BMC Public Health,* 7: 298–298.

Sweeting, H., Young, R. and West, P. (2009) GHQ increases among Scottish 15 year olds 1987–2006. *Social Psychiatry and Psychiatric Epidemiology,* 44: 579–586.

SWRB. (2011) *Standards for Employers and Supervision Framework, Social Work Reform Board* (http://media.education.gov.uk/assets/files/pdf/standards%20for%20employers.pdf)

Sylva, K., Melhuish, E., Sammons, P., Siraj-Blatchford, I. and Taggart, B. (2004) *The Effective Provision of Pre-School Education (EPPE) Project: Findings from the Early Primary Years.* Nottingham: DfES.

Sylva, K., Melhuish, E., Sammons, P., Siraj-Blatchford, I. and Taggart, B. (eds) (2010) *Early Childhood Matters: Evidence from the Effective Pre-school and Primary Education Project.* London: Routledge.

Tanner, J.M. (1990). *Foetus into Man.* Cambridge, MA: Harvard University Press.

Taylor, A. (2007) Decision making in child and family social work: The impact of the assessment framework, PhD thesis, Durham University.

TCSW. (2012) *Professional Capabilities Framework,* from The College of Social Work at www.collegeofsocialwork.org/pcf.aspx.

Thomas, N. (2000) Putting the family in the driving seat: Aspects of the development of family group conferences in England and Wales. *Social Work and Social Sciences Review,* 8 (2): 101–115.

Thompson, L. J., and West, D. (2012) Professional development in the contemporary educational context: Encouraging practice wisdom. *Social Work Education, iFirst Article,* 1–16.

Thompson, N. (2009) *Understanding Social Work* (3rd edn). Basingstoke: Palgrave Macmillan.

Tisdall, K., Wallace, J., McGregor, E. Millen, D. and Bell, A. (2005) *Seamless Services, Smoother Lives.* Edinburgh: Children in Scotland.

Tomlinson, M., Walker, R. and Williams, G. (2008) Child poverty and well-being in the here and now. *Poverty,* 129: 11–14.

Townsend, E. (2007) Cognitive-behavioural interventions for young offenders. In P. Vostanis (ed.) *Mental Health Interventions and Services for Vulnerable Children and Young People.* London: Jessica Kingsley Publishers, 110–120.

Trawick-Smith, J. (2010) *Early Childhood Development – A Multi-cultural Perspective* (5th edn). Columbus, OH: Merrill.

Triebenbacher, S.L. (1998) Pets as transitional objects: their role in children's emotional development, *Psychology Rep* 82(1), 191–200

Turiel, E. (1983) *The Development of Social Knowledge: Morality and Convention*. Cambridge: Cambridge University Press.

Turney, D. (2009) *Analysis and Critical Thinking in Assessment*. Dartington: Research in Practice.

Turnell, A. and Edwards, S. (1997) Aspiring to partnership: The signs of safety approach to child protection. *Child Abuse Review*, 6:179–190.

Turnell, A. and Edwards, S. (1999) *Signs of Safety: A Solution and Safety Oriented Approach to Child Protection Casework*. New York: Norton.

Twigg, R. and Swan, T. (2007) Inside the foster family. What research tells us about the experience of foster carers' children. *Adoption and Fostering*, 31 (4): 49–61.

UNICEF (2007) *Child Poverty in Perspective: An Overview of Child Well-Being in Rich Countries*. Florence: United Nations Children's Fund Innocenti Research Centre.

Utting, D., Monteiro, H. and Ghate, D. (2007) *Interventions for Children at Risk of Developing Antisocial Personality Disorder*. London: Policy Research Bureau.

Van Ijzendoorn, M.H., Goldberg, S., Kroonenberg, P. and Frankel, O. (1992) The relative effects of material and child problems on the quality of attachment: A meta-analysis of attachment in clinical samples. *Child Development*, 63: 840–858.

Ventress, N. (2009) *Child Neglect: Reference Manual*. London: Community Care Inform.

Vincent, S. (2008) *Child Protection Statistics: A UK Comparison (Briefing Number 3)*. Edinburgh: The University of Edinburgh/NSPCC Centre for UK-wide Learning in Child Protection.

Vostanis, P. (2007) Therapeutic services for homeless families. In P. Vostanis (ed.) *Mental Health Interventions and Services for Vulnerable Children and Young People*. London: Jessica Kingsley Publishers, 149–164.

Vygotsky, L. (1978) *Mind and Society: The Development of Higher Mental Processes*. Cambridge, MA: Harvard University Press.

Vygotsky, L. (1986). *Thought and Language*. Cambridge, MA: MIT Press.

Wade, J. (2003) *Leaving Care* (Quality Protects Research Briefing). Dartington: Research in Practice.

Wade, J., Biehal, N., Farrelly, N. and Sinclair, I. (2010) *Maltreated Children in the Looked After System: A Comparison of Outcomes for Those Who Go Home and Those Who Do Not*. London: Department for Children, Schools and Families/Department of Health.

Walker, J. (2008) The use of attachment theory in adoption and fostering. *Adoption & Fostering*, 32(1): 49–57.

Walker, J. (2009) Family life in the 21st century: The implications for parenting policy in the UK. *Journal of Children's Services*, 3 (4): 17–29.

Warman, A., Pallett, C. and Scott, S. (2006) Process and outcomes in the Fostering Changes programme: Foster carers learning from each other. *Adoption and Fostering*, 26: 39–48.

Warren, W.H. (2006) The dynamics of perception and action. *Psychological Review*, 113: 358–389.

Warren-Adamson, W. and Lightburn, A. (2010) Family centres: Protection and promotion at the heart of the Children Act 1989. *Journal of Children's Services*, 5 (3): 25–36.

Weare, K. and Gray, G. (2003) *What Works in Developing Children's Emotional and Social Competence and Wellbeing?* London: Department for Education and Skills.

Webster-Stratton, C. and Reid, M.J. (2010) Adapting The Incredible Years, an evidence-based parenting programme, for families involved in the child welfare system. *Journal of Children's Services*, 5 (1): 25–42.

Weikart, D. and Schweinhart, L. (1997) High/Scope Perry Pre-school Program. In G. Albee and T. Gullotta (eds) *Primary Prevention Works*. Thousand Oaks: Sage, 146–166.

Wellman, H., M, and Hickling, A., K. (1994). The mind's 'I': Children's perceptions of the mind as an active agent. *Child Development*, 66: 754–763.

Wellman, H.M, Phillips, A.T. and Rodriguez, T. (2000) Young children's understanding of perception, desire, and emotion. *Child Development*, 71 (4): 895–912.

White, C., Warrener, M., Reeves, A. and La Valle, I. (2008) *Family Intervention Projects: An Evaluation of their Design, Set-up and Early Outcomes*. London: Department for Children, Schools and Families.

WHO (2009) Growth charts, developed by Royal College of Paediatrics and Child Health, World Health Organisation and Department of Health http://www.rcpch.ac.uk/child-health/research-projects/uk-who-growth-charts/uk-who-growth-charts

WHO (2001) *Mental Health: Strengthening Mental Health Promotion*. Geneva: World Health Organization.

Wilcox, A., with Hoyle, C. (2004) *The National Evaluation of the Youth Justice Board's Restorative Justice Projects*. London: Youth Justice Board.

Wilkinson, R.G. (2005) *The Impact of Inequality: How to Make Sick Societies Healthier*. London: Routledge.

Wilkinson, R.G. and Pickett, K.E. (2009) *The Spirit Level*. Harmondsworth: Penguin.

Williams, J.M., Muldoon, J., and Lawrence, A., (2010) Children and their pets: Exploring the relationships between pet ownership, pet attitudes, attachment to pets and empathy, *Education and Health*, 28(1), 12–15

Wilson, D. (2006) The prison trick. *The Guardian*, 17 June.

Wood, L., Gilies-Corti, B.,and Bulsara, M., (2005) The pet connection: Pets as a conduit for social capital?, *Social Science and Medicine*, 61(6), 1159–1173.

Woodhouse, S.S., Dykas, M.J., and Cassidy, J. (2009). Perceptions of secure base provision within the family. *Attachment and Human Development,* 11 (1): 47–67.

Woodman, J., Pitt, M., Wentz, R., Taylor, B., Hodes, D. and Gilbert, R.E. (2008) Performance of screening tests for child physical abuse in Accident and Emergency Departments. *Health Technology Assessment,* 12: 1–118.

Woolley, H. (2006) *Inclusion of Disabled Children in Primary School Playgrounds.* London: National Children's Bureau.

YJB (2004) *Cognitive Behaviour Projects.* London: Youth Justice Board.

YJB (2005) *Mentoring Schemes 2001 to 2004.* London: Youth Justice Board.

YJB/MJ (2011) *Youth Justice Statistics 2009/10. England and Wales.* London: Youth Justice Board and Ministry of Justice.

Zaff, J.F., Moore, K.A., Papillo, R. and Williams, S. (2003) Implications of extracurricular activity participation during adolescence on positive outcomes. *Journal of Adolescent Research,* 18: 599–630.

Index